SECURE IN THE GREEN ZONE:

Guarding the U.S. Embassy in Baghdad

By James Shuman

Gotham Books

30 N Gould St.
Ste. 20820, Sheridan, WY 82801
https://gothambooksinc.com/

Phone: 1 (307) 464-7800

© 2024 *James Shuman*. All rights reserved.

No part of this book may be reproduced, stored in a retrieval system, or transmitted by any means without the written permission of the author.

Published by Gotham Books (October 31, 2024)

ISBN: 979-8-3302-9627-9 (H)
ISBN: 979-8-3302-9625-5 (P)
ISBN: 979-8-3302-9626-2 (E)

Because of the dynamic nature of the Internet, any web addresses or links contained in this book may have changed since publication and may no longer be valid.

The views expressed in this work are solely those of the author and do not necessarily reflect the views of the publisher, and the publisher hereby disclaims any responsibility for them.

TABLE OF CONTENTS

Chapter 1 1

Chapter 2 32

Chapter 3 57

Chapter 4 126

Chapter 5 241

Chapter 6 314

Chapter 7 383

Chapter 8 466

Chapter 9 492

Chapter 10 512

Chapter 11 553

Chapter 12 601

CHAPTER 1

Holy Crap! How in the hell had I gotten myself into what I can only describe as an extraordinary, mind blowing, life-altering mess? In my own defense, the insurgents usually only shot a couple rockets at us at any one given time. I certainly was not expecting to be able to count by salvos instead of individual rockets. This was where I found myself, in Baghdad, Iraq, running for my life through the P.X. parking lot dodging rockets on Easter morning, 23 March, 2008. But I think I am getting ahead of myself.

They called me Rooster, I was a Physical Security Specialist with a contracting company providing protection for the Department of State and the U.S. Embassy in Baghdad, Iraq. My assignment, at the time, was to manage the guard force providing security for the camp that housed all the bodyguards, and convoy security specialist, who were employed by the State Department; protecting the guys, and girls, who provided protection for the diplomats and emissaries in Iraq. Do you see the irony here?

Commonly called the "Whips Camp" (whips is how you pronounce the acronym WPPS, which stands for Worldwide Personal Protection Specialist), it lay in the shadows of Saddam Hussein's palace on the Tigris River. Although this may sound picturesque, and conjure up all kinds of romantic images of "The Prince of Baghdad", "Aladdin", and other Arabian Nights fantasies, I was beginning to find out it really meant all the rockets that did not quite make it to the Palace tended to fall somewhere around us.

I worked the night shift, which was usually a quiet and uneventful shift, but as they say all good things must come to an end. It was getting close to 6 am, the end of my shift, on Easter morning and I had been cleaning up around the office, putting things away, and getting ready for shift change when the C-RAM alarm went off. C-RAM stood for Counter – Rocket, Artillery, Mortar. Normally pronounced "See Ram", it was basically a radar unit that detected, yes, you guessed it, in-coming rockets, artillery, and mortar rounds (referred to as IDF, a shortened term for indirect fire – Pay attention, there will be a test later). Do not get alarmed, no pun intended, I am not going to give away any classified information here.

With that in mind suffice it to say that the C-RAM could detect shells and rockets, calculate from where the rounds were being fired and, more importantly, determine where they were supposed to impact.

In addition to being able to detect IDF, there were also a series of localized alarms plugged in to the system designed to sound a warning when the unit detected incoming rounds. Being localized meant the loudspeakers were wired so the alarm first sounded in the generalized area where the C-RAM predicted the rounds would impact. The alarm started with three LOUD gong-like blasts, followed by the words "In-coming! In-coming! In-coming!". The volume of the alarm alone was loud enough to scare the crap out of anyone when it first went off. Knowing the alarm meant something was seconds away from falling out of the sky, and exploding close by, gave a little extra emphasis for your heart to try and jump out of your chest. This time the alarm sounded like it was right next to my office.

I knew that meant the camp was probably within the intended impact area, so I bolted out of the soft-sided trailer containing my office, and headed, hell bent for leather, straight for the front gate shack. The gate shack was not so much a shack, as it was an inch thick steel container, with ballistic windows. My office trailer, on the other hand, was constructed of the same material which ordinary trailer homes were made. The gate shack seemed like the best place to be at the time. Unfortunately, the door to the trailer was on the side opposite from the front gate, so making the transition required a bit of dodging and weaving. I sprinted out of the office, scrambled around the corner of the trailer, dashed across the driveway, and had almost made it to the door of the gate shack when the initial salvo hit.

At the first sound of the alarm, the main gate had initiated lock-down procedures. Those who were inside stayed inside, those who were close enough sprinted inside, and the front and back doors were closed. I say doors, but they were more like inch thick, solid steel bulkheads, and weighing over one-hundred pounds. They were not so much slammed shut as they were closed at a tectonic pace.

Rounding the corner of the trailer I saw the smallest of the guards struggling to get the behemoth door in motion. Yelling for him to hold the door I poured on more speed. Having just gotten the monstrosity up to speed, he slammed his entire body weight into slowing it for me. As I closed the distance three or four rockets exploded in front of the Palace, and a few more landed in the P.X. parking lot just in front of the camp. All of the impacts were within one hundred yards of the gate shack. Throwing my hips and shoulders sideways I bounce my back along the side of the shack, jump behind the guard, and forced myself through the narrowing gap between the guard and the door jamb.

Even before the echoes of the explosions had faded away my guard posts began checking in by radio. Initial reports related no rounds had impacted inside the WPPS camp. Pretty Damn close, but nothing inside, and as the reports continued a light breeze brought the scent of smoke and cordite wafting over the camp. Once all posts had checked in I quickly relayed the report of "no impact, no damage" up the chain of command.

We had not been getting shot at very much lately, and with the impacts of the morning's attack having been so close, so very close, I needed to get out and check my team to make sure everyone was holding steady. Distant explosions were an everyday occurrence, but rockets on our doorstep had not happened in a long time, and I was worried it may have had a significant, negative effect on the mental state and moral of my guards. I needed to ensure everyone was handling the situation as best they could, and the most effective way to do that was to walk among them.

Calm was returning to the camp as more of the WPPS leaders and managers began receiving reports from their teams that the attack had missed us. Tentatively, morning activities were returning to some sense of normalcy.

Having already checked on the Main Gate, I checked the Side Gate next. Having been just as close to the explosions as the Main Gate, I needed to make sure they were holding up. As I approached I noticed the guards were looking a little nervous, and a bit frazzled. Eyes scanning the sky for the smallest indicator of incoming, their ears were trying to pop off their heads so they could hear just a little further, but they were still holding their ground.

Crossing the compound to the Back Gate, I had closed to within twenty yards when the C-RAM alarm went off, and the guards standing around the gate scattered for cover like cats to a thunderclap. I broke into a sprint to cover the remaining distance. Unfortunately, the gate shack at the back gate was not much bigger than a phone booth and, unlike the front gate, was only made of prefabricated building material, not metal. To make matters worse, there really was not a whole lot of open space around the back gate, so hard cover was sparce. Consequently, we were trying to cram four guys, me and three guards, between the concrete outer wall of the camp and a short "Jersey curb" style barrier that had been placed next to it. That was it. That was all the space available to build hard cover; a space barely big enough for three normal sized people. Ever seen those pictures of people trying to stuff as many folks as they could into a phone booth? It was a lot like that.

The guards we employed were mostly from South and Central America; Peru, Honduras, Nicaragua, places like that, and they were usually not very tall, or very big. I, on the other hand, was almost six and a half feet tall, and weighed close to 250lbs. Needless to say I made a big target, a really BIG target, and you can imagine how space could become rather limited when you were trying to hide from a rocket. Fortunately, one of the guards realized we were running out of room quickly, and dove into the empty shell of an armored assault vehicle the motor pool had left abandoned on the other side of the street. If I lived through this, I was damned sure going to address this lack of hard cover.

We were still trying to sort out the issue of where to take cover when the second barrage of rockets impacted. They hit so fast I could not tell how many detonations there had been, but by the intensity of the explosions they sure did sound like they had impacted even closer than the first set. Before the first echoes of detonation had faded the radio came alive with reports of impacts right outside the front gate in the P.X. parking lot.

The sky was still dropping little bits of gravel and shrapnel as I untangled myself from the others sharing my little piece of safety, stood up, checked the condition of my immediate surroundings, and took off running for the parking lot. I zigzagged my way around the buildings in the camp, and ran straight through the front gate to a chorus of guards yelling in Spanish and pointing at the parking lot in front of the camp.

As I approached the gate separating the camp's parking lot from the P.X. parking lot, the guard stationed there peeked his head around the corner of the bunker next to the shack, and caught a glimpse of me bearing down on his post. Not wanting to have his machismo questioned, he pulled his head back around the corner, took a second, and then sauntered around the corner of the sandbags like he did not have a care in the world. In his hand he was bouncing a piece of metal the size of a shot glass. I slowed down as I got closer, and he tried to pretend he was just noticing me for the first time. I could tell that even though his brain was doing its best to make his body act like this was an every-day occurrence, the small tremors in his shoulders and the wobbliness of his steps were not keeping faith with the story. I walked up to him and placed a reassuring hand on his shoulder, looked at the shrapnel he now held in a less than steady hand, and asked what had happened.

It was like someone had inflated a balloon in his chest, replaced his spine with a ramrod, and vaccinated him with a phonograph needle. He held up the piece of shrapnel like a trophy, and lit off with a burst of machine gun fast Spanish that left me staring at his palm and wondering what had just attacked my eardrums. Even though I had been brushing up on my Spanish for the past year or so, the last time I really buckled down and studied was back in High School, almost twenty-five years ago. Eventually, I was able to get him to calm down to a point where he could explain, so I could understand, that he had dove into the bunker at the first sound of the C-RAM alarm. No sooner had he landed inside the bunker when the first of the rockets exploded in the parking lot, sending several pieces of shrapnel bouncing around inside the bunker with him. The piece he currently held in his hand had skipped off a couple surfaces in the bunker, struck him in the helmet, and dropped to the ground next to his face. Just talking about it seemed to drain his shakes away.

Once he had settled down a bit I shifted my attention away from the guard, and focused my sight over the expanse of the parking lot laid out in front of the camp and the P.X. I could see faint trails of smoke and dust drifting up from impact craters, and hear the sharp, piercing wails of a couple car alarms that had been triggered by the concussion of the blasts. My eyes focused on the opposite side of the lot where one of those columns of smoke was very close to the main bus stop. Not knowing if anyone had been waiting for a bus at the time of the attack, I headed over to see if there were any injuries.

One or two rockets at a time was the norm for those guys to shoot at us. For them to shoot two separate salvos at us was unusual, but had happened before, so I was not all that concerned there would be a third when I began to jog across the parking lot toward the bus stop. When the C-RAM alarm went off for the third time, it not only caught me very much by surprise, it also caught me very much exposed, and very much in the open.

The first horn of the alarm blared from every speaker surrounding the parking lot, and my heart thumped a beat so hard I thought it had just doubled in size. Beating that hard has got to put scar tissue on the heart muscle. The closest hard cover bunker was beyond the bus stop, a good thirty meters (a bit over 30 yards for you Americans) to my front, and I took off toward it at a dead sprint. No pun intended. I had barely covered half the distance when the first rocket impacted somewhere just off to my right. Something did not sound quite right about the impact, but I was not about to check it out right then. Instead, it was the second rocket hitting with a thunderous explosion that inspired me to channel my inner Carl Lewis. Just saying the word boom does not convey the force of the explosion produced by this rocket, to fully understand the force, effect, and saturation of these detonations you would have to experience the word boom.

It was a bit like standing in front of a huge speaker playing the loudest bass note ever. Combine that with standing in the surf while a huge wave passed by. A wall of sound slammed into my right side, flowed through my body, and exited the other side. I felt like my brain had been punted up against the side of my skull and, for just a second, both of my eyes went out of focus as they wobbled in their sockets. The pressure wave forced my guts to jump around inside my stomach, and like a good, hard stomach punch it drove the air from my lungs. My heart felt like a fist had just grabbed and squeezed it. The force tried to push me off balance, and I staggered for a second. A couple forced, quick gulps of air helped refill my lungs, and steady my vision. With newfound motivation I was able to kick my legs into overdrive, and burn a path toward the bunker.

As I drew closer, I realized I had no idea who might be inside, and with all the excitement and adrenalin going around I certainly did not want to surprise anyone by stampeding in. (Getting shot while running into a bunker to get away from being rocketed would simply be embarrassing). Thinking it bad form to yell "Fat guy running!", I announced myself to the bunker by yelling "One coming in!" I slid around the corner of the end cap and found there was already one of the South African dog handlers laying on the ground beside his dog, and one of the guards from the parking lot scrunched down next to the wall inside the bunker. Feeling the need to reacquaint myself with Mother Earth, I found a nice patch of ground to lie down on as well.

No sooner had I less-than-gracefully thrown myself to the ground when two more rockets slammed into the parking lot just outside the bunker. The ground trembled as the rockets detonated, and I could hear the crack and ping as small pieces of shrapnel hit the side of the bunker chipping off small pieces of concrete as they hit the outside wall. After the booms had stopped, I took a second to check myself to make sure I had not been given a few extra holes by any of those rockets. I repeatedly rubbed my hands down my torso, lifting them in front of my face after every pass so I could look at them and make sure they were not covered in blood. Next, I used the same process to check my legs and arms to make sure they were not leaking anything vital either. But why?, you say, if I had been hit with any of that shrapnel I would know it, right? Not exactly. Adrenaline and endorphins, combined with shock, have the ability to block out pain and fatigue, and can mask those tell-tale signs trying to tell you that you have been wounded. Other than being incapacitated by the wound, physically wiping your hands across your body, and visually inspecting them, was the best way to make sure you were not bleeding.

    Having completed my self-check, and coming up clean, I waited for a couple more seconds before poking my head out of the bunker to see what was going on. Finding the most explosive part of the excitement had passed, at least for now, I crawled out of the bunker and went toward the front entrance of the parking lot looking for anyone who may have been injured or needed assistance. So far there had been a five-to-eight-minute pause between salvoes. Not a long amount of time in the grand scheme of things, but remember, everything is relative. Take thirty seconds to gaze at the most beautiful person you know, the time will pass in an instant. Place your hand on a hot stove for thirty seconds, and it will feel like eternity. Each small window of opportunity between strikes provided time to search for anyone who may have been wounded. Anyone enduring their own eternity.

As I got closer to the vehicle search area (commonly called the search pit) just inside the front entrance to the parking lot, I saw two U.S. Army soldiers telling everyone to clear the area around the duck and cover bunkers next to the pit. The guards assigned to the Pit were quickly fanning out away from the bunker toward the perimeter of the lot, and one of the explosive detecting dog teams was heading in my direction. Everyone was moving with a sense of urgency, but both the dog and the handler were the only ones that had a look of shocked, confused fright on their face.

"Back off a bit, mate." The handler said as they got a little closer, "That last rocket shook my dog up something terrible." I did not think the dog was the only one shook up. Both of them had been inside the bunker when a rocket struck it. They had gotten lucky when the rocket struck the thick base of the bunker's end cap, and had not impacted directly on the thinner side of the bunker itself. Probably due to the angle of trajectory, and the thickness of the end cap's base, the rocket had glanced off and plowed a six-foot-deep hole in the parking lot pavement before exploding. At least we thought it had exploded. This must have been that first rocket impact that sounded so peculiar.

The dog team needed no further encouragement to get out of the area, but you would be surprised at how many other people had shown up, wanting to crowd around and watch the Explosive Ordinance Disposal guys (E.O.D. for short) pull the rocket out of the ground. Having taken cover in other bunkers around the parking lot, or riding out the strike hunkered down in their armored vehicles, people were starting to show up to watch the recovery now that things had quieted down.

One of the E.O.D. teams had been conducting their morning equipment and vehicle check in the parking lot when the first strike hit. By the time the second set of rockets impacted, they were all geared-up, ready to answer the call, and respond to wherever they were needed to deal with unexploded ordinance. It was only when the third salvo had been delivered that their work was, quite literally, dropped right at their feet. They never had to move their truck from its parking spot. That sure cuts down on commute time, doesn't it?

The closest E.O.D. Tech stopped my progress and challenged the necessity for me to be in the area.

"Are you the Security Manager for the parking lot?" He asked.

"No, I manage the WPPS camp." Not knowing exactly where the Parking Lot Manager was, I added, "I'm sure he's dealing with some of the other impacts. What can I do to help?"

He quickly brought me up to speed on the dud impact, and asked for assistance in getting the rubber-neckers and lookie-loos cleared out of the area. They wouldn't leave! I gathered the guard supervisor and several guards to move people back, and they still wouldn't leave! It was not until we told them we were not sure if the warhead had exploded, or not, that they remembered they were late for an appointment, any appointment, anywhere else!

As the clock ticked, E.O.D. worked on extracting the rocket from its burrow, so they could defuse the warhead. Ten minutes passed after the last attack without any more rockets. Twenty minutes passed, and no new badness had happened. After thirty rocket free minutes had passed, E.O.D. was done with their task, and the Parking Lot Manager had arrived, relieving me of my need to hang around.

By the end of the morning attack, the palace grounds and parking lot had been hit with three salvos of rockets damaging seventy-five vehicles. A few were completely destroyed. One truck in front of the palace had taken a rocket right through the windshield. Not sturdy enough to detonate the war-head, the rocket had punched through the glass, and impacted on the armored floor under the back seat blowing all the windows out, pushing the roof up, the rear quarter panels out, and generally making the whole destruction of the vehicle look like a giant popped kernel of burnt popcorn.

I later learned the warehouse behind the palace had also been hit, and set on fire, burning up most of the office supplies and toilet paper for the IZ. It is funny how, when you are a young warrior, the words of Conan the Barbarian reverberate through your head. What is best in life is to crush your enemies, see them driven before you, and hear the lamentations of their women. But as we get older, and possibly wiser, those priorities tend to shift a little until what is best in life turns into a warm place to sleep, dry socks and soft toilet paper. These insurgents really knew how to hit right where it hurts. A couple rounds had dropped short, and landed in the river, and a few had gone wide, and hit Helicopter Landing Zone (H.L.Z.) Washington. None of those had caused a lot of damage, and so far no one had been injured. However, the day was not yet over.

All of the security managers had agreed we were going to get a couple rockets shot in our direction today; it was Easter after all, in a Muslim country, in the middle of a war. But none of us had expected to receive three full salvoes! Once this last round of rockets was over, I figured we had gotten all the excitement we were going to get for the day. Pumped up by adrenaline and excitement, I deliberately walked back through the parking lot, with measured and purposeful strides, in an attempt to slow the dump of endorphins that had been pouring into my system. By the time I reached the office, my heart rate had dropped back to something resembling normal, and I was breathing more regularly. Fortunately, the day shift security manager arrived soon after, and we were able to conduct our shift change before I bottomed out. I brought him up to speed on the morning's excitement, made sure my guards had been relieved from their posts and were on their way home, and then headed for home myself.

Because Saddam's palace had been built for him to rule from, as an administrative headquarters, and not for him to live in, there was not a lot of living space inside the building. To remedy this, the State Department had a whole fleet of trailers brought over to house the people who worked in and around the Palace. They were not much, but they worked. The basic trailer looked like a mobile home on the outside and consisted of two rooms, one on either end of the trailer, with a bathroom and shower in the middle. Hundreds of them had been placed around the vast expanse of ground between the river and the back of the Palace, and were arranged in small groups. Yes, the Palace had trailer parks. Directly behind the Palace was the trailer park known as "Embassy Estates" and the group surrounding the pool had been labeled "Pool Side". Imagination did not seem to run rampant in the State Department. "Palisades" was the area east of the Palace, and I lived in the trailer park on the southeast side known as "Edgewood." To get maximum occupancy, with the minimum number of trailers, four people were assigned to each trailer, two to a room. I shared my room with the guy who was working the day shift at the camp. It turned out to be a pretty good arrangement. I got the room to myself during the day, and he had it at night.

As I walked through the front gate of the camp, and began my trek through the same parking lot that had been raining rockets so recently, a sense of contrast struck me so hard I had to stop so my brain could catch up. Where minutes before rockets had been whistling and roaring in their final flights, birds were now singing and chirping. Where detonations and explosions had been ejecting shards of steel and asphalt to rip through the air, beams of the newly risen sun were now meandering their way through the tree branches and leaves to illuminate individual patches of earth. The wail of the car alarms and C-RAM sirens that had pierced the early morning calm had now become the low rumble of traffic and the commotion of people as they began their daily transition to work.

The adrenaline rush, brought on by the chaos and excitement of the morning's onslaught, had finally bottomed out. As I gazed across the landscape, so familiar because of my daily crossings to and from work, unexpectedly thrown into havoc by the intensity of the past few hours, only to be returned to the serenity to which I had grown accustomed. I noticed my fingers and palms were turning cold, and slightly numb, as my hands began to shake. My legs were slowly turning to rubber, and were threatening to fail as the final dregs of the endorphins surrendered the last of their influence. I had been running high on adrenaline all morning. Now was the time for the bill to come due, and I was not positive my credit card would be able to cover it. The fatigue that now invaded my mind and body was so pervasive it made it more than a chore just to drag myself back to my trailer.

In a dull haze I changed out of my work clothes, and flopped onto my bed. Rocket strikes during the day had been very rare, mostly happening during the morning and evening, so the thought of getting hit again before late afternoon did not occur to me. Laying there, I did my best to clear my head of everything that had happened that morning until sleep overtook me. It felt like I had just dozed off when I was suddenly, and quite rudely, awakened by the sound of a couple very loud explosions, and my trailer being shaken like a British secret agent's martini. A key thing to remember here is that when you were in a combat zone you did not go to bed wearing anything you would not want to be seen wearing in public or, for that matter, be caught dead in. For me it was a simple pair of shorts and a t-shirt.

Jolted by a fresh kick of adrenaline, I immediately rolled out of bed, fell flat on the floor, and waited for a pause in the booms. Since this morning's attacks had come in groups, I figured this was not going to be the only set of explosions. That the explosions had shaken my trailer was also a good indication the impacts had been a lot closer than the definition of comfortable allowed for. On the flip side of that, can the word comfortable ever really be used when people were shooting rockets at you?

Information tid-bit. If you are a tobacco user, I would suggest keeping your cigarettes and lighter, or if like me a can of dip is your preferred nicotine, right next to your bed. If not, have something that will help pass the time. You never knew how long you would have to remain undercover, and if you put them in the same place every time you will be able to grab them without thinking as you make a mad dash for the bunkers.

Realizing I was never going to be able to determine the difference between a pause in the rockets, and the last rocket (movie stars can do that because they get a copy of the script, the lucky bastards), I heaved myself off the floor, ripped the door to my trailer open, and sprinted around the corner toward the concrete bunker. Having received three separate salvoes of rockets this morning, I felt it was quite possible this was only the first set in this engagement. Six of us hunkered together in the bunker, and since none of us had been privy to that script mentioned before, it took us about ten minutes to realize the last explosion was, in fact, the last rocket in this attack. A couple minutes later the "all-clear" was given over the loudspeakers, and we departed each other's company, and the safety of the bunker, for the comfort of our trailers. Now came the really hard part, since it was only 10:00 in the morning I had to try to go back to sleep!

Eventually, I was able to drift off to something resembling sleep. The kind of sleep that did not really feel like sleep but, on the other hand, you knew you were not awake. I had been floating in this "in-betweeness" for only a couple of minutes when the silence was shattered by another alarm. Immediately, I vaulted out of bed in the direction of the door. Somewhere in mid arch my brain clawed its way through the cloud of sleep, and recognized the alarm for what it was; my alarm clock. Sheepishly, my body surrendered its flight response to the authority of my brain, and I slowly trudged back across my room to turn off the alarm. It was 1530, 3:30 pm for you civilian types. I turned on the lights and the TV (yes, the rooms had TV, with cable from somewhere in Europe), flipped on the coffee maker, and went back to bed for a snooze alarm. Fifteen minutes later I lay in bed sipping coffee, and watching a little TV. Now THIS was how I preferred to wake up! Shift change was at 1800. Yes, we worked twelve hour shifts but, hey, it's not like there were very many other things to do around there, and the time finally came for me to get ready. I piled out of bed, again, and drug myself into the shower. About half way through my shower, covered in soap, I thought I heard something that sounded a lot like the C-RAM alarm going off again. "Three times in one day? No way." I thought to myself. Not sure if I was really hearing an alarm, I stepped out of the water stream, stood still, and started moving my head around to try and distinguish the sound a little better. "Did I just hear the C-RAM go off?" BOOM! "Yah, it was the C-RAM!" Crap, my luck just kept getting better and better!

Understand I was not an overly modest type of guy, but I would be damned if I was going to run out of my trailer buck naked, covered in soap. I was not, however, too proud to curl up on the floor of my bathroom, and hope like hell the rockets did not hit my trailer. If you have never done this before try getting dressed, completely soaked, lying on the floor, trying to be as tiny as possible, as fast as you can – it gets a bit tricky. I drew on my shorts, crawled into a t-shirt, and took off out of the trailer like a shot, heading for the cover of a bunker. I was still soaking wet, but at least I was modestly clad. A couple more rockets exploded before I made it to the bunker, but they were not nearly as loud as the first explosion.

When I got to the bunker there were two soldiers, an Army guy and girl both wearing their armor, already inside. Both of them looked pretty shaken up. Of course, they were not nearly as shaken up as they would have been had I come racing around the corner in my "alltogetherness", though. They could barely keep their hands steady enough to smoke a cigarette, and they seemed to think the first explosion had been very close.

Even though it had been loud, I did not think it had sounded all that close.

"Come over here and take a look." One of the troops said as they pointed out their side of the bunker. I walked to the other side of the bunker, well, not so much walked as hunkered since I am more than a foot taller than the bunker is high, and looked in the direction they had been pointing. It appeared I may have been a bit mistaken in my first assessment. The first rocket had struck the sandbags in front of the trailer two rows in front of mine. Read that as about 30 feet (just under 10 meters for you Europeans) from my nice comfortable shower. Had that rocket hit an up-draft, or had a little more fuel, my shower would have ended a whole lot differently. It did not seem to have done a lot of damage to the sandbag wall, but looking in the opposite direction, you could see the shrapnel holes all along the backs of the trailers on the other side of the sidewalk.

Trailers in the living area were lined up in opposite facing rows. The front of your row of trailers faced the front of another row of trailers and the back of your row of trailers faced the back of another row, with ten to fifteen feet between the backs. The part I found incomprehensible was the sandbag walls were only built along the front of the trailers, between the trailer and the sidewalk. The backs of the trailers were not sandbagged at all. Since one of the backwards facing row of trailers had been longer than the forward-facing row, and the sandbag wall had not been extended, the shrapnel from the rocket blew past the sandbagged front of one row of trailers and tore holes in the backs of the longer row of trailer behind it.

Another rocket from the second salvo had hit the base of a duck and cover bunker down the road as well. Three of our guards, an American contractor, and an Iraqi had taken cover there when the alarms went off. The rocket impacted at the base of the bunker wall. The explosion had torn a two-by-two foot hole through the concrete, right behind where the Iraqi had been squatting. Needless to say, the Iraqi did not fair too well. He had been squatting down, leaning up against the wall of the bunker, when the rocket impacted right below him, literally blowing his ass off. Everything from the top of his buttocks, down the back of his thighs, and down his calves had been turned to hamburger. The overpressure from the detonation had also thrown two of the guards out of the bunker, and set everyone's ears to ringing for the next couple of days.

Being at the Palace had a couple of advantages, and a couple of disadvantages. The biggest of the disadvantages was pretty obvious; we got targeted for the rockets. One of the advantages, though, was regardless of who you were, if you got injured in an attack on the Palace you got Army medical treatment. For those of you who do not understand the significance of this, think of it this way. If you had just suffered a traumatic injury, would you rather go to a hospital that dealt with that kind of injury every day, all the time, or would you rather go to a hospital that rarely dealt with that kind of situation. Army doctors here got really good at what they did, really quick, get it?

Eventually, the "all clear" was given, and I rushed back to my trailer to finish getting ready for work. Ready for my shift I made my way through the palace grounds, out the main gate, and walked across the street between the Palace and the camp, right through the parking lot where the rockets had hit that morning. I entered the camp, and met up with the day shift guy in front of the office. Since the rockets from this afternoon had all landed in or around the palace grounds there was not much for him to pass on to me. We completed the change a little after 1800 and I settled in to work for the night. The order had come down from higher for everyone to wear their helmets and vests until further notice. That meant it was not going to be a comfortable night, but I was hoping it would be a quiet one. When I say everyone was wearing their armor, I actually mean all of my guards were in helmets and vests. Being a bit taller and larger than the normal guard, a set of armor had not yet been located that did not look like a postage stamp strapped to my chest, and until this morning there had not been much of a sense of urgency to find one.

Distant explosions and random gunfire had been pretty common ever since I first came to Baghdad. Up until today, no one ever paid much attention to it, and things would settle down around 2100 (9 pm for those still not good with military time). As you can imagine, there was not a whole lot of night life in the greater Baghdad area, and it seemed the insurgents liked to get their shut-eye. With this in mind, I surmised that if we could make it to 2100 the rest of the night would be quiet.

No such luck. The clock had not quite struck 2100 when the booms started all over again – go figure. I guessed the insurgents had a few more rockets lying around, and wanted to get rid of them before bedtime. The explosions were quite significant, but way off in the distance. I had not gotten any word on where they landed, but I was sure I would. So far, you could probably say this had been a fairly normal Easter Sunday, as much as Easter in a war-torn Moslem country could be categorized as normal.

Holy Crap. How in the hell had I gotten myself into this?

CHAPTER 2

This all started about the time I decided to retire from the Army. My battalion had rolled over the berm, into Iraq, behind the main invasion in March 2003, and we had spent the next year in the Tikrit area before returning to Ft. Hood, Texas in 2004. I returned to Iraq at the beginning of 2005, with the same battalion, and this time was teaching Iraqi police at the Baghdad Police Academy. During both deployments I had met a large number of contractors who were doing the same jobs I had been doing, but for a whole lot more money. Since I already had over 20 years on active duty, I figured it was time for a career change.

Do not get me wrong, the Army was a great career. It had given me many opportunities to travel to places I would never have seen otherwise, and provided chances to do a great number of things I never would have gotten to do without being on active duty. I originally enlisted in 1983, and spent the majority of my career as a military policeman conducting operations in law enforcement, SWAT, hostage negotiations, physical security, and a myriad of combat support roles. I enlisted during the Reagan years, a time when some military members would tell you was the best time to be in the service. The cold war was in full swing, and we had a clear purpose.

Almost all of the Noncommissioned Officers (NCOs) in my first unit were Vietnam Veterans, and they were training us for the confrontation with the Big Russian Bear we all knew was going to happen. Over the next twenty plus years much would change. Operations were conducted in Grenada. The Berlin Wall came down and the city, and eventually the country, would be reunited. The Soviet Union collapsed, and the Iron Curtain disintegrated forever. Actions were taken in Panama, called off at the last minute on Haiti, and run throughout the mountains in Afghanistan. Throughout this entire time, one thing remained constant for everyone involved; being a soldier was an affair of the heart, not of the checkbook. Defending a nation did not pay very well. But I digress, and those are stories for another time.

Shortly after leaving active duty, in the summer of 2006, I dipped into my GI Bill and enrolled in a couple of college classes to finish an associate degree I had been putting off. Pro Tip – While in the military, use their tuition assistance program to get as much college as possible. The more you complete on active duty, the more G.I. Bill you will have when you get out, and the more money you will have for higher education. Toward the end of the semester, I began to realize I would not be able to afford a life of retired leisure on a military pension, so I dusted up a resume, put it out to all the web sites that favored former military, and began cruising the job fairs in the greater Ft. Hood area. Do not let anyone fool you; embarking on a major career change at forty years old is neither a fun adventure, nor a stress-free process. Fortunately, Operation Iraqi Freedom was still going full tilt boogie, and traditional methods of conducting campaigns were changing.

For years, the U.S. Military had been undergoing a series of drawdowns, and cutbacks. With the size of the force reduced by almost 500,000 troops, during my career alone, many jobs and tasks once accomplished by service members were being outsourced to civilian contract companies. I am not going to climb on a soapbox and pontificate over the intelligence, or stupidity, surrounding this reduction in force. Nor will I offer an opinion regarding the wisdom, or lack thereof, for bringing non-military companies to the fight. I am simply going to point out the opportunity this policy provided for people who had honorably hung up their uniforms to extend a career to which they had dedicated a significant portion of their lives.

Eventually, I was given an opportunity to sign on with a little security company that had been started by another group of former soldiers (not to be confused with the little security company started by a former sailor. You can figure it out.) and I was hired as a security manager for a small force of guards protecting the U.S. Embassy, and other Department of State property in Baghdad. This would be my opportunity to extend my career, as well as continue to serve my country.

It was a cool morning in December when I boarded a plane in Killeen, Texas, switched planes in Dallas, and flew on to Dulles. When I left, Texas was recovering from winter. It had lasted the better part of last week; it was brutal. D.C. on the other hand was still knee-deep in it. Once outside the airport I met up with the rest of the prospects who would be training and competing for a position in the Baghdad Embassy Security Force

(BESF, we pronounced it Bee-sef). In the beginning, there were sixteen of us. On the ride to the training site, a little raceway on the outskirts of Winchester, Virginia, I began to get familiar with the others with whom I would be spending the next couple of weeks. Most of them were former military, with several having served in the Army, a few from the Marines, and a former sailor. Their backgrounds were also very diverse ranging from Special Forces to infantry, on the Army side of the house, and recon to rifleman on the Marine side. I did not have a lot of experience with the Navy, so I never figured out what his job had been. The few remaining, without military backgrounds, all came from somewhere in the civilian law enforcement community.

December in the northern reaches of Virginia was a lot different than December in the central part of Texas. For one thing, when Texas had winter, it tended to only last for about a week at a time, and mostly consisted of a lot of freezing rain. Above the top end of the Shenandoah Valley, on the other hand, snow was a real possibility, and having spent the last six years stationed at Ft. Hood, with most of that time spent deployed to southwest Asia, the Middle East, and northeast Africa, I had lost a lot of my acclimation to the cold. Fortunately, most of our training would be conducted indoors, and the only time we would be outside was during range week. For those of you with military backgrounds, I am sure you are getting the same visual I started to get, "range weather". For those of you who do not know what I am talking about, it simply means this: if it ain't raining, we ain't training; if ain't snowing, we ain't going; and if the sun should show its face, we're inside some stink'n place.

The first week kicked off with classroom training. The curriculum consisted of the basic guard duty training any soldier would be familiar with and, we found out later, was the same training given to the guards we would be supervising. Not exactly the most exciting or challenging, it was still important because it gave us the base of knowledge we could expect from our guards. For the most part, the weather behaved itself. There were a couple of days when blizzard conditions had been forecasted for the mornings, but since we were training in classroom conditions light flurries were the most that hit us.

With the worst of the weather staying at bay we headed into week two, range week. Week one had not resulted in much competition, since the material had been pretty basic, and everyone's test scores were pretty close. We were still sixteen strong.

Week two, on the other hand, would consist of qualifying on several different weapon systems including the Glock 19 pistol, M-4 rifle, M-249 Squad Assault Weapon, M240 Machine gun, and shotgun. Again, for those of you with prior military experience, these qualification tables will be old hat. For those of you without, the pistol, rifle, and shotgun qualification tables were pretty straight forward. The silhouette target (Cardboard cut in the outline of an upper body and head) was planted on a stake at the end of the range, and you shot at it, with a designated number of rounds fired within a specified amount of time, from different distances. The 249 and 240, both machine guns, required hitting much smaller silhouettes, called tombstones, with short bursts of fire from a fixed position. Although these may sound like simple tasks, remember we were also wearing our entire kit, to include body armor with steal chest plates, and failure to qualify on any of these weapons would result in our being released from the course; meaning we would not get the job. So, no pressure.

The competition for top shot was as difficult as any I had ever shot. In my entire career I never qualified less than expert on any of these weapons and, shooting against the company I was currently keeping, I was willing to bet nothing less than my A game would keep me above middle ranking, let alone on top. Qualifications came out pretty much the way I expected, almost all of us qualified expert with every weapon. We only had one person fail to qualify with one of the machine guns, and to everyone's surprise our former sailor had never fired the M-4 in his career. Coming to this course with a certain amount of proficiency in a specific set of skills had not exactly been laid out, but it had been heavily implied. No one saw the failure to qualify with the machine gun coming, especially since the guy had been an infantryman, but no one was willing to send the sailor home without a chance. To the credit of our instructors, after a little instruction and a practice round of qualification, our "web-foot" became a wonder by qualifying two shots short of expert.

Of course, when you got one Type A personality together with more Type A's do you know what you got? A competition, and we shot the shit out of that range! One on one, group eliminations, and team shooting. Pistols, rifles, and shotguns. Timed fire, timed holster to holster, and two gun. My ego wants me to tell you I was able to rally a last minute, come from behind, dare-to-be-great victory over some of the best shooters from the special operations community I had ever competed against – it's my story, right? But I can't. The way it really went down was this: in a field of fifteen, remember we lost one after machine gun qualification, I ended up fifth. The fact that these guys were some of the best shooters from the special operations community I had ever competed against still stands. Oh, and remember all that snow that had been forecasted? I did not know if we had compiled enough good karma, or the gods of war had found our pre-combat offering of blood, sweat, lead, and gunpowder satisfactory and they chose to give us clear skies so they might better observe and bestow blessing on our training, but the temperatures during range week had risen into the high fifties, and the snow clouds never materialized. Great weather, shooting lots of guns, all in all it had been the best range week ever.

With class rankings fleshing out, we drove on to the last week; more classroom. Our first week had been about putting us through the basic guard training course; snore, boring. Week two had been shooting and scooting; energy and excitement. This week, however, was focused on supervisor training, and slammed into us like jamming a race car at full speed down to second gear.

Once again, we faced off with the greatest adversary ever confronted by mortal man in a classroom environment: the dreaded Z-monster. Many of you have already locked horns with this formidable opponent without ever realizing the true nature of your encounter – some have won, some have succumbed. For those who have never crossed swords with this vile creature of sleep, let me tell you a little about them. Stealth and camouflage are their primary method of infiltration. So good are they in their techniques that, to date, no one, victim or observer, has ever spotted one. And due to their mythical ability to remain "invisible", little documentation exists regarding their stalking habits or attack methods. I have been assured research is on-going. One thing that is known for sure is that the victim is completely unaware they are being stalked until the attack is well under way, and they begin to feel the effects of the onslaught.

Experts disagree as to whether the Z-monster is a lone hunter or hunts in packs. Evidence taken from attack scenes, combined with post-attack interviews conducted with victims, gives weight to the theory they may be pack oriented due to the fact that there is seldom a single sleep victim in any one classroom. Further evidence suggests more than one beast participates in the attack as victim testimonials regarding the initial minutes of the assault remain very consistent. Victims state their head begins to feel very heavy, possibly due to the weight of multiple Z-monsters amassing on their cranium, their vision begins to tunnel and blur, possibly due to the Z-monster's primary weapon; sleep, and they are unable to keep their eyes open. Usually, if a victim is going to realize they have become prey this is when it will happen, and the decision will be made to fold or fight. Battles of epic proportion have been known to erupt as a result of the direct contest with a Z-monster. Common martial techniques, used with varying degrees of success, include; vigorous head shaking, as if to dislodge the creature; powerful rubbing of the eyes, in an attempt to dilute the monster's sleep inducing saliva; and pinching of the skin. The only move known to thoroughly defeat the creature, and render it harmless is to stand up and move to the back of the class. It seems Z-monsters are startled by sudden movement, and are afraid of heights, causing them to immediately jump off their prey. Alternatively, losing this battle usually resulted with the prey falling into a deep, coma-like sleep. Additional ego damaging injuries like uncontrolled drooling, snoring, and being left to the mercy of the rest of the class (who are still awake) can also result.

    The last week of training proved to be a campaign of skirmishes pitting the forces of training against the legions of sleep. The instructors, steadfast and valiant, boldly lead sorties and excursions through curriculum dark and dreary. Us, their guerillas of learning, battled clash and conflict through droves of fanged and foul monsters of Z. The engagements became things of legend as class after class we went galumphing through a quagmire of State Department sanctioned material, encountering the red eyed beasts of sleep at every turn. Their jaws, they did bite; their claws, they did catch. If any fell, not a single comrade was allowed to doze for long. Not without receiving a fraction of humiliation prior to waking them, of course.

At long last our training came to an end, and we were certified as State Department trained Security Managers. We had only lost that one candidate, during range week. The competition we had all been feeling throughout our training had served the purpose to which it had been intended; our training was as much a course to teach us what we needed to know to do the job as it was an evaluation of us by our instructors. We all loaded our gear into the vans, and began the trek back home. Now that we were all certified, the next step to get us to the worksite would be a security background check. Known as a Medium Risk Personal Trust (MRPT), it was one of the lower-level security checks conducted by the State Department before allowing a contractor to deploy. Having carried a secret clearance for over twenty years, I was not worried about the outcome of my check. The thing I was curious about was the length of time it would take. With the pool of contractors ever increasing, we had been told this could take as long as six months.

When I arrived at the airport ticket counter, I asked the attendant if I could be assigned an aisle seat, for the leg room, since I was a bit taller, and a bit larger than the average person. I handed my ticket across the countertop, and the lady began to look it over. She looked it over some more. As she was about to look at it a third time, she looked up at me with a puzzled look and said, "Sir, you're in first class. I can't get you much more leg room then that." Well, imagine that – coach to training and first-class home. I was beginning to like this company more and more. Of course changing planes in Dallas/Ft. Worth, for the final leg to the Killeen Municipal Airport, put me in a plane not much bigger then my Jeep, so no first class on that leg. Not knowing how long it would take to complete my background check, I left town the next day to make the Christmas rounds. It was the 21st of December.

I made the family Christmas visits, and was back in Killeen by the 20th of January. I think that had been the longest I had ever been on vacation in my life. I settled in for the long wait by getting my old job at a local tactical retail store back, and set about getting my routine going again. Everyone from the class was bouncing emails around asking if anyone had heard anything, but so far there had been no word. One of the guys had gotten ahead of the power curve, and started his paperwork back in August. I did not know how he was able to do this but he was able to get his security clearance while we were still in class. He deployed a couple days after we graduated. Looking at the amount of time it took for his clearance to be complete, I figured mine was going to take up to March to be finished.

The company gave me a tease phone call the middle of the next week. Originally, I had told them I could deploy with 72 hours advance notice, and they called to confirm I could still do that. They still did not have my paperwork, they just wanted to know. Wouldn't you know Texas was having winter that week, and if they sent word for me to go it would have taken me a few extra days to get out of town. By Wednesday of the next week I got a call telling me all my paperwork was complete, and I would be flying out post haste. Boy, did I underestimate the time I needed to get everything done to leave. When on active duty you had a whole support network of people helping you deploy. When a civilian, it is just you. Well, I got it all done. I had pre-staged all the paperwork I needed to send out; Power of Attorney (POA), checks, change of address cards, stuff like that. Packed a bag, and a follow-on box, and got ready to go.

I left Killeen on 25 January 2007, to begin my life as a defense contractor. I flew from Killeen to Dallas/Ft. Worth, then on the Chicago. Remember the first-class ticket they had given me after the course, it was coach this time. When I arrived at O'Hare airport I had to find my way around all the terminals. Royal Jordanian Airlines was the carrier I was supposed to fly across the pond, and when I arrived at the check-in counter another American was already waiting. The clock ticked on, and as we waited for the counter to open more people began to show up. Contractors are fairly easy to spot once you know what to look for. The pants, the shirts, the way they carry themselves.

Not looking forward to a fourteen-hour flight stuffed into a little seat in coach, I upgraded my company provided ticket to business class. A thousand dollars to have some leg room, a reclining seat, and a fully stocked cheese plate sounded like a good investment. When you are as big as I am, you take all the cheese plates you can get, right? We landed in Amman, Jordan, more than half a day later, and the upgrade had been well worth it. We left the plane and were met at the ramp by a local guide the company had employed to help expedite us through customs. His help was invaluable, and within minutes we were walking through the front doors, bags and baggage in hand, and loading up the bus that would take us to our hotel. This was my first trip to an Arab country as a civilian, and so far it had been nothing like arriving on a military transport.

The drive from the airport was also a different experience. The desert stretching away from the highway was not much different from any other view in this part of the world. The rock outcroppings and hills covered in short, scrub trees were also a rather familiar scene. What took a little time for my brain to detect was, beginning with the highway we were traveling on, and extending to the houses we could see, everything looked well taken care of and very modern. This may sound a little odd if you have never traveled to this neck of the woods, so I will try to explain. My experience in the Middle East and Northeast Africa had been that they were filthy with litter. I mean it was everywhere. Paper, trash, rubbish, the whole lot of it was just left to blow around. On my first deployment to Egypt, I watched one of our Egyptian counterparts crumble up an empty cigarette pack, and toss it on the ground. When he saw me staring at it he simply shrugged his shoulders and said, without a care or concern, not to worry, the wind would take it away. As we drove on, into Amman proper, it became difficult to remember we were in a Middle Eastern country. Unbelievably, most of the signs were in English as well as Arabic.

Built on a hilly expanse separating the desert from the Jordan Valley, Amman spanned almost nineteen different hills, from top to bottom, and was one of the oldest cities in the world. We wound our way up hill and down, through ultra-modern sections, and ancient ruins until we arrived at the hotel in which we would be overnighting. I have to say the company had pulled all the stops with this one. We would be spending the night in five-star splendor, at The Meridien Hotel in downtown Amman. There were ten of us, with our company at least, on our way to Baghdad.

We were due to leave the very next day, on another RJ flight into Baghdad International Airport (BIAP, pronounced bye-op), the civilian side. I had already been to Iraq twice, courtesy of Uncle Sam and the US Army, but never as a civilian. On my first time we had driven over the berm, since that is what you did when you are invading. The second time I had flown in on a Military Airlift Command (MAC, surprisingly pronounced Mac) C-130. That flight had been in early 2005, toward the end of the second year after the invasion, and the pilot had taken a lot (read that as LOT) of evasive maneuvers on his approach to the airport. I had no idea what I would be in for on a civilian flight.

We left the hotel at 0430, local time, still jet-lagged, and made our first attempt at Baghdad around 0900hrs; only missed it by 30,000 feet. Baghdad had been socked in by a dust storm for the last three days, and I was not sure why anyone thought that would change during a two-hour flight. We circled the BIAP once, staring down into a red-brown haze, and headed back to Amman.

Nice airport in Amman, even if it was a little on the small side. We busied ourselves for a couple hours while options were weighed, and decisions were made, before they decided to put us back on the plane and try again. Like cows into a cattle car, we shuffled back into the plane, found our seats, stowed our baggage, and tried to get comfortable for the short flight. We never taxied away from the gangway. Once more, again, we got the word this flight was going to be a no-go. So sorry, we'll try again tomorrow, please collect your bags and deplane. Coming from America, we were not used to dust storms being intense enough to close down flights, and you could imagine the frustration curve infecting all the Type A personalities who had been on this plane, trying to make it to Baghdad so they could start working their contracts. Adding to the emotions was the fact that, now that we were going to spend more than one night in Jordan, we had to buy visas. A few of the contractors who could not quite keep their knuckles from dragging on the ground exchanged hot words with the ground crew, giving me and mine a great diversion to skirt the crowd, and be the first ones in line to get our visas. I guessed that boys would be boys, and proved that knuckles-draggers could be good for something outside a combat environment. With freshly stamped passports we boarded the bus for the hotel, and took the rest of the afternoon to try to kick the jetlag.

The next morning we tried the dance again, with the same results; get on the plane, get off the plane. You would think someone would have picked up the phone by now, and called Baghdad to see about the weather. After a few more hours of sitting in the terminal, we were loaded back onto the plane, and this time we actually took off. Halfway into the flight the pilot got on the intercom and told us there had been a general agreement in Baghdad that the storm was dying out, and it looked like we had a better than average chance of making it. Now, I was not a pilot, I had never worked at an airport either, but as we circled Baghdad I looked out my window, and was not all that sure that I could tell the difference between the intensity of the dust I saw yesterday and what I was seeing today. So, we circled the airport, and then we circled it some more, they kept us in a holding pattern for over an hour, and I was beginning to wonder if we were going to land or if we were going to run out of fuel and crash. Fortunately, we landed.

Remember all those evasive maneuvers I mentioned the military planes do? This civilian plane did not do any of them. The first time I flew into Baghdad was in the back of a C-130, packed in like sardines, and the flight crew had handed out airsickness bags to everyone. Even if you did not want one, you got one. If you have never flown like this before it is an experience you were not likely to forget, especially when people started losing their lunch. Imagine a rollercoaster ride where you get thrown around like a ragdoll, and you could not see anything outside of your own little space. Your guts got bounced all over the place as the plane climbed and dove. Sometimes you were crushed down into your seat, other times your butt floated off the cushion.

All it took was one person to get the puke flowing. After the first person blew chunks came those who had been holding it back by sheer force of will. Then the border line up-chuckers began to spew, and last but not least, the sympathy heavers let go. Oh, the good old days. This time? Nothing. The only thing that marked we were landing in less than friendly conditions was the airplane nosed down at a much steeper angle than usual when we started our dive for the runway.

Once on the ground, the stairs were pulled up to the plane, and we were off-loaded onto the tarmac. Another company rep met us as soon as we had gotten inside the terminal, and he walked us through customs; literally, right through. Sweet!

BIAP was in the Southwest corner of a complex of Forward Operating Bases (FOBs, pronounced fob, like the things that used to be attached to old pocket watches) known as Victory Base Complex, or V.B.C. for short, and on the West end of Route Irish, the highway running between BIAP and the Green Zone. Sometimes called the highway of death, or IED Alley, it was probably the deadliest stretch of road in the world. I had run this route more than a lot, when I was on active duty, and had gotten my fill of being shot at and having IEDs blown up at me during the trip. Thank God we would not have to ride on it this time. The Rep took us to the helipad on Victory and signed us up for a flight into the Green Zone. The flow of people to and from the Green Zone had become heavy enough, and steady enough, that helicopter shuttles had been established to supplement the workload of the ground shuttles. I did not know how they prioritized who went, and in what order, but it took us several hours before we were manifested on a flight.

Having been an MP, I was used to doing most of my traveling in wheeled vehicles of one kind or another. Patrol cars on post, and hummers for combat. This did not mean I had never ridden in a helicopter before, having been involved with the Army's version of SWAT for over 15 years we had used helicopters quite often, but those rides had been fairly short, and we had not always waited for it to land before we got out. Two helicopters touched down on the VBC pad, and we all loaded up for the trip. By this time the sun had set, and we would be making the trip in black-out conditions: no interior white lights, no running lights, no nothing. We loaded in the glaring light of the helipad, and took off into the darkness. The lights of VBC dropped away below us, and we were able to see the sprawl of Bagdad spread out in the distance.

Still climbing, the helicopter banked and started to make its run for the Green Zone. We had been in the air for all of five or ten minutes when I heard three loud pops and the airframe shudder. Even though we were all wearing ear plugs, the noise was still loud enough to be heard clearly over the chop of the rotor blades, and the clamor of the engine. The helicopter shuddered and the sky lit up in a bright flash of light. I wrapped my arms around the only available object to help me stay stable in my seat. Unfortunately, that was my luggage.

By the second flash I realized we were still airborne, bonus, and by the third flash I realized what was happening. As we crossed over the Tigris River, and entered the Green Zone, the pilot had popped flairs from the side of the helicopter. Bright, white balls of magnesium chained to parachutes; flairs were deployed as countermeasures to heat seeking missiles. Nothing reached up from the ground to try and knock us out of the air, and it was not until well after the third flair I was able to coax my heart to start beating again. Welcome to the Green Zone.

CHAPTER 3

The Green Zone, also known as the International Zone, or the IZ, was the central area in Baghdad for officials from the American State Department, the Government of Iraq (also known as the GOI), and the majority of the Command Group for the Multi National Forces – Iraq (MNF-I). The term "Green Zone" came from a military designation that used the color green to imply the area had been occupied, and declared safe and/or secure. Of course, this only applied for a given value of the words safe and secure, but when contrasted with the rest of Iraq, designated as the "Red Zone", I guess it could be considered a bit safer.

Taking up most of the southern half of the Karkh District, the Green Zone roughly occupied four square miles of west central Baghdad. Although the boundaries surrounding the Green Zone tended to shift from time to time, the one border marker that remained constant was the Tigris River. Flowing down the east side of the IZ, then curving to run along the southern side, the river bent around the largest of Saddam's palaces, and the seat of his power; The Republican Palace. The remainder of the Green Zone, not bordered by the river, was ringed with steel reinforced concrete walls (T-walls), razor wire, and chain link fences. Access was only possible by passing through a small number of highly fortified checkpoints scattered around the perimeter, and manned by a mix of Coalition Forces, American Forces, and Defense Contractors. Due to the intensity of the security protecting the IZ, the Green Zone had come to be known as the ultimate gated community.

Prior to the invasion, the area that would come to be known as the Green Zone had been the home of several government ministries, and the administrative center for Saddam's Ba'ath party. The party headquarters, along with numerous villas and other living accommodations for the more important party members, were spread out among military bases, and a small number of palaces for Saddam and his family. After the invasion, these same buildings would become the homes and offices for Paul Bremer and the Civil Provincial Authority (CPA), Coalition Embassies, military forces, and numerous other Iraqi Government agencies.

As American and Coalition forces were advancing on Baghdad many of the villas, apartments, and other houses that had become abandoned by the fleeing Ba'athists were soon occupied by Iraqis who had lost their homes due to the conflict, had been homeless in the first place, or just saw an opportunity to get out of the slums. Yes, there were normal Iraqi citizens living inside the Green Zone alongside the American forces. Most of them were just normal people; trying to make a living, feed their families, make a life for themselves. Others were not so benign in their intents.

I am sure you heard all the news agencies refer to the International Zone as "The heavily fortified Green Zone" in almost every report about Baghdad. It had gotten to the point this was the only phrase anyone ever used when mentioning the area, but it was only accurate up to a point. The "heavily fortified" part referred to the size and strength of the perimeter, as well as the complex and thorough screening and search processes everyone had to endure prior to entering. The result of all these features was a slightly higher degree of security. Soldiers did not wear their armor or helmets when walking around the IZ, although they still carried their weapons. Military vehicles and personal were required to unload and clear their weapons upon entering (it was referred to as "placing your weapon in green status." See, there's that green thing again).

The entire Green Zone was constantly patrolled as Army Military Police, Air Force Security Forces and combat patrols continually moved in, around, and through the IZ. Even still, IEDs (Improvised Explosive Devices), suicide vests, and the occasional rocket still managed to find their way inside. The Green Zone itself would probably be best described as one big military compound with shops, homes, offices, and a ton of people living and working inside. Within the big Green Zone perimeter could also be found smaller, more specialized compounds surrounded by their own walls and razor wire, requiring their own security. Picture small islands of safety in a lake of green, surrounded by a sea of red. Providing security for those islands was the job of the physical security specialist. Providing safety in the middle of a war zone was the job of the defense contractor.

I had been working this mission for over two years; guarding the U.S. Embassy, U.S. Mission facilities, residences, and the Chief of Mission (Ambassador).

Providing access control operations at all access points, many guards and I provided an environment for U.S. and coalition personnel, military and civilian alike, to live and work secure in the Green Zone.

25 March 08 – Early this morning, around 0100hrs or 0200hrs, I sat in the office on the WPPS camp, doing a little research, and it looked as though the Army and GOI had conducted some raids on Saturday to round up a bunch of the Mahdi Militia, a loose knit militia directed by exiled Shi'a cleric Muqtada Al-Sadr. It appeared this got al-Sadr's panties in a bunch, and he instructed his militia that, even though they should still observe the cease fire he had arranged with the GOI, they should defend themselves if anyone came to arrest them. It sounded like the Mahdi Militia decided the best defense was a good offense, and this was why they were shooting at us again.

A little background information would probably come in handy. The Mahdi Militia, also known as Jaysh Al-Mahdi, was a paramilitary group/militia created by the Shi'a cleric Muqtada al-Sadr. It would seem, in this part of the world anyway, if one wanted to be regarded as a person of power and influence, one needed to have their own militia. Hey, all the fashionable people were doing it. Sidebar; both Shi'a and Sunni Muslims believe in The Mahdi. Loosely defined, The Madhi will appear with Christ at Armageddon, fight along-side him in the final battle against evil, then bring peace and justice to the whole world. Can you see the implications and significance behind naming his militia Mahdi?

Initially formed from a small group of hard-core followers to "defend the faith", they first came to the attention of the world in 2004 when they began a major armed offensive against US and Coalition forces in retaliation for the banning of al-Sadr's newspaper, and subsequent attempts to arrest the cleric. After the invasion, factions of the Militia began to broaden and establish themselves as the authority in a number of southern Iraqi cities. A major contingency also moved north and began occupying a large Shi'ite community in the northeast corner of Baghdad originally call Al-Thawra, later renamed Saddam City. Against a large U.S. Army presence, the Mahdi Militia had been fighting for control of this area since 2003, and once they felt they had solidified their control over the community, even though they did not fully control the ground, they renamed the area Sadr City. Ironically, they renamed it for Muqtada's father, Ayatollah Mohammad Mohammad Sadeq al-Sadr (Not a type-O, one Mohammad wasn't enought), not him. On active duty, my platoon and I often patrolled Sadr city with some of the Iraqi police we had trained. Pictures and posters of the Ayatollah had been posted everywhere; pictures of Muqtada were much less frequent.

For the rest of 2004 the Mahdi Militia conducted attacks on US forces in cities like Najaf, Kut, Nasiriya, and Basra. More often than not, these attacks consisted of hit and run strikes, ambushes, or harassment style attacks. Eventually, al-Sadr would present himself to the cameras, addressing the political community through international new agencies, and with a great show of religious power and political posturing would call for a ceasefire. But the ceasefires never seemed to last very long, especially in the southern regions of Iraq where Sadr and his Mahdi Militia were getting only a small amount of support. On the other hand, in the Baghdad area, Militia members were gaining great influence due to the influx of Shi'a support for the battles in, and on the outskirts of Fallujah.

In the 2005 elections candidates loyal to al-Sadr in the National Independent Cadres and Elites, the United Iraqi Alliance parties, ran for office. However, the al-Sadr loyalists did not do quite as well as he had hoped, even though a few of them won elections to the Transitional Legislature, extinguishing al-Sadr's aspirations of becoming a political player and direct influence at the national level. In the two years following the election, al-Sadr and his Mahdi Militia continued to engage Iraqi Security Forces and police units in several battles, often times coming away from these skirmishes as the clear victor.

Drawing confidence from their victories over the Iraqi Forces, the Mahdi Militia began to grow strong enough, and popular enough, that al-Sadr was starting to gain the political influence he sought during the elections and was able to influence governments at the local level, control certain police forces, and become a credible bottom-up threat to the authority of the elected Iraqi leadership. Evidence was also surfacing that the Mahdi Militia, quite possibly, was becoming the driving factor behind the majority of the sectarian violence occurring in the country, and was trying to push Iraq down the road to a religious civil war. It had been in response to one of the engagements with the Iraqi police in Karbala that al-Sadr had called for the most recent cease fire between both sides, and had told his Militia to stop fighting. This was the ceasefire that was supposed to still be in effect.

Big Army had decided, even though the insurgents were shooting rockets at us, they would not fire counter-battery artillery because of the possibility of collateral damage. Instead, they had drones, UAVs (Unmanned Aerial vehicles), up and flying for the past couple of days looking for the launch sites, but this had not stopped the rockets. They hit us again today. Around 1000, I was asleep in my trailer when I heard the Duck and Cover alarm go off. To be honest, with the little bit of sleep I had been getting over the last couple of days, I was surprised I even heard it at all. On went the shower shoes, into my hands went the Skoal and cell phone, and off to the bunker I sprinted.

The Duck and Cover alarm was a little different from the C-RAM alarm. First, the C-RAM alarm started with three loud klaxon bursts, followed by the word "In-Coming!" repeated three times. This sequence was then repeated several times. The Duck and Cover alarm, on the other hand, started with the words "Duck and Cover!" repeated three times, followed by the words "Seek Cover!" Secondly, whereas the C-RAM was an area and event specific localized warning, the Duck and Cover alarm was a more general warning, and was manually initiated as a non-specific call to seek cover for any number of reasons, not just in-coming. Since this was only the Duck and Cover alarm, I did not have the great sense of urgency that would accompany a C-RAM, but I was not taking my time either.

I did not hear any booms for the next four or five minutes, so I figured it was clear to head back to my room. When I got there, I noticed something extremely unusual – silence. The AC, a buzz and hum so constant and ubiquitous my brain had eventually dismissed it, was no longer running and the lights would not turn on. Great, no power, ergo, no AC. This had happened the other morning, and a faulty circuit breaker had been the cause. I checked the circuit box, but everything there was in order. Unknown to me at the time, a rocket had impacted in my housing area right before the alarm had gone off, and I had slept right through it. The rocket was launched from across the river, and had flown directly toward row

55; I lived in row 44, a mere 9 rows beyond the intended impact site. Instead of impacting in someone's trailer, the rocket had struck a pole, cracked the top of the pole off, and been deflected right into the generator that powered the Edgewood trailers, and the chow hall. Why the duck and cover alarm had gone off, and not the C-RAM alarm? I had no idea. Welcome to the confusion of a combat zone. It looked like every silver lining truly did have a dark cloud.

Realizing there was nothing I could do about the power problem I went back to bed. Around 1500, the C-RAM alarm went off, and this time with a great sense of urgency I did the bunker run one more time. For the next hour we played this dance off and on. The "All Clear" would sound, I would head back to my trailer, and about the time I got comfortable the C-RAM alarm would go off again. Of course, the power was still out, and things were starting to warm up a bit. Surprisingly, the trailer had remained fairly cool during the coolness of the spring morning, but now that it was reaching the afternoon heat the cool was quickly starting to wear off.

Another information tidbit... The palace was located in the southeast corner of the Green Zone, and was nestled up against the right bank of the Tigris River, right where the river curved around to the west. Surrounded on three sides by water, Iraqis claimed this location had been chosen because the bend in the river created a microclimate that kept the building and grounds slightly cooler than the surrounding city during the summer. This may have been true, but without air-conditioning the inside of my trailer was turning into an easy-bake oven, and was starting to get uncomfortably warm.

Without power, the water pumps were not working either, which meant there was no running water in the trailers as well. Great! No shower! Washing with bottled water was nothing new for me; we had to do it for the first few months after the invasion, but it seemed it was the fine details that always slipped the mind first. For those of you lucky enough not to have encountered this before, let me explain. The shower was in the bathroom, of course, which was in the center of the trailer. There were no outside windows in the bathroom so when the power went out they got dark. Really dark! Additionally, room temperature water tastes like it is warm, right? Wait until you dump that water over your head. Only one word describes it – shrinkage! We used to set camp shower bags and/or water bottles out in the sun to warm them before washing. In Iraq, it did not take long for that to happen. Taking the water right out of a dark closet, well, you get the idea.

Stripped down, I stepped into the shower stall, uncapped the first bottle, and poured the contents over my head. Soap and washcloth in hand, I began at my shoulders, thankfully not with my face. Almost immediately, the C-RAM alarm began blaring, and the place started to go boom again. I thought it a good idea to change my shower time for the next couple of days. Dropping straight down, I rode out the storm curled up on the floor between the shower and the toilet, squeezing myself up toward the front of the trailer in an attempt get as close to the sandbag wall on the other side as I could. I lay in the dark and the heat until the rockets stopped exploding, and the alarm stopped wailing. I lay there long enough to become reasonably certain the rockets had stopped falling. It took just a little bit longer for me to get my nerves under a sufficient amount of control so that I could finish my bottle shower, get dressed, and get the hell out of Dodge.

Leaving my trailer I walked down the sidewalk, passed the bunker, and began to weave my way through the other trailers as I headed for the chow hall. I had almost made it all the way there when I realized I had not seen anyone else walking around; a bit strange for this time of day. As I rounded the last corner I saw a large group of people standing around one of the bunkers outside the back door of the chow hall. It seemed the "All Clear" had not yet been sounded after the last C-RAM Alarm. Oh well, I had come this far, and I did not see a reason to slow down now. Keeping with the idea that if you looked like you knew what you were doing people were not going to question you, I strode past the bunker and walked into the chow hall. With the power still out, they had not been able to prepare any hot food, and the dinner menu consisted of sandwiches and sodas; not much but at least it was something. Sitting in the chow hall there were two more alarms accompanied by several far-off booms, a rather busy afternoon. Finishing my room-temperature repast, I did the bunker shuffle to the side entrance of the Palace.

If I have not described the bunker shuffle yet, here is how it went. A duck and cover bunker consisted of an upside-down U-shaped piece of steel reinforced concrete, about six feet wide, under six feet tall, and ten feet long with pre-formed concrete barriers placed a couple of feet in front of the openings to cover the ends from blasts and shrapnel. Together, these pieces made up the interior of the structure, and the rest of the bunker was supposed to be built around it. The harder bunkers, the ones that had been completed, had been covered with layers of sandbags to help absorb the impact. The bunker shuffle consisted of looking out of the bunker you were in, or standing next to, finding the next bunker along the route you wanted to walk, and heading straight for it. Before starting your transition, though, you needed to identify the half-way point between the two. As Flight Attendants will tell you, the closest exit may be behind you. This process was repeated until you made it to your destination.

I decided it would be safer for me to get to the office by cutting through the Palace, instead of doing three to five second rushes across the palace grounds. Smart for cover; not for time. Once inside the Palace, they would not let me back out again until the "All Clear" had been sounded after the last alarm, and I did not remember hearing it. Oh well, at least I was inside under hard cover. Eventually, I was able to make it the rest of the way to work where I found one of the rockets from earlier today had scored a direct hit on one of the helicopters parked on the HLZ. Shrapnel from the explosion had ripped through a couple more birds parked on the apron, causing varying degrees of damage, and the contracting company responsible for the choppers would be flying the rest of them over to BIAP for the rest of the night.

At last, a bunch of Army teams finally showed up, and would be heading out tonight to try and scoop up the guys who had been shooting at us. Al-Sadr had threatened to take the leash off his Mahdi Militia if we started to pick any of them up, and since I doubted the raids on the launch sites were going to stop anytime soon, I guessed things could wind up getting a little interesting over the next couple of weeks. My question was; when was the Iraqi government going to put a leash on al-Sadr?

26 March – This was not all that much fun anymore. We had a 107mm rocket impact and detonate on the WPPS camp this morning.

Once again, I was out making my last round of post checks before shift change when the C-RAM alarm went off. The thing to understand about the WPPS camp was there was a whole lot of stuff; buildings (prefabricated type, not hard construction), MILVANs, equipment, vehicles, etc., packed into a really small camp. The problem was, with all this stuff there was not a lot of room for things like walkways and bunkers. It was through one of these areas, an area without bunkers, I was walking then the alarm went off.

If you ever happen to find yourself in a war zone, one of the things to keep catalogued in your brain was the location of the bunkers, and other forms of hard cover around you. The WPPS camp was small enough, and the bunkers were sparse enough, that it was not difficult to remember the location of every one of them, and I was nowhere near any of them. CRAP! I did the only thing I could do. I squatted down next a big block of cement, stuck my fingers in my ears, tucked by head down between my legs, and prepared to kiss my ass good-by.

I was hunkered down somewhere between the side gate and the back gate when the rocket came in and detonated somewhere around the back gate. Shit, that was loud! I waited a few more seconds to make sure this rocket did not have any friends following close behind, and took off for the back gate. At the sound of my approach the guards poked their heads out from behind their cover, like prairie dogs, gave me a thumbs-up to say everything was good, and started pointing around the corner toward the logistics warehouse. It was early enough in the morning I was pretty sure there would be no one inside.

As I rounded the corner of one of the MILVANs I got my first look at the impact site. The rocket had detonated roughly twenty feet up in a tree, right next to the side of a building. With the rocket exploding that high off the ground, it had sprayed shrapnel a lot further than a normal ground burst would have. Leaves, twigs, and branches lay strewn everywhere. Great chunks of aluminum siding had been torn from the side of the warehouse, and all the windows under the eaves were shattered. The MILVANs surrounding the impact site had taken the lion's share of the shrapnel, and the sides facing the explosion looked like they had been shot with a shotgun, about a hundred times each.

Hearing movement off to my right, I shifted my gaze away from the destruction, and headed toward the commotion. My worst fear was one of the Loggy Doggies, logistics folks, had arrived early for work, and caught some shrapnel. Unclipping the radio from my pistol belt, I called my Guard Supervisor, and instructed him to bring a team to secure the scene. Leaving the blast sight I walked down the long end of one of the containers, drawing closer to the noise I had heard. As I walked I noticed this one did not appear to have any damage to it. That was a good sign. Clearing the end of the MILVAN I caught motion out of the side of my eyes. Glancing down to my left I found three people, two women and a man, huddled up against the big, aluminum doors of the container, packed together in a tight bunch, with their fingers in their ears.

They had not heard me approach, and the woman closest to me almost jumped out of her skin when I squatted down, placed my hand on her shoulder, and asked, "You guys alright?" Slowly recovering from a second shock to their system, they hesitantly stood up. Heads nodding, and murmuring to themselves, each attempted to take inventory of the situation, and evaluate their status within it.

Having not really gotten a definitive answer yet, I asked again. "You guys alright?"

"It looks like it." The first woman answered in a more confident voice.

Now on their feet, I recognized them as three members of the camp's logistic team. They had decided to show up for work a little early and catch up on a backlog of work that had been stacking up. One minute earlier, their dedication may have cost them their lives.

"Can you guys conduct a search of your warehouse for me?" I asked. "Check and make sure no one is inside and hurt?"

"Yah." "Sure." "No worries, we got it." Came their responses, and off they went.

With the immediate need to check for wounded met, I turned my attention to the next task. The Operation Center in the Palace needed to be notified of this impact, so I pulled out my cell phone and called our company representative in the TOC. "Impact on the WPPS camp, next to the logistics warehouse. Right now it looks like property damage only. I need EOD and RSOs to respond, I'm establishing a cordon at this time."

The Operation Center, also known as the Tactical Operation Center (TOC for short, pronounced tock), was the central controlling station for all tactical operations involving State Department property and personnel. They tracked the attacks, dispatched responders, and generally kept tabs on everything going on in the State Department's area of responsibility. With my notification complete, the TOC started getting the initial responders moving, and I started getting my guards into position. This was about the time things started to get a little complicated. Up until about a month ago, the company with the WPPS contract had also been providing security for the camp as well. For some reason, the State Department had pulled the camp security portion of the contract away from them, and had awarded it to the company I was working for. I would like to think that, even though we worked for different companies, we could still work together as professionals. Yah, right.

No sooner had I gotten the cordon established, to secure the blast site, than the first of the people living in the camp started to show up wanting to "sight see" the damage. "But I live here; I should be allowed to look at it," was the first explanation they tried. "Not until the RSO and EOD have cleared the site."

"But I'm a first responder and I need to make sure no one is injured," was another common excuse they would try. "The guards and I have already cleared the area, and the warehouse has been cleared. No one was in there. Unless you are an RSO, EOD, Head of Logistics, or the Program Manager, I need for you to clear this area, and make room so those folks I just mentioned can get in and do their job." No matter how much we told them to stay back, they just kept trying new reasons to get inside the blast site. Fortunately, the RSO arrived rather quickly, and folks soon realized they were not going to be let in. I understood they lived here, and they wanted to help, but enough was enough. To add insult to injury, all the MILVANs that had been damaged were refrigerator units storing food for the camp. Not only were the refrigerators destroyed, but all the food inside of them had to be dumped since there was no real way to determine what had shrapnel in it and what did not.

Last night the Iraqi Army conducted raids on the Mahdi Militia in Basra. Reports said they were looking to round up the main instigators of the rocket problems we had been having. They may also have been looking to put the habeas grab-ass on al-Sadr himself. Rumor had it al-Sadr had told his field commanders to go on alert, and get ready to strike against the "occupiers." Well, his headquarters in Najaf told them to do that anyway. It was still not clear if al-Sadr was still in Iraq or hiding out in Iran.

We had an alarm activation, or an explosion, almost every two hours today while I was trying to sleep. About the time I would get comfortable, and was about to fall asleep, the C-RAM alarm would activate, and I would have to grab all my crap and head out to the bunker.

This bunker I had been running to all week was about 25 feet from the front door of my trailer, but of course it was not in a straight line, or over smooth ground. The routine went something like this: sit up in bed, slip on my shower shoes, grab my cell phone and Skoal (all in one scoop), run out the door, hang a right, and head down the sidewalk between the sandbag walls. Just before getting to the end of the wall of sandbags was when I usually heard the rocket fly overhead. Falling flat on my face, I would stick my fingers in my ears, and lay prone. This was usually all the further I would get before the first rockets impacted. Then I would wait for the ground to stop bucking, and crap to stop falling, pick up, run over loose gravel, and throw myself sideways into the bunker. Again, I had to do all of this in shower shoes, and within the first couple of seconds after waking up. It usually took around fifteen minutes for the "All Clear" to be given before I could head back to my room, and the process would start all over again.

At one point today, the Operation Center had to come over the loudspeaker and tell people to clear off of the second-floor balcony over the front entrance to the Palace, and take cover. A rocket had detonated in the parking lot in front of the Palace, destroying another vehicle – same place as the popcorn explosion, different truck this time. A bunch of people inside the Palace had run out onto the balcony, and started taking pictures of the wreckage, only to have to stampede back inside when the next set of explosions happened. What the hell were these people thinking? This was probably a self-correcting problem, though. Let one more rocket land on the palace after they had run outside, and we would see how many of them ran back inside, if any of them were able to run at all.

I was finally able to fall asleep this afternoon, and slept until 1500hrs, when I was awakened by yet another explosion. You know it was getting bad when I thought since the rocket had already detonated, was there really a reason to get out of bed? I rolled over and went back to sleep for a few more minutes.

I was still without a helmet and vest, so this afternoon I drove over to the administrative office to see if I could pick up a set of body armor. As I suspected, they still did not have anything in my size, so I returned to the Palace, and headed over to the palace grounds office to catch up with the Palace Day Shift Security Managers. Collectively, we decided our best course of action would be to head over to the chow hall before the five o'clock fusillade started. That way we would already be under cover when the booms began.

While we were eating, the TOC (if I have not already told you, it is pronounced like the opposite of Tick) came across the PA system to announce they would start shuttling people over to the N.E.C. (New Embassy Compound being constructed on the other side of town) if anyone wanted to sleep in the hard buildings they were building over there. Great idea for the night sleepers, but what about us day sleepers? I did not think anyone was thinking about us.

Fortunately, later in the afternoon my boss brought me a set of body armor big enough to fit me, so now I had some armor. The Five o'clock fusillade was a little late today, it hit a little after six. In all the confusion and excitement that followed one of the WPPS guys backed his truck into one of his teammates, pinning him between the truck and a MILVAN.

If all the rockets today were not enough, Iraq was playing Kuwait in a soccer tournament tonight, and around here they took their soccer VERY seriously. A warning had gone out to everyone saying if the Iraqis won, expect celebratory gun fire. Here is how this one worked; in celebration of, well, just about anything, these people tended to shoot guns up into the air. The bigger the event, the more people would be shooting, hence more bullets going up. They called it "Allah's fireworks", although I did not know where Mohammed ever spoke of the holy AK-47. We called it happy fire. In their opinion, when the bullet came down, where it landed was in God's hands, and if you should get struck by one it was God's will. Basically, it fell into an old Arabic saying, Insha

Allah or, "if God wills it." A little more on this quaint little saying a bit later, but for now, if this was not the epitome of not taking responsibility for one's own actions, I did not know what was. I am also not going to comment on the wisdom, or more specifically the lack thereof, in this particular practice. Suffice it to say, do not wonder why these people were not world leaders. Thankfully, Iraq lost. No happy fire tonight, guys.

With only three hours of sleep today, tonight was going to be a long night. I had a bad feeling a nap was coming on.

27 March '08 – And the hits just kept on coming. I never did get that nap last night. I had been able to close my eyes a couple of times, but was never able to fall asleep. What rest I did get was enough to help recharge my batteries. It was not enough to top them off, but it did take a bit of the edge off. It was a good thing too, since dealing with all the madness and mayhem I had been getting a little on the twitchy side. I think the problem was a little more about having sleep deprivation than it was about getting shot at. Chief, one of the other Security Managers, seemed like he

was doing a bit better today as well. He had been looking a little twitchy too.

Chief, a retired Air Force Chief Master Sergeant, was one of the grand old men of the project. Standing a little shy of six feet, you could still see his military background in his posture and stride. To look at him, you would not guess he retired almost twenty years ago, and was well into the back half of his fifties, that was until you got to the much more salt than pepper hair on his head. Normally, he had a great sense of humor on him, and was more than willing to pass on tidbits of information, as well as some of the tradecraft skills he had acquired along the way. Someone call a jeweler, Chief is dropping gems of wisdom! Lately, though, he had been showing the signs of getting just a little stressed. But then again, so were almost all of us.

There had been a couple of times yesterday when we had heard a loud thump that sounded an awful lot like a launch. Chief would get a wild look in his eyes, and pretty much run right over the top of anyone standing between him and hard cover. He had been getting a little spooked since he was the day shift Security Manager for the Palace Grounds, and most of the rockets had been falling on his venue. Not only had he responded and delt with all the impacts during the day, his trailer was also in Edgewood, and he had to react to anything coming in at night. Needless to say, he had been seeing just what those rockets could do. For me, it was one thing when I was working over at the N.E.C. last year, knowing back then the rockets were coming in, but not having any of them drop close. It was a completely different thing to be working, and even more so sleeping, where those rockets were landing.

They did not shoot at us this morning. Yah! Fine by me! We were expecting the "Good Morning, Baghdad!" rockets, but they never showed up, and we began to kick around the idea that the insurgents may have decided to call this whole thing quits; yah, right. The bad guys had settled into a routine for when they would shoot their rockets at us. Usually, they hit us around an hour, or so, after the morning call to prayer had finished wailing, and since they had broken that pattern today, we could only hope. I went back to my hooch, and was asleep by 0800. It was around noon all the noise started again, with most of the rockets landing in places other than where my trailer was, which was alright by me. Something got hit pretty well, and sent a lot of black smoke wafting up into the sky for a while. The explosion had been pretty loud, and we thought that it may have hit the fuel tanks over by the helipad. I forgot to ask at shift change, but since there was not a big, smoking crater at the end of the runway, it looked like it was not the tanks.

We had three or four more alarms between noon and fourteen-hundred today, but they were all somewhere else, and I was able to get a short nap before the alarm clock went off at fifteen-hundred. Boy was it a chore just to get out of bed, turn on the coffee pot, the TV, and the lights. Snooze alarms could be so friendly. It was nice to just lie in bed and drink a cup of coffee, take my time in the shower, all the usual morning stuff. I still did not wish to push seventeen-hundred, just in case they decided to launch the Five o'clock fusillade, and was up and dressed a little before.

I stepped onto my front porch, and pulled my cell phone from my pants pocket so I could call Lippy, my roommate and day shift Security Manager at the camp. When the rockets first started falling, the order had gone out for all of us to wear helmets and vests until further notice. Since the order had already been in effect for about a week, I wanted to see if there had been any updates. No sooner had Lippy answered his phone when I heard three distinct thumps that sounded suspiciously like launches. "Don't worry, it's outgoing, dude." Lippy said.

I was about to reply when my ears were assaulted by what sounded like a 747 trying to land on my trailer as one of the rockets flew overhead. With instant realization I screamed into the phone "Bullshit! That's incoming!" and bolted off the porch in the direction of the bunker. I had not made it more than two steps when the first rocket slammed in, and detonated. The force of the explosion rocked the air, and sent dust and dirt flying off the sandbag wall on either side of me. The concussion hit me hard enough to knock me off my feet, and sent me sprawling across the sidewalk, only stopping when I slid up against the side of the sandbag. I rolled flat on my stomach, dropped my forehead to the ground, shoved my fingers in my ears, and waited for the rest of the impacts.

The next two rockets hit like freight trains. Oh, for the love of God, they were loud! I picked myself up off the ground, and sprinted the rest of the way to the bunker. As I rounded the corner, and headed inside, I realized I still had my phone in my hand, and had not hung up. "Lippy! Lippy! Impacts in Edgewood! Send the extraction teams and first responders!" Those explosions had been just too loud to have landed anywhere else.

Hanging up the phone, I sat in the bunker for a couple of seconds before realizing it was going to take a while for anyone else to show up. The longer it took help to arrive decreased the chances for anyone wounded by those blasts to survive. Doing the math, I figured no one was going to respond faster than I could, so I gave up the safety of the bunker. At least I could get a start on looking for survivors, assess damage, or help direct first responders when they arrived.

The All Clear had not yet sounded when I ran back to my trailer, strapped on my helmet and vest, and took off in the direction of the explosions. As I headed for the impact site a group of Air Force Security Police showed up, with a few RSOs, and a couple of medics in tow. Preparing ourselves for the worst, we fanned out and headed toward the back of the trailer park. We only had to go a couple of rows behind my trailer before encountering debris splayed out on the ground in front of us. Turning the corner, entering one of the rows, we caught our first glimpse of the carnage. One trailer had taken a round right through the roof. The explosion had torn the trailer in half, throwing one half up onto the top of the sandbag wall, and tossing the other half backwards.

Since the only protection the trailers had were five-foot-tall sandbag walls along their front, the explosion had pushed the back half of the trailer a good ten feet back, to crash into the back of the trailer behind it. Shrapnel had ripped and torn gaping holes throughout the adjoining trailers. Two of the RSOs climbed into the broken pieces, while the rest of us searched underneath. Within a few seconds it was easy to determine this trailer had been empty, and no further search was necessary.

The stench of high explosives hung heavy in the air, and black smoke drifted low across the carnage as more First Responders began arriving on the scene. Without needing to be told, small groups of men and women began forming into breaching and extraction teams. Once gathered, they started busting down doors to get into the damaged trailers. We were looking for anyone who may have been inside at the time of the strike. At the worst, we were looking for anyone seriously injured and trapped. At the best, there would be no wounded, and we would only find the trapped, or the dead. Considering this to be the best scenario probably does not sound right to anyone who has not been to war, or worked in a hospital, but in the medical field they call it triage.

Triage is the process medics use to determine the priority of patients for treatment, and evacuation. It was also the same system we used to achieve the same goal. Casualties with wounds that threatened life, limb, or eyesight got the most attention from the medics, and were prioritized as the first to get evacuated to the hospital. Casualties with wounds that did not present an immediate threat, whose wounds were minor, or needed less immediate treatment were moved accordingly down the scale. Casualties with wounds so severe they would most likely die, regardless of the amount of medical care they received, or how fast they received it, and those who had already died, well, I hate to sound callous, but they were beyond our help, and went to the bottom of the list. I know this sounds pretty heartless, but First Responders could not devote time to a casualty who was going to die anyway when they could focus that attention on a casualty whose life they could save. We did find one guy in a trailer that had taken the brunt of one of the explosions.

Needless to say, he was triaged at the low end of the scale, and set aside for later recovery.

One of the rockets had slammed through the rear wall of his trailer, before punching through the floor, and detonating on the ground underneath. Most of the floor had been blown up, and away from the foundation. Chunks of the walls were ripped away, and scattered pieces of ceiling tile and insulation lay strewn about, smoldering and smoking. Bits and pieces of furniture had been launched by the detonation, and we found one of the bed frames sticking through one of the sidewalls. The other bed had been tossed against the front of the trailer. It was under the mattress we found him.

Since the rockets had started falling, some folks had taken to wearing their helmet and vest pretty much all the time, even when they were sleeping. This guy had been one of those people, and the areas covered by his armor had been well protected, and remained uninjured. Unfortunately, the other areas of his body had not fared so well, and the sheer number of wounds to the exposed areas were more than life could handle. The pattern of his wounds suggested he had been lying in bed, hopefully asleep, when the rocket detonated. I truly hoped he never knew what hit him.

By this time enough First Responders had arrived on scene we were able to clear several rows of trailers at a time. When a rocket impacted inside one of the trailer parks, shrapnel tended to rip through several trailers at a time. Due to the presence of the sandbags the destruction usually remained focused, and localized to only two rows. When multiple rockets blew up inside a trailer park the carnage got spread around, a lot, and all over the place. This meant we had to get into a bunch of trailers, and get into them quickly, if we wanted a fighting chance to save anyone's life.

I would like to tell you the process of clearing a trailer after a multiple rocket strike was a well-choreographed operation, but not so much. The pure size of the endeavor, combined with the urgency to rescue anyone injured by the detonations, or trapped by debris thrown around by a butt load of high explosives and shrapnel tended to make prior planning a little difficult. Organization happened at the team level, and teams moved around the dance floor following the tempo of their own band. The situation dictated the cadence and the beat. Coordination between teams controlled the flow. The dance was comprised of a few tactics, loose enough to allow for a small amount of personal expression, and executed with the use of a couple special tools.

The first, and most basic tool we used was one that should be familiar to just about everyone. The long handled five-pound sledgehammer. When applied correctly, there were very few things that could withstand its direct attention. The second tool in our arsenal was a piece of equipment every Fire Fighter and SWAT Officer has affectionately come to know as the hooligan tool. The proper name for it is The Halligan Bar, but hooligan tool speaks to the soul and purpose of this piece of equipment. It was designed as a prying, twisting, punching, or striking tool. It did to doors what food processors did to vegetables. Imagine a three-foot-long, fifteen-pound steel bar. Imagine that bar topped with a three-inch adze attached at a ninety-degree angle. Imagine a four-inch spike offset to the adze. The other end of the bar ended in a forked claw, like on the back of a claw hammer. This was the hooligan tool. Chances were better than good anything that could stand up to the sledge, would fall to the hooligan.

The simplest tactic we used for clearing a structure, or area, was to start at the beginning, and stop when we were done. Sounds easy, almost Zen like. Right? Trust me, it could get very confusing. The key words to remember here were systematic, and thorough. For an area search, start searching from the greatest destruction, and work your way out. If enough search teams were available, have others working from the outside in. Clear trailers in a straight line, one right after the other (dare I say, systematically?), and do not jump around. It was a rookie mistake to break off your search because someone else found something, and you wanted to go help. You would never be one-hundred percent certain exactly where you broke off when you returned to search your area.

Search your area completely and, here it comes, thoroughly. The area you skipped over may just be the place where someone was lying unconscious, and bleeding out. As each trailer was searched, and found empty, it was clearly and plainly marked as having been cleared. Usually with spray paint. The team then gathered up their gear, and moved off to the next trailer. And so it went until every trailer was searched. It was kind of like eating an elephant; one bite at a time.

Each search team usually consisted of an R.S.O. (I will tell you more about these guys in a little bit), a medic or two, an Air Force Security Policeman, and/or one of our Security Managers. This was why Chief had been getting so twitchy; lately he had been the Security Manager at every incident. When the team arrived at the door to one of the trailers to be searched one person would yell, "Is there anyone inside?" while they pounded on the door. If someone answered the door, mission accomplished. We got them out of the area, and drove on. If no one answered the door, we went to step two.

Step two basically consisted of getting into the trailer by any means possible. Checking to see if the door was unlocked was always a good start. If so, you were in. If not, that was when things got difficult. Since the door frames were made out of metal, it usually took a couple of good applications of the sledgehammer, or hooligan tool, to pry them open. Once the door was open, everyone piled into the room, and bounced everything inside. All the closets were opened, the beds turned over, and anything stacked high enough to hide a body got torn apart. Quick and thorough were the key words here when someone's life might be hanging in the balance. Subtlety pretty much went right out the window.

We were still knocking down doors, and looking through trailers, when the C-RAM alarm went off again. Great! Bad juju time for everyone! There were a couple dozen, thirty or more, people currently clearing just this row of trailers. At the sound of the klaxon everyone scrambled out of the trailer they had been clearing, instantly jamming the sidewalk with people. Every head scanned left and right, frantically looking for the closest, most direct way out of the corridor of sandbags. The realization of our predicament became apparent. I could almost see the exact instant everyone crammed onto that sidewalk came to the same conclusion I had. There was no way we were all going to make it off this sidewalk, and into a bunker before the rockets hit. Total clarity can be a real bitch sometimes.

Having no other option, each one of us unceremoniously threw ourselves to the ground. Wiggling around, like a bunch of worms, everyone squirmed to make room for the next person. Desperately, I hoped the sandbags would be able to withstand another strike, and we could ride out the worst of the attack lying prone on the sidewalk. Once again, the jet-like roar of a rocket engine drowned out the shriek of the alarm as the first missile screamed over our heads, and crashed into a trailer just behind me, and off to my right. The force of the detonation caused the majority of the trailer to instantly disappear. The thunder crack of the explosion was deafening, even though I had my fingers stuffed in my ears; all the way up to the first knuckle.

Shrapnel and debris slashed through half a dozen trailers on either side of the impact site, destroying everything inside them, including most of the trailers. The concussion wave struck. With the force of the shock the sidewalk underneath me bucked and heaved, like a bronco crossed with a bulldozer. Dirt, dust, and debris erupted into the air adding a brown tinge to the black acrid smoke produced by the explosion. And the sandbags held! They absorbed the majority of the shrapnel that had been heading in our direction. The rest, along with most of the detonation force, had been blown down into the ground, or deflected back into the air. Hot metal, dirt, plywood, aluminum siding pieces, and other sundry bits of junk came raining down on our backs. I cringed, waiting for the bathroom sink to drop.

The trailer that took the direct hit disappeared. It simply disappeared. One second it was there, and the next it was gone. Completely. The concussion of the blast had blown down, toward the ground, and the shrapnel had blown up, into the trailer. As the shock waves hit the ground they had bounced back up, and blew the rest of the trailer across several rows. Where there had once been a relatively smooth row of trailer roofs, there was now a big empty space filled with sky, and the pungent stink of high explosives.

Up until now the insurgents had been shooting 107mm rockets at us. The 107mm was a rocket with roughly a seven-inch diameter (exactly 107mm), capped by a fairly decent sized warhead containing approximately three pounds of explosives (1.3 kilograms for you Europeans). Debris later retrieved identified this had been a 240mm rocket, which was why the damage had been so widespread, and devastating. A 240mm rocket, as you guessed, had a 240mm diameter, and packed a 45-kilogram warhead. You math geeks can figure out the inches and pounds.

The sky continued raining down on us as two more shock waves rocked the ground, indicating two more rockets had finished delivering their bad news. For what seemed like minutes, but was most likely seconds, I waited to see if any more bad news was going to arrive. Nothing bad happened. I heaved myself up, off the pavers, and started to make good my escape. Several others had decided this was a good time to get off the X, and were beginning to pile out of our impromptu cover too. Ensuring I did not run over the guy in front of me, or get run over by those coming up from behind, I looked down to notice someone was still lying face down on the concrete. Hands clasped over the base of his neck. It was Chief.

"Hicks!" I yelled "We are leaving!"

I reached down, slid my left hand under the base of his armor, grabbed the scruff of his vest with my right, and lifted him off the sidewalk, onto his feet. Everyone else was already up and moving, and I did not want him getting trampled by the throng of people stampeding to vacate the area. Information tidbit: without proper training and experience, a regular person might succumb to the effects of adrenaline and excitement, and seriously underestimate the amount of strength they were applying to a situation. Fortunately, I have had them, and when I picked Chief up off the ground, I really did not throw him all that far down the sidewalk ahead of me... regardless of how he tells this story.

Aided by the additional momentum Chief got his legs underneath himself, and we tore down the sidewalk, exiting the bullseye with a quickness. For a man in his mid to late fifties, all the girlies say he's pretty spry, for an old guy. I was ten, maybe a bit more, years Chief's junior, and not all that out of shape myself, but I found it tough just keeping up with him as every living soul trapped on that sidewalk heaved themselves off the ground, and took off running for the nearest bunker. Charging into its safety, gasping for air, our entire group panted for breath like we had just sprinted a marathon.

Bent forward, gulping down breaths of air, hands gripping his thighs just above the knees, Chief turned his head to look at me as I hefted my arms over the top of the bunker's endcap, hung my head between my shoulders, and tried to feed my oxygen starved lungs.

"Fall back and nuke 'em from orbit. It's the only way to be sure."

Something else never seemed to fail. Why was it during any highly emotional, adrenaline-charged situation there was always that one guy who had to yell "GO, GO, GO, GO!" as fast and loud as humanly possible? That Guy was there too.

It was hard to say just how many rockets had fallen on us in the last few salvos. I was a little too busy to count at the time, and my attentions had been elsewhere, like centrally focused on keeping my butt alive. I found out later a couple rockets had gone long, and landed by the Controlled Access Center (CAC, pronounced kack) behind Edgewood. The guards and Security Manager there were dealing with that mess. A few had also flown over the grounds, and landed outside the walls, exploding harmlessly on the banks of the Tigris.

When the second strike hit, we were already finished with the primary search of the trailers, and most groups were working on their second look when the alarms went off. The two-forty that sent us scrambling landed right in the middle of a row of trailers that had already been cleared, so there was not much of a need for us to go back and clear them again.

Once the "All Clear" was given, I walked out of the bunker. Others, who had also sought shelter, were wandering now off, in their own directions, in pursuit of their own objectives. As I was milling around the entrance, one of the other Site Managers who had been helping clear trailers lumbered from the bunker, and walked over to me. His call-sign was Lunchmeat, or just Meat for short. He was new to the project, having been here for only a couple of weeks. I had been told of his arrival, since both of us were retired MPs, and that he had been assigned to the P.X. Parking lot as the Security Manager. It was Easter morning when I first had the opportunity to meet him, and that had barely lasted more than a few minutes. The attack that morning came while he was taking over from his night shift counterpart, so he had in fact been off dealing with another incident when E.O.D. had asked. When he finally showed up, my briefing to him had basically been; "Unexploded rocket there, E.O.D. there, perimeter there. Good luck with that. I'm out."

This time, we had more time to walk and talk. Extreme, emotionally charged events spun your senses into overdrive, especially when the event was spread over a long period of time. Seconds, minutes, and hours become interchangeable, and the fight or flight induced mindset could make events blur and meld. Adrenalin is one hell of a high, especially when you had been getting frequent shots of it. I could see how thrill seekers became adrenaline junkies. But, for every high there needed to be an equal low, and bringing that rush to my mindset, my emotions, and my senses back down to a more stable level was a process best done over time. Think of it this way. When riding a speeding freight train, it was much easier, and more controllable, to allow that train to stop over time and distance than jamming on the brakes. To give ourselves that time and distance, Lunchmeat and I decided to walk and talk. The walk would provide time for the adrenaline to slowly fade, and dissolve out of our systems. Talking would give us a chance to take our minds off the recent chaos. New surroundings would give us a real, as well as emotional, distance.

Traveling alone can be a risky business, even in a safe environment. Walking around in a combat zone, by yourself, was not only an unwise practice, it could also become downright hazardous to your health when the rockets started flying. Not only was it a little difficult to watch your own back, but applying first aid to yourself could get more than a bit tricky. Remaining conscious was a basic necessity for that to work. To increase survivability in these conditions, the Army had developed, and strenuously advocated, a concept known as the battle-buddy. This covenant could be as short-lived as a walk across the compound, could develop into a mutual support bond for the duration of a mission, or evolve into a life-long alliance of trust and reliability. Police, Firefighters, combat vets, anyone who has found themselves in a position where they had to place their life in the hands of another, and had the life of another placed in theirs, knows what this means. At the front end of this scale, soldiers refer to their counterpart as "Battle." Reach the top end of the scale, and they simple became Brother.

Without much thought our training kicked in, and subconsciously we fell into the old battle-buddy routine. We had only taken a few steps when the Security Manager for all the CACs, call-sign Finch, came over the radio. While dealing with the impacts around the CAC behind Edgewood he had been receiving distress calls from one of the other access centers for which he was responsible. Being just a bit overloaded, he asked Meat to help him out by heading over to the Service CAC at the back of the compound. The issue seemed straight forward enough, check on the status of one of the local nationals who worked as a screener/interpreter there. Having a long history as being a bit of a drama queen, the CAC Supervisor had called for some assistance in dealing with her hysterics.

As we approached the CAC, we found one of the rockets had impacted out in front of the building, in one of the vehicle approach lanes, and not detonated. E.O.D. was already on scene dealing with it. Entering the building we checked on the screener, and found she was only shaken up, in full drama mode, but still only shaken up. Yah. Right. Who wasn't? After several minutes of trying to calm her down, with no success, we changed tactics. What was the best way to deal with a child throwing a temper tantrum? Do not acknowledge it, and get them engrossed in something else. And that was what we did. Reminding her she was needed to process people through the CAC, and they were depending on her to do that seemed to interrupt her, and she was soon back to work.

The excitement appeared to be over for the time being. No longer pressed for the immediate need of a battle-buddy, I left Meat to follow-up with E.O.D., and started on my way back to my room so I could pick up the rest of my work gear. Sticking to the main road I walked to the far side of Edgewood, instead of cutting through. As I rounded the corner into the trailer park I ran into Chief and Zombie, Chief's night shift counterpart, taking stock of the afternoon's activities. With all that had been happening today, Zombie was expecting an exceptionally long change over, and had arrived very early. Early enough I had time to join the conversation. Standing next to a bunker, we regaled each other with stories of the last two attacks. Do you know the difference between a fairy tale and a war story? Fairy tales start out with "Once upon a time," and war stories start with "No shit, there I was." In mid-story, we heard the distinct launch of three more rockets.

Never had a telephone booth been stuffed with as many people as we crammed into that duck and cover bunker. I did not remember seeing very many people wandering around the area while we were talking, but once those rockets launched, and the alarms went off, they came out of the woodwork. Everyone did their level best to be the one person in the safest place in the bunker: the very center. The rockets exploded off in the distance, and no one was sure where they had hit. Since it was not anywhere around us, we decided they were someone else's problem. With the threat passed, we untangled ourselves out of the bunker, and everyone went about their business, keeping a wary eye toward the heavens.

Checking my watch, I realized it was getting very close to shift change, and I would be pressed for time to get to the camp prior to formation. At the beginning of every shift we conducted an accountability formation, with the guards, to ensure everyone had arrived for work, they were all in proper uniform, and had all of their equipment. If you ever spent any time in the military, you know the drill.

I went back to my trailer, collected up my work kit, and headed off to work. As I approached the bunker, where I had been spending so much of the time I should have been sleeping, I heard that distinct, low bass boom in the distance again, more launches. A hop, skip, and a jump later I gained the safety of the bunker, with only a little time to spare before the rockets impacted. This time they sounded close. The launch to impact time on this set had been extremely short. Too short, I think, for the C-RAM to react to their flight. That was the only thing I could come up with to explain why the alarm had not been activated. I was further confused by the close proximity of the detonations. Wondering if acoustics had played tricks on my ears, and those rockets had really landed further away than I thought, I stuck my head around the corner of the bunker, and looked for signs of explosions. Smoke was rising in the direction from where I had left Chief and Zombie, and without an alarm activation to warn them of the incoming, I could only imagine the worst.

My heart skipped a couple of beats as I tore out of the bunker at a dead run. Turning the corner around the last trailer I pulled up short, and stopped. I could see the rockets had impacted further away than I had initially thought. The area around the bunker where we had been standing was empty of people, and damage. Breathing a heavy sigh of relief, the scramble of feet running on gravel broke the moment as Chief and Zombie ran past me yelling the rockets had impacted close to our guard's barracks. The same place where the guards and Security

Managers for the entire Palace Complex held their formations.

With shift change coming up, I could only imagine all the CAC guards, Grounds guards, and Palace guards would be lined up in neat formation ready for roll call. The devastation would be unbelievable. When I arrived at the impact site, it was worse than I could ever imagine. All the guards had scattered at the sound of the launches, and were able to make it to hard cover before the impacts. The rockets had fallen short, and instead of landing in the formation area, they had detonated on the tin roof of the bar the State Department had here on the grounds. Oh, the horrors of war! Fortunately, it was late afternoon, and no one was in the bar yet, so nobody was hurt by the explosion. The liquor cabinets, on the other hand, received multiple wounds, most of which were fatal to their contents.

Things quieted down for a while, after that last salvo, and it seemed like that was going to be the last of it for a while. Having no need to hang around, I began the long walk to the office so we could conduct our shift change. I had barely made it to the front gate of the Palace grounds when the C-RAM alarm went off yet again. Just can't get enough of them rockets, ya' know? These landed a ways away, over in the FOB next to the camp, I think. They were close enough to our camp, though, that some of the shrapnel landed inside, leaving little divots in the asphalt.

You may have noticed how I refer to the other Security Managers by nicknames. It was not like they did not have real names, they did. It was because we got branded with a call-sign when we first arrived on project, and most of us continued to use them, even when we were not talking on the radio. There were a couple of ways to receive your call sign.

The first way was to already have one when you got there. I chose to revive my call sign from the days I was the only Army instructor at an Air Force ground combat skill school in Europe. Being the only soldier in a group of airmen, they claimed I would continually "crow" about the Army. Hence, my call-sign became Rooster. At least that was their story. I still believe they were trying to call me a giant cock, but I could not prove that. Most guys who retired from the military brought a call-sign with them. Sometimes it was based on their rank, like Chief or

Gunny or Top, other times it was based on their favorite call-sign from a previous mission.

The second way to receive your call-sign, and you really did not want this one, was to have one given to you. Usually, it was awarded because of something you had done. Something you would rather forget had happened. One Security Manager wanted his call-sign to be "Professor" because he had a PHD. That lasted right up to the time someone realized the way he kept his hair made him look like the cartoon character Jimmy Neutron. You can probably guess which name stuck. Another Site Manager had been teaching Salsa dancing at the Palace, in the evenings after his shift was over. I cannot remember what call-sign he started out with, but it instantly became Tiny Dancer as soon as that little tidbit of information leaked out.

Around 2300, the P.A. over on the Palace Grounds began talking. Because of the distance between the Palace and the Camp, combined with all the echoes caused by concrete walls and what not, I couldn't understand what was being said. I called around to a couple of the Security Managers at the Palace, and found out the announcement was to let everyone know there was a threat of indirect fire in the International Zone, and everyone should stay under hard cover for the night. Really? You don't say. Thanks for the update Captain Obvious. About five minutes later, one of the WPPS managers walked into my office, and asked me to make a P.A. announcement to the Camp. He wanted everyone out of their trailers, and under hard cover because of the announcement at the Palace. Well, there was a twist. The day shift folks were getting their sleep messed with. Welcome to the party.

I think I had about as much of living in an impact area as I was able to take for a while, too. Five days of sleeping where the rockets were landing was pushing my luck about as far as I thought it was going to go. Tomorrow, I was going to find a place inside the Palace to sleep. Even though I knew this was the best decision for my own safety, I could not shake the feeling that I was giving up. I was letting the insurgents win. I knew it was stupid to think like that, but there it was.

Most of the Palace day workers had already moved, and for the second night in a row were sleeping inside the Palace, mostly finding sleeping space in their offices. You would have thought they were having a slumber party. I cut through the Palace, on my way to midnight chow, and a bunch of folks were still up, walking around in their P.J.s, chit-chatting. This was turning into a big social event for them. We would see how they did during the day, when the rest of us were trying to sleep.

I did not know why Big Army was not hunting down the rocket launchers, and killing them. Do not ask my why the Apaches were not on station, flying around the I.Z. during the day, killing anything that launched a rocket. I did not know why the Iraqi Government, Army, Police, or general population were letting this stuff happen in their neighborhoods either. One thing was for sure, there were no more innocent civilians. Until these people stood up, and took control of their country, they were just letting the insurgents have it.

28 March – Finally, I was able to get a full day's sleep. Last night, day shift had pulled out some cots and stretchers, and set them up in the two rooms on either side of the main entrance doors to the Palace. At least, that way, everyone was under hard cover.

Yesterday, an official directive had been put out for all Chief of Mission employees to limit all outdoor activity, and strongly advised no one slept in the trailers. I had already moved some of my stuff into one of the rooms day shift had set up, and even though the stretcher I was sleeping on was surprisingly comfortable, it still took me a while to fall asleep. The irony of sleeping on a stretcher did not help. With everything I had already been sleeping through lately, it was also surprising how the quiet, repetitive squeaking of a small table fan kept me awake. It must have been close to 0900 before I finally fell asleep.

Around 1430 I was woken up by the distant sound of an explosion, followed by the Duck and Cover alarm. I guess the alarms were starting to get tired of all the rockets too. I know I mentioned the difference between the C-RAM and Duck and Cover alarms earlier, but let me clarify a little better how the Duck and Cover alarm was different. Where the C-RAM alarm was activated when the system began tracking in-coming missiles, the Duck and Cover alarm was manually activated. It was the back-up alarm. Where the C-RAM alarm was localized to the predicted impact site, the Duck and Cover alarm was more generalized. The idea was to let others know indirect fire rounds were impacting somewhere in the I.Z., and everyone should take cover just in case the bad guys decided to shift fire. The C-RAM alarm announced itself with three loud, heart stopping klaxon blasts. The Duck and Cover alarm started with a series of high-low tones, like the police sirens in Europe, and then just yelled at you in a staccato, mater-of-fact tone of voice. "Duck and cover. Duck and cover. I.D.F. rounds are impacting in the I.Z."

It was nice to be able to think the boom was someone else's issue to deal with, roll over, and go back to sleep for a change. And that was what I did. By the time I woke up again, it was a little too close to five o'clock to go back to the trailer for a shower, so I got a cup of coffee from the little deli style café inside the Palace, and waited for the chow hall to open.

True to form, the Five O'clock Fusillade was right on time. Now I knew why these rockets had not been a big deal to most of the people working in the Palace. While the Duck and Cover alarm was broadcast over the Palace's internal P.A. system, the C-RAM alarm was not. Inside the Palace I could hardly hear the C-RAM alarm, and the explosions were so faint that if I had not been paying close attention, I probably would have missed them. They did send us a bit of a change-up though. Around 1730hrs, and again around 1745hrs, while a group of us were eating in the chow hall, the C-RAM alarm had gone off. No explosions though.

Armed with a good day's sleep I wandered over to the camp, and began to settle in for work. Lippy had joined us in the chow hall, so we had conducted our changeover while we were eating. I had just gotten a cup of coffee from the Camp's chow hall, and was walking back to the office when the C-RAM alarm activated. It sure was funny how my mind worked. I ran the whole way to the bunker with the cup in my hand. I was even more surprised to find, when I finally arrived under cover, there was still a good amount of coffee left in the cup. The rockets impacted on the hospital's helipad, just down the road from the Camp, and as the echoes of their explosions faded away everything got quiet again. I decided I would be wearing my armor for the rest of the night.

I almost forgot. During my quest for coffee this afternoon I had run into Lunchmeat. Sometime during the day he had been chatting with one of the R.S.O.s, and learned they had been keeping count of the week's rocket activity. So far they counted just over one hundred rockets had been shot at the I.Z. over the past five days, with the majority of them falling on, or around the Palace grounds. We both agreed it felt more like the majority had been impacting in, or around the Edgewood area. Yes, I think I had pushed my luck far enough.

Early in the morning, like zero-dark-thirty, before the insurgents woke up and started shooting at us, I was going to head back to my trailer, get some clean clothes and my shower stuff, and head to the showers behind the Palace Security Office to clean up a bit. Even though we had not been getting hit at night, I was not sure I wanted to try my luck by showering in my trailer, especially since people had taken to calling that area Deadwood instead of Edgewood.

29 March – I decided to shower in my trailer last night anyway. Not only was it an eerie feeling, but I now have a better understanding of P.T.S.D. The whole time I was in the shower every noise, every new pitch of sound, every new tone would register in my brain as the C-RAM alarm. By the time I turned the water off I was so high

strung I could barely stand it. Had the feeling been even a little bit stronger, I probably would not have been able to stay.

Having spent the last two days in full kit, it was nice to get a little soap and water on the grimy spots, but I could not help but feel a little isolated, vulnerable, the longer it took to get clean. I never realized just how loud the spray of water through a showerhead could actually be. How much the sounds of the drops splashing off the sides of the shower, pelting against the shower curtain and my body, drowned out the ambient noises from outside the shower stall. Having been caught right here, twice, rocketed in the middle of taking a shower changed my entire perspective of this simple, mundane task. Naked meant exposed. Exposed meant vulnerable. Vulnerable meant defenseless. So, I scrubbed. The shower got louder, and I scrubbed faster. The spray became a roar, and with frantic zeal I scrubbed even faster. I scrubbed so fast, I was not sure if I was attacking the dirt or my own insecurities. I think I scrubbed a few spots raw.

Finished with my shower, I was still not all that comfortable about being in the trailer. Stepping out of the stall, with the water now turned off, my feelings of isolation began to subside. The cascade of noise had been silenced, and with it the little voices that had been whispering danger in my ears had been washed down the drain. Well, most of them had been. I dried off as quickly as I could, put my pants and shoes on, and opened the front door of the trailer while I finished dressing. Maybe I could shoo the rest of those voices out.

Being 0300hrs, no one was moving around outside, and the atmosphere was graveyard quiet. I figured, if nothing else, and with as quiet as it was, if I left the door open I would probably be able to hear any launches. If not the launches, I would definitely hear any rocket flying in, and the longer I stayed the more comfortable I felt about being there.

Roughly an hour later I was clean and dressed, had gathered up some clean clothes for the next day, and picked up that all important fresh can of tobacco. Locking the door behind me, I walked out of the trailer park with a great sense of relief, like I had just gotten away with something. Of course, that was until I walked around the corner of the trailers, and almost ran over two of our guards on patrol. By the way we all jumped, you could tell everyone was on edge.

After shift I went back to the room in the Palace where I had recently taken to sleeping, set up my stretcher, and laid down. For a change, it did not take long for me to fall asleep. The first rockets of the day were later than usual, around ten-hundred I think. I did not know if I was just that tired, or if I had just become that comfortable with my new room, but it was nothing for me to roll over, and go back to sleep. I slept all the way to 1600hrs. Waking up, I put on the clean clothes I had picked up last night, straightened up the area, and went in search of coffee.

As I walked toward the Deli Café, I ran into a couple of the other Security Managers. They told me there had been two strikes this morning, totaling eleven rockets. Most of them had impacted in other areas, not the Palace, but a couple had landed in the compound. One had impacted pretty close to the North Drop Arm, the barrier that blocked the north side of the road that ran directly behind the Palace. The majority of the guards there were able to make it to their bunker before it hit, but the last one had gotten his bell rung pretty well from the concussion. Running for a bunker was kind of like running from a bear. You did not need to be the fastest, but you certainly did not want to be the slowest. They had taken him to the hospital to have his head and ears looked at.

It looked like we were finally starting to shoot back. The Apaches had been up all day, and a couple of them had even engaged a few of the launchers with missiles of their own. It was about time. The two morning attacks were all that had happened. Now that we were getting some air cover, I thought I would try heading to the gym tonight, and then head back to the room to wash clothes and shower.

The P.X. was still having a run on plastic foot lockers, and clean underwear. Last night there were twice as many Rhinos (armored buses) in the convoy to BIAP than usual. The allure of the big money that could be made by contracting in a war zone had brought a lot of people to Baghdad. The reality of what happened in a war zone was sending them back home. I guessed some people had not read the warning label before taking a job over here. It said: War – This product may contain rockets, mortars, bombs, bullets, and other substances the Insurgent General has deemed likely to cause death, or grievous bodily harm. Your mileage may vary, no purchase necessary to enter, see your local retailer for details. (May contain nuts)

30 March – It had been a week since the rockets first started falling, and maybe things were starting to slow down a little. We only had five rockets hit the I.Z. today, and none of them impacted around the Palace, or on the Palace grounds. They hit us in three salvos this morning, and that was the end of it. The news was saying al-Sadr had instructed his people to stay off the streets, and protest their concerns through other political means. Since when had shooting rockets at people been a political means?

Since moving into the Palace there had not been much excitement for me. During the day, at least. I heard the C-RAM alarms, or the explosions, and was able to roll over and go back to sleep. It did mean I had to head into the impact area late at night so I could shower, and put on clean clothes though. That tended to be a little nerve racking in its own right, but since we had not been getting hit in the early hours of the morning, I found the more I went into the belly of the beast the more comfortable I got with it. I only hoped that comfort did not wind up biting me in the butt, and we got hit one morning while I was in the trailer. If it happened it happened, I guessed. Dwelling on it only made it worse.

31 March – We were settling into our new routine. We would get a salvo or two of rockets in the late morning, a salvo or two early in the afternoon, after which it would quiet down for the rest of the day. I did not know how the helicopters and drones were missing those launch sites. I could only guess the insurgents were getting more creative. The day shift Security Managers were getting up early, and meeting at the shower trailer behind the Palace Security Office. In classic military fashion, half of them would shower while the other half pulled security, listening for rockets or alarms. Then they would switch.

    I woke up in the afternoon, dressed, shaved, and brushed my teeth in one of the bathrooms inside the Palace, then went to work. Despite the name, the bathrooms did not have baths in them, only sinks and toilets. By 0300hrs, I would head back into Edgewood to shower, and put on clean clothes. It only took around thirty minutes to get everything done, and I was on my way out of the impact area.

More sandbags were starting to arrive. A couple of flatbed trucks loaded up with them showed up at the Palace today. The WPPS guys (a collective word, since the company providing WPPS also had women) were able to get their hands on a few of the bags as well. Of course, all the WPPS guys stacking sandbags spent the day further hardening the already hard bunkers they jumped into, instead of spreading the wealth around. They did drop off small loads of sandbags at the areas where my guards were, but nobody was stacking them. I only had so many guards at any one given time, and could not stack sandbags with the same guys being used for security. Besides, if any of the R.S.O.s found out I had done that, they might decide to push a contract compliance issue. Something, by the way, I found out was a much bigger issue than I would have expected…. especially with this being a war zone. I would have to figure something out. The last time I threw sandbags around I was so sore I could barely walk for the next two days.

At the beginning of the week, when all this was just starting, I had told my guards that if they wanted to take their brakes inside bunkers, instead of their unarmored break room, that was fine by me. Additionally, there were a couple hardened watch towers along the walls of the compound they could use. Built out of steel, they were concrete reinforced, and had an A.C./heater in them. Last night one of my guards had climbed the stairs to take his break in a tower, and found a couple of the WPPS guys (guys this time) had already set up cots, and were sleeping there. As we walked around the camp, it became apparent all of the towers, including most of the duck and cover bunkers, were filled with WPPS guys and girls trying to get some sleep.

The containers that made up their hootches had been stacked three high, with stairs and walkways at every level. The hard, overhead cover built above them was only as wide as the trailers themselves, providing no overhanging protection for the balconies, or roadways between rows. Not too bad if you were dealing with mortars, since they tended to fall at a rather steep angle. But, we were dealing with rockets, and they tended to slide in from the side.

CHAPTER 4

1 April – So far, today had been our first day in over a week without any rockets. It looked like al-Sadr had finally gotten a hold on his guys, and you could see a marked relaxing in everyone around the Palace. We would see if this cease-fire held.

Well, so much for that idea. I was sitting in my office on the WPPS camp, around 2145hrs, when the C-RAM alarm went off. That was a bit late for those guys. Could that have been a false alarm? Not really wanting to gamble on it, I grabbed my helmet, walked out of the office, and down the steps. During the last week I had come to the realization the front gate was just a little too far away for me to make in one full sprint before the rockets arrived.

Looking around the trailer for alternatives, I had noticed a large concrete block off to the right from the steps leading up to my office. The block had been cast as a base for one of the I-beams supporting the overhead cover sheltering the stack of living trailers next to the office. There was plenty of room between the block and the concrete wall of the compound for a couple of people to take shelter. I had gotten into the habit of squatting down next to the block, until the first of the explosions were over, and then going on the Main Gate to await the "All Clear." As I was standing next to the block, two rockets exploded somewhere in the direction of the FOB behind the camp. Here we go again! I guess these guys had not gotten al-Sadr's memo.

So far, the rocket count had been as follows: over one-hundred-fifty rockets shot at the I.Z., over one-hundred-twenty impacts in the I.Z., and over eighty impacts in the Palace complex. It had been a very busy week and a half. One thing I had not been able to figure out yet was, where did the insurgents keep getting all those rockets? It had been suggested they may be coming from Iran, and I was rather inclined to believe that line of thought. A rocket was not the kind of thing you could pop around to the corner store, and pick up like a six pack.

2 April – Again, we went all day without any IDF (in-direct fire. This included mortars, as well as rockets). YAH! Tonight was a different story. At 2140hrs, almost the same time as last night, rockets hit the hospital two-

hundred yards away. I guess that rocket crew did not get the memo either.

Once again, I was sitting in the office, finishing up some paperwork, when I thought I heard the sound of rockets launching. It had been so faint I hardly noticed, and did not really pay much attention to it. I think my brain cataloged the thump as someone slamming a door on the other side of the camp. No alarm. No warning. Just wham! Once more unto the breach dear friends. At the crack of the explosion grab the helmet. Get out of the office. Pause by the cement block. Head straight over to the main gate, and get the status of all my guards. And this used to be such a quiet neighborhood.

With the frequency of rockets decreasing in the last few days, I had begun to hope I would be able to move back into my own trailer soon. I guess I would have to re-start that countdown clock. The stretcher had been O.K. to sleep on, but was starting to get a little on the old side. Not to mention a little uncomfortable. The fabric was stretched pretty tight between the two support poles, but it was still a stretcher, not a mattress. My hips and back were starting to complain, rather loudly and painfully I might add.

I was able to make it to the gym again tonight, around 0200hrs, when everything was quiet. I went this early because it gave me enough time to get back to my trailer, and get a shower way before boom time began at 0530hrs. Each time I returned to my trailer and showered, without anything bad happening, the oppressive sense of vulnerability I once felt dwindled a little bit more. I was certainly not, by any stretch of the imagination, completely comfortable when I stepped under the spray of water. Not yet. The feeling of foreboding had eased off enough though that it did not raise much higher than a general sense of uneasiness.

Tonight, I had just stepped out of the shower when the alarm went off. Once again, my heart tried to pound its way out of my chest from the adrenaline injection. My mind scrambled for cover. My legs prepared for the sprint. My hands grabbed for the towel. Again. There I was. In the bathroom. Butt naked. Rockets inbound. Seconds away from exploding. But this time the alarm sounded just a bit different. It took my mind a second or two to realize this was not the C-RAM alarm. Nor was it the Duck and Cover alarm. It was my smoke alarm. Oh, for the love of God!

I did not know if it had gone off because I left the bathroom door open while I showered, and the heat from the water had rolled into the bedroom. Maybe the batteries were signaling they were about to die. Or maybe karma had a really messed up sense of humor. I can tell you this much, it scared the shit out me. With a long, slow exhale, I gathered together the little shards that once had been my nerves, grabbed a towel, and wrapped it around my waist. In wet, slippery shower shoes I carefully made my way out of the bathroom, across the bedroom, and reached up to grab the smoke alarm. Just as it shut itself off. Really? Really! Hanging my head, I started to take long, deep breaths to help combat this new frustration as I tried to relax. Enhance your calm Edger Friendly. OK, I could try to get dressed now.

Through sheer force of will I contained the effects of the adrenaline, bottled my frustration, and wrestled my dread to a point where I could stop shaking. Seizing my pants from the bed, I was able to stab one foot through the first leg. I was stepping into the second leg when another alarm screamed through my trailer. It was loud. It was piercing. It was a short blast of chaos. The restraining straps flew off my panic, and it was all I could do to keep from falling flat on my face. Grasping the waist of my pants in both fists, I bounded across the trailer on one foot. My other foot still wrestling with the other pant leg. Only to realize the alarm was my cell phone ringing.

I had been coming to my trailer, in the middle of the night, to shower because that had been the only time we had not received rockets. Each time I had taken the precaution of keeping the door open so I could clearly hear the sound of any alarm, or the rockets coming. Every night it had been graveyard quiet, and I had been the only one making noise. I had been coming back here for so long I was starting to get a bit anxious, thinking I had pushed my luck to the breaking point. But, with every night of success I grew more confident in my safety. Now, twice, piercing alarms had gone off. Scaring the ever-loving crap out of me. I thought I had about as much excitement as I could stand for one night. Without even answering the phone, I grabbed all my stuff, and stormed out of the trailer. Whoever had called would just have to wait until I was in a better emotional head space.

3 April – One more time, they threw us a change-up. For the past two nights they had shot at us around 2100hrs,

but tonight they waited until almost 2300hrs before taking their shot. If everything went as normal, now that they had shot at us, the rest of the night should have been quiet.

Tonight, while out on my rounds, I got to talking with a couple of my guards, and found out the I.Z. had taken two rocket strikes this morning as well. After last night's shift was over, a group of my guards had gone over to FOB Prosperity, on the west side of the I.Z., so they could use the gym. They had finished with their routine, and were walking toward the front gate when the C-RAM alarm on Prosperity had gone off. None of them could tell me exactly where on the FOB the rockets had impacted because they were too busy bobbing and weaving their way toward the gate. I guess that meant I would be resetting the clock, yet again, before I got to move back into my trailer. The R.S.O. had not rescinded the order for full body armor yet either, and since the office on the WPPS Camp was not even close to being hard cover, I was still wearing my kit in the trailer, as well as out walking around.

Yes, I can see the confused look on your face. Who are these R.S.O.s of which I keep speaking? The letters R.S.O. stood for Regional Security Officer. A badged, Federal Law Enforcement Officer, The R.S.O. was a Special Agent assigned to the State Department's Diplomatic Security Service (D.S.S.), and served as the law enforcement and security advisor to the Ambassador. Basically, he was the Sheriff.

Just like a Sheriff would have an assortment of Deputies, The (notice the capital T) R.S.O. also had a number of deputies, or assistant R.S.O.s (A.R.S.O.s). Here is the part that gets a little confusing. Where the Sheriff would be addressed as "Sheriff," and the deputies referred to as "Deputy," all of the R.S.O.s were referred to as "R.S.O.," regardless of whether they were the top agent or an assistant. From here on out, if I refer to someone as an R.S.O., it would most likely be one of the A.R.S.O.s. If not, I will give you a signal I am talking about the boss. Keep an eye out for the capital T.

Being the Top Cop on the Embassy, The R.S.O. was in charge of security for all personnel, buildings, residences, and outlying properties that fell under the authority of the Chief of Mission – That's the Ambassador. With an operation as large as the Embassy in Baghdad, you could see how it would take a lot of people to make this mission happen, but I am only going to touch on a couple of those groups.

The largest group of R.S.O.s encountered by anyone on the Embassy was the department which conducted all the investigations here. At any other Embassy, these investigations would be few and far between, usually involving things like passport or visa fraud. Baghdad, on the other hand, was a whole different animal. It was my understanding this was, by far, the largest embassy complex for the U.S. State Department, and related personnel. That meant there were a lot of people living and working on these grounds. With a population that large, the additional incidents the agents here may have to investigate could range from simple loud music complaints in the living areas to negligent weapons discharges. They could even go all the way up to more serious, felony criminal activities.

The division we, the Security Managers, dealt most directly with was a smaller department made up of four R.S.O.s. Known as the Southern Operating Branch (that's right they were called the S.O.B.s). They had been assigned the dubious task of overseeing us, and directing our mission of securing the Embassy. Normally, we operated within the guidelines of standard operating procedures (known as S.O.P.s), State Department Directives, or CoM policies (CoM – Chief of Mission. Pronounced "calm" without the L), but these were not always thorough, and they certainly could not cover every situation.

Actually, most of our procedures had evolved through the process of conducting the same operation day in, and day out. They had developed, on their own, into the most efficient and effective way of doing business. Normally, the Security Manager was all who was needed to get business done. When something new or important happened, or we ran into a particularly bothersome troublemaker and needed to put a little teeth into our procedure, we called the S.O.B.s.

The last office we interacted with was the group of R.S.O.s with the task of overseeing any and all State Department convoys that left the Embassy grounds. They were the ones who rode out in the convoys, responsible for their operation, and directly supervising the WPPS teams.

By now, you have probably asked yourself "Hey, aren't there supposed to be Marines guarding the

Embassy? What's the deal with all these contractors?" Another very good question, and I'm glad you asked. The simple answer was yes, there were Marines here, and they did guard the Embassy. The complex part of the answer was their mission only extended to controlling access to some of the secure areas inside the Embassy, protecting the Ambassador in residence, and were the fighting force to defend the embassy should it be attacked on the ground. They did not man the towers along the walls of the compound. They did not man the gates around the perimeter of the grounds. They did not search vehicles entering the compound. Nor did they search people entering, or leaving the grounds. These, and many other similar tasks, were done by us, Security Specialists.

6 April – It had been a couple of days since I wrote anything, and as you can guess that meant it had been pretty quiet.

Around 2100hrs last night we did get a C-RAM alarm activation, but there had not been any explosions. They called that alarm a 'False Positive." I did not understand that one. Anywhere else I had been we would have just called it a false alarm. Around 2250hrs the C-

RAM alarm went off again, but this time there were some booms. Would that be considered a "positive positive?" Two rockets impacted over by the CaSH. Sorry, I did not mean to confuse again. CaSH (pronounced just like it is spelled) is the acronym for Combat Support Hospital. I know, why didn't I just say hospital, right?

The hospital was originally called Ibn Sina, and was located just a couple hundred yards north of the WPPS camp. Opened in the 1960's, it originally served as the hospital for Saddam, his family, and the Ba'ath party elite. Fun fact: Ibn Sina was a Persian (Those were the people who came from the area that had become Iran, and no, Persians are not Arab), born around 980AD, and was renowned in the medical world as one of medicine's greatest scholars in all history. Known in the west as Avicenna (the Latin version of his Persian name), he wrote over one hundred treatises, papers, and canons on medicine. One of them, *The Canon of Medicine*, became the standard medical text in both Europe, and the Islamic world, up until the eighteenth century. He also has a crater on the moon named after him, but I think that is getting a little off topic.

Once American forces had secured Baghdad, the hospital was taken over by the Army, and turned into the primary trauma and emergency treatment facility for wounded soldiers (American or other coalition forces), civilians (contractors, third country nationals, and Iraqis alike), captured insurgents (whether suspected or confirmed), and anyone else needing emergency medical treatment. You may remember this facility from the show *Baghdad ER*.

The N.E.C. guys later told us they had heard those rockets flying over them, so it looked like the insurgents were moving to new launch sites. Part of the reason could be that U.S. and Iraqi forces were currently moving into Sadr City. Well, the southwestern half of the city anyway. The range on the smaller 107mm rockets, the common ones they had been shooting at us, was not long enough for them to reach the Green Zone if they were launched from the north side of Sadr City, so the two Armies were moving in to occupy the southern part of the city. Denying the Mahdi Militia the use of the ground. The big controversy was engineers were going to construct a tall, cement wall to seal off this part of Sadr City. It could also have had something to do with the fact that some of the old launch sites, along with a few launch teams, had been getting shot up by our helicopters too.

We had not been having much in the way of booms during the day, so I moved back into my trailer today. My hips and lower back were preparing to file for divorce if I slept on the stretcher any longer, so I figured I would give sleeping in my trailer another try. This morning it took me quite a while to fall asleep. Lying in bed I realized the coffee pot had been sitting, unused for the last couple of weeks. Since I was only staring at the ceiling anyway, I decided to get something productive done with my time. I plucked the pot off the machine, grabbed a clean rag, and headed into the bathroom to clean out all the dust and coffee stains that had taken up residence. With hot water streaming out of the tap, I slid the pot under the flow to dampen the inside. As soon as water touched the glass, the thing exploded in my hand. It just shattered, right there in the sink. This was not going to be a good day. I cleaned up the mess the best I could, and not wanting to risk any further destruction headed to bed.

Around 1530hrs my alarm clock went off. I rolled a sleepy arm over, and smacked the snooze alarm.

Strange, I knew I hit the button, but I could still hear an alarm. Lifting my head out of my pillow, I looked toward the clock to try and figure out what was wrong. It was not just the alarm clock that had woken me up, the duck and cover alarm was going off too. CRAP! Here we go again! I grabbed my stuff, jumped into my shower shoes, and took off out of the trailer. I sat in the bunker for a couple of minutes, trying to get my heart back under control, when I realized nothing was going boom.

Mumbling to myself, I slogged my way back to the trailer. The alarm clock had already gone off so, technically, it was officially time to get up, and get a shower. I may as well get it over with. Get in, get wet, soap up, rinse off, get out, get dry. Ba-da-bing, ba-da-boom. No pun intended. Done. The rockets had caught me in the shower enough times I had learned to do this quickly. Shower heads in these trailers were not like the ones most people would be used to. They were not fixed to the end of a pipe sticking out of the wall. They were the kind attached to a handle on the end of a hose so you could lift them out of their bracket, and direct the water where you needed it.

Finished with my part of the shower I had taken the handle out of the bracket, and was using it to spray down the stall when the shower head came off. Plop. It just fell off. There I was, holding the handle, a stream of water as big as my thumb shooting out of the end, and the shower head lying on the floor of the stall. Great! First the coffee pot, then the alarm, and now the shower head. What next?

There was not much I could do about the shower head. I just needed to put a work order in with the maintenance guys, and then bide my time until they came to fix it. On the other hand, there was something I could do about the coffee pot. I finished getting dressed, and headed off to start the work order paperwork, and pick up a new coffee pot from the P.X. The walk to the P.X. was pretty much the same route I took to work. Out of the Edgewood trailer park, around the chow hall, down the side of the Palace, across the front lawn of the Palace, through the Main CAC, across the street, and through the parking lot where I had dodged all those rockets a few weeks ago. The P.X. compound butted up against the back wall of the WPPS camp, and was only about a ten-minute walk. It felt much longer than that, especially when you walked this far just to find out the P.X. did not have any more coffee pots in stock. Things just kept getting better and better. Fortunately, I remembered there was an extra coffee maker in the office at the Palace. I stole the pot out of it.

Wanting to put all my frustrations behind me, I dropped my new coffee pot off at my room, and set out to get something to eat. A good dinner, breakfast as it related to my work schedule, would right the balance of my misfortunes. Additionally, today was Sunday, and on Sundays the chow hall served Prime Rib. I swung back around to the Palace Office, rounded up the day shift crew, and we joined the stream of eager diners heading toward the feast. With our sights set on one of the few luxuries we had, we crowded our way into the chow hall, and scrubbed the filth and dirt from our hands. We selected the sturdiest trays we could find, to support the thickest cut of meat we could get, just to find out they were not serving Prime Rib tonight. They were having turkey loaf. Since the insurgents had started their most recent rounds of trouble, the convoys bringing rations into the I.Z. had not been getting through regularly, and the cooks had been forced to make do with what they could get.

Disappointment was not the right word for what we felt. Chagrined came close, but still fell short of the mark. So, vexed, with equal amounts of resentment and fury, we started to complain. We started. As one, minds focused on wreaking havoc and destruction, we drew the first breath that would give life to our grievances. Having been denied this one simple pleasure our lungs expanded, filling themselves with the righteous indignation that beef could never be replaced by turkey loaf, only to be brought up short. Chief was just a heartbeat ahead, and made a connection none of had spotted, and at this point were never going to see without a little help.

"Guys," he said. "I think we can live with this."

Each of us stopped in mid breath and turned, jaws hanging open, to look at Chief in disbelief. Could he be serious? One of the very few things we had to look forward to in this dirt-infested heat box, and it had been taken away. Prime Rib had been replaced with turkey loaf, TURKEY LOAF, and they expected us type-A personalities, red meat eaters, die hard carnivores, to be O.K. with that? Our lungs contracted, preparing to expel a tempest of verbal abuse and retribution. Once aimed at the chow hall staff, now directed toward Chief.

"No, really guys. I think we can *LIVE* with this."

And the wind was immediately robbed from our sails. With everything we had endured over the past two weeks, we had missed one simple reality. There had once been people here who now would never eat another meal again. Those resupply convoys had been running gauntlets to bring us food, and not everyone had made it every time. Focused on our own survival, responding to rocket strikes, and explosions, dedicating our attention to the task of rescuing the trapped and wounded, we had lost a bit of our professional perspective. Although all of us had responded to numerous rocket impacts, the only one who had been to all of the attacks had been Chief, and now he was bringing that perspective back to us. Yah, with all things being equal, he was right. We could live with that.

7 April – Al-Sadr was calling for a million-man march on the ninth, to protest a few things that had upset him. Things like the U.S. conducting air strikes on the teams, and launchers, that had been shooting rockets at the I.Z.,

and that the Iraqi Army, at the direction of their Prime Minister, had been conducting joint raids with the U.S. Army on his people in Sadr City. How dare we defend ourselves.

Everyone was a little skittish about this march. Popular consensus was we were going to have more rockets than usual shot at us in support of the protest, and opposing groups would attack the march with car bombs and suicide bombers. Enough people had become concerned to the point that tall, concrete barriers, known as T-walls, were being placed directly in front of all the windows and doors at the Palace to shield them from the explosions.

Since we had not been receiving the normal Five o'clock fusillade, there were a lot more people than usual in the chow hall tonight for dinner. The first time that had happened since the rockets had started falling. To understand the significance of this, you need to understand our chow hall. The Palace was a very big, very thick, and very protected building. The chow hall was not.

The chow hall had been constructed by contractors hired by the State Department, not an original stone building repurposed as a Chow Hall. It was built a couple of years ago, and was constructed as its own independent building behind the Palace. The materials used had mostly been prefabricated in nature. Steel I-beans for support, prefabricated insulated/aluminum siding for the walls, metal cable for reinforcement, that kind of thing. Once the building had been finished a hardtop, pavilion styled cover had been built over the top of the whole thing. The roof of the pavilion was constructed from hard, heavy materials, designed to protect the top of the building from the explosion of rockets, and mortars.

T-walls had been placed around the outside of the building to shield the side from any blasts close enough to spray them with shrapnel. The problem was they were not quite tall enough to link into the overhead cover. This created a five-to-seven-foot gap between the two where a rocket could directly hit the soft side of the chow hall. Realistically, given that anything is possible, but some things are less probable, the chances of a keyhole shot were pretty slim. Even still, most of the State Department folks had become reluctant to leave the safety of the Palace since the rockets started coming. Putting it into perspective though, most of these people were the same ones who thought a walk across the parking lot, to the P.X., was to take a walk in the Red Zone. There were people who had not left the Palace the entire time they had been there. We called them Palace-ites.

The security posture had been downgraded yesterday, and we were allowed to take off our armor for the first time in a while. Tonight, they reversed that, and issued another warning telling everyone to put it back on at midnight. For the next two days we were to wear armor any time not under hard cover. The directive came down because there was still a general belief we were going to get the bejesus kicked out of us during the million-man march al-Sadr had called for.

We were still getting rockets in the I.Z., but not so much at the Palace anymore. Because of the lack of incoming, and the constant aches and pains sleeping on the stretcher had caused, I had been sleeping in my trailer for the last two days. Well, trying to sleep anyway. More often than not I would lay in bed for a couple of hours each morning, waiting for the C-RAM alarm to go off, before I could actually nod off. The clincher had come the other morning when the pain of sleeping on the stretcher had become so bad it took great time and effort, not to mention a lot of aspirin and ibuprofen, just to roll off the stretcher and stand up. Present, real pain had greater swaying power over future, and only possible pain. Although, with al-Sadr's march coming up, I would probably be moving back into the Palace tomorrow.

The lack of sleep was starting to get to me too, and this time I went looking for a cot. The stretcher had been O.K., but it was just a little too narrow, just a little too low to the floor, and over the long run had proven to be quite uncomfortable. Just trying to get onto the thing had become its own set of problems. The legs were only a couple of inches long, instead of the longer cot legs, and the process involved me sitting on the floor, rolling onto it, then trying to find a comfortable position. I am not even going to comment on the irony of sleeping on a stretcher, in a war zone, with so many explosions, and so much destruction going on.

Since the rockets had started falling none of the State Department, or Reconstruction Teams, had been leaving the Palace to meet with their Iraqi Government counterparts. That meant all the WPPS Teams who protected them while they were out and about had been getting a lot of time off too. With no missions going on, there had been a lot of poker games going on in the camp chow hall, and more folks in the gym in the evenings.

8 April – So much goings on. Nuri al-Maliki, Iraq's Prime Minister, had called for the disbandment of all militias in the country, and was barring al-Sadr from being allowed to enter politics while the Mahdi Militia existed. On the other hand, al-Sadr was pushing back by proclaiming he would only disband his militia if the clerics in Iran told him to, and he was still calling for his million-man march tomorrow. Expecting a lot of trouble, all Iraqi Government offices were going to be closed for the day. U.S. Military, and State Department offices would remain open, however we had all been instructed to stay in our kit until tomorrow night.

I had also moved back into the Palace, for the next couple of days at least. Laying in my trailer, waiting for the alarms to go off, or the roof to explode, had started to become a bit too much for me to endure. Stretched out, under the covers, trying to get comfortable, my mind would start to wander, and fill with thoughts both curious and dark. Would I hear the explosion if a rocket actually hit my trailer? Normally, you could hear the roar of the rocket when the missiles flew overhead. Would I be able to hear the engine of the rocket that hit me? Or would it have outflown its own thunder, like a bullet racing ahead of the sonic boon it created as it pierced the air, flying faster than sound. Stop! Stop that! Clear your mind. Try to relax. Close your eyes. Empty your thoughts. Oh, this pillow was so fluffy. Yes. These sheets were so soft. Would I hear the sound of the shrapnel as it pinged through the wall of the trailer? Like they show in the movies. Or would the crack of the explosion drown out the bedlam of accompanying noises with the ferocity of the blast? Knock! It! Off! Go to sleep! But wait, what about…? Brain, I said that's enough. Now quit. It was kind of like that, until I finally nodded off.

This evening, I arrived at the camp a little early, and was able to get myself settled into the office prior to shift change. My guards arrived on time, and they hustled into formation so we could conduct accountability and inspection quickly. Even though the time around the evening formation had become relatively quiet lately, none of us were feeling overly comfortable about being in a large crowd. Especially when that crowd had to gather in the open, at a predictable time. Finding everyone present, and properly equipped for work, all new and relevant information was announced. Receiving no questions, or requirements for clarification, the guards were released to head off to their assigned posts, and relieve the day shift.

Watching my guards police up their gear, and depart the formation area, I realized I had some extra time before my first set of checks needed to be conducted. I headed over to the chow hall to hit the latrine, and grab a cup of coffee. My office did have a bathroom in it, but the plumbing had never been hooked up. This forced us to use one of the two public latrines on the camp. Remember, security for the camp used to be provided by a guard force who lived on the camp, and if they needed a bathroom break they just went back to their trailer. Not having our own living trailers on the camp, my guards and I had to use the latrine in the gym, or the one in the chow hall. Being in full kit all the time also presented its own set of challenges when nature called.

For all you more senior vets, you probably remember the old style L.B.E. Short for Load Bearing Equipment, the L.B.E. consisted of a shoulder harness (suspenders, if you will) that connected to the front and back of a pistol belt. Pouches, pockets, and small packs to hold all your equipment were clipped around the entire assembly, including the straps. This piece of kit could be worn by itself, or in conjunction with body armor. The most commonly issued set of armor, up until recently, had been the flak vest, A.K.A. flak jacket.

Actually, it was a bit misleading to label the flak jacket as armor. It was originally designed only to give protection against secondary projectiles, debris kicked up by an explosion, not defend against bullets and shrapnel. At the time of the invasion, if you were not assigned to a unit like Special Forces or Rangers, the flak jacket was what you were issued. When my unit and I first rolled over the berm, behind the main invasion force, that was the kit we were wearing.

Advances in the technology of individual body armor had led to the mass development of stronger armor, with lighter pads and plates, resulting in greater protection. With the increase in their availability, the military had been able to collect up all the old flak jackets, and issue these new vests to deploying units.

Not to be left behind, the vests that carried the pads and plates had undergone their own evolution as well. Having started as a simple cloth or nylon outer shell, straps and loops had been added to the front, sides, and back of the carriers. This gave the wearer the option of taking all the pouches once clipped to the L.B.E., and affix them directly to the vest. Making the armor, carrier, and equipment one giant kit. The down side was the combined weight of the entire ensemble was no longer divided between two pieces of equipment, and it became a matter of all or nothing when it came to wearing your kit. Additionally, when nature called for an extended sit down, prior planning needed to be conducted to determine where you were going to drop this monstrosity, and still be able to keep an eye on it. Q.E.D., big toilet stalls should be a standard feature for any construction projected for a war zone.

Having more space than the stalls over at the gym, the only real option that came close to fulfilling the above-mentioned criteria was the latrine at the chow hall, and I walked into the bathroom to find a bank of empty stalls. Standing outside the cubicles I wrestled my way out of my kit, and having freed myself from its encumbrance sloughed it in behind me. Locking the door, I leaned my kit up against it, got situated, and seated myself on the throne. No sooner had I gotten comfortable than, wouldn't you know it, the C-RAM alarm went off. In my entire life, I do not think I had ever experienced a feeling of such complete and utter helplessness as I did at that moment. Options? I only had one. I reached over to my kit, grabbed my helmet, and smashed it down on my head. With both hands I grabbed my armor by the shoulders, and slung it across my back. Leaning forward in the saddle, I tried to make myself as small as possible by laying my chest on my legs.

"Please, oh please." I begged. "If I have any karma left, please don't let me get hit on the toilet."

The alarm continued to scream, and the rockets slammed into the FOB next to the camp. The detonation were strong enough to rattle the chow hall, and knock loose dust that had accumulated on the rafters, allowing it to drift down and fill the air with that familiar reddish brown haze. Milliseconds later, the concussion from the blast caused the floor to tremble, made the toilet shake, and rattled the mirrors over the sinks. At least I thought that was caused by the concussion. As the old saying goes, first you say it, then you do it, and if you are scared enough at the time toilet paper would not be necessary afterwards. Thankfully, the rest of the evening was very quiet.

9 April – In a great display of when the right people to make a decision were too scared to make the right decision, the last couple of days had been spent putting more T-walls all the way around the Palace. Not just in front of the doors and windows, but all the way around the building. Now, the Palace, a two story structure with thick – and I do mean thick – walls, and a strong roof was completely ringed with twelve-foot tall T-walls.

I mentioned these T-walls before, but I do not think I explained exactly what they were. A T-wall was a four-foot wide, ten to twelve-foot tall, sixteen-inch thick, steel reinforced concrete wall. They were constructed to be portable, but only if you had a crane big enough, and could be locked, end-to-end like Legos, to provide protection from direct fire weapons, or shrapnel from indirect fire weapons. Every camp, FOB, and compound was ringed with these walls, as well as most of the checkpoints. Basically, you could not go anywhere in the I.Z. without seeing them. The only problem with them was everybody wanted them, and the supply just did not seem to be keeping up with the demand.

I could understand why they had been placing them in front of the entrances, doors, and windows around the building. My bewilderment came from when the Duck and Cover alarm went off the announcement clearly stated, "move away from all windows and doors." I guess that instruction was a little too difficult for some people to follow, since I knew they were not so dedicated they refused to leave their desks during an attack.

I was further puzzled by the act of erecting these barriers along the thick, stone, windowless walls. These T-walls would have done better service if they had been placed around the soft trailers out in the trailer parks, but since the Palace-ites were not going out there anymore, why would they want to do that?

Not much else happened today. This morning, around 0830hrs, the C-RAM alarm had gone off. I heard a bang, rolled over, and went back to sleep. Around 1515hrs, the alarm went off again, but this time the bang came before the alarm.

Al-Sadr's much anticipated march had been a no-go today as well. Rumors had it the march had been postponed, or possibly even called off. I did not know which one was true, but I would be more inclined to believe the whole thing had been cancelled. Someone finally figured out that bringing so many people together, in one place, would make such a great target of opportunity no self-respecting terrorist would be able to pass it up.

Helicopters and fast movers (fighter jets) had been pretty busy all last night, and most of today as well. There had never been more than a couple of minutes when you could not hear the sound of one or the other flying overhead. From time to time last night the ignition flare of a missile launch could be seen as it jumped to life, off the side of a helicopter, after being fired at some far-off target. I hoped they would be up and around tonight as well.

I was still sleeping in the Palace during the day, but since the rockets had been coming later in the morning, I had taken to waiting until after shift to go back to my trailer for a shower instead of heading over in the middle of the night. Either way was still a little nerve racking, but nothing bad had happened so far.

10 April – Today had been pretty classic. We had been wearing full kit for the last two days, in preparation for al-Sadr's march. Now that it had been called off, we were still wearing armor. This evening, my normal group was in the chow hall, eating dinner, when the P.A. started talking.

"Mandatory P.P.E. (Personal Protective Equipment. Helmets and vests) is no longer in effect." It said. "Personnel are reminded that there is still a threat of I.D.F. in the I.Z. and P.P.E. should remain ready/available at all times."

For the first time in what felt like forever, we all pushed away from the table, stood up, and stripped out of our kit before sitting back down (in much greater comfort, I might add) to finish our meals. Throughout the chow hall the din of conversation slowly returned as everyone else divested themselves of their own gear, got settled back into their seats, and resumed eating. I had just taken a stab at some brown in color, meat like substance the cook was trying to pass off as meatloaf when, yes, again, the C-RAM alarm went off, blasting throughout the chow hall. Chairs screeched and skidded as people threw themselves away from their tables, and dove onto the floor to get as small as possible. By now, everyone knew the C-RAM alarm activating inside the chow hall meant this building had been calculated as being within the intended impact site. With no time to run, and nowhere to go, we lay prone…waiting for the explosion. And then, we waited some more.

It was a full minute before anyone lifted themselves off the floor, poked their head over a table, and looked around the building for an answer. The alarm had stopped screaming, and one by one heads popped over the tabletops to see what was going on. As silence continued to pour over us, people slowly regained their feet, righted their chairs, and made the decision whether they were going to finish their meal, or give it up for a bad idea. We had gone all last night, and all today, without a single rocket and now, within minutes of the announcement canceling mandatory P.P.E, we had gotten a C-RAM alarm. Things that make you go, hmmm.

12 April – And the madness continued. The I.Z. was still getting rocketed, once or twice a day, but the rockets were now being concentrated over by the Chancellery. Also called the Chancery, this building housed the actual,

official Embassy, and was located further upstream, politically and as the Tigris flowed. The Palace, while still called Embassy, was actually where the majority of the bureaucrats worked. A little confused? Let me explain. Diplomatic relations between the U.S. and Iraq had been an on-again, off-again thing dating all the way back to the early 1800's, when the region was still a part of the Ottoman Empire.

Let me give you a real quick, very condensed, overview of our diplomatic history to help put a little perspective on this. In 1831, the U.S. started the process of political relations with the Empire by making its first diplomatic appointment to the Ottomans, a Charge d' Affaires, to serve American interests. That office was in Constantinople. As relations prospered, the U.S. expanded its representation to the Ottoman Turks by appointing additional representatives to the Mission. The Ottoman Empire would soon dissolve, and the office that would eventually become the Embassy in Iraq was spun off from the Constantinople Headquarters. Initially entitled the American Consul for Baghdad, its first political appointment was assigned in August 1888. This department would serve as the official U.S. presence in the region until 1931.

The United States formally recognized the independence of Iraq in January 1930, but it was not until 1931 initial diplomatic relations were established with the creation of The American Ligation at Baghdad. The final step to full diplomatic relations would not be accomplished until December 1946, when the U.S. upgraded its representation in Iraq from Ligation to a full-fledged Embassy. This Embassy would remain open until Iraq decided to sever relations with the U.S. in response to the 1967 Arab-Israeli War.

Communications between the two countries remained murky for quite some time, until President Reagan and Iraqi Foreign Minister Tariq Aziz came to a decision to reestablish diplomatic relations in 1984, and reopened the American Embassy in Baghdad. Moved into a different building, not the one that housed the original Embassy, this Embassy would only remain open seven short years before closing its doors in 1991 following Iraq's invasion of Kuwait. With this severing of ties only a small department, known as an Interests Section, of the Embassy would be left in Baghdad. It was this office, maintaining a small footprint in the same building, which would establish the foundation for the return of diplomatic relations.

Stay with me here, we are just about caught up, and this next part is going to move a little fast. U.S. and coalition forces invaded Iraq on 20 March 2003, and pushed up to take Baghdad on April 9. By the middle of May, the Coalition Provisional Authority (C.P.A.) had been established, under Paul Bremer, with a mandate to move Iraq in the direction of reconstruction, and sovereignty. It was during this time Saddam's Palace on the Tigris River was first occupied. Later, a building inside the Green Zone, not the Palace and not on its grounds, was designated as the U.S. Embassy in Iraq. Located upriver, and around the bend, the actual Embassy building sat in the northeast corner of the I.Z.

At the end of June 2004, The Iraqi Interim Government was established. Signaling that once again, Iraq had become a sovereign state. The C.P.A., having fulfilled its purpose, was dissolved, and diplomatic relations were once again restored between the U.S. and Iraq. The reopening, and staffing of this Embassy building would later prove the structure and grounds were too small to house all the organizations necessary to complete the combined mission of the State Department, and U.S. Military in Iraq. To facilitate their need to expand, the Palace was eventually brought under the umbrella of the Department of State, and made an annex to the Embassy. Both of these would remain the official Embassy and Annex of the United States until the New Embassy Compound (NEC) would be completed further down river, and opened for business. Clear as mud, right? Keep reading, there will be more explanations ahead.

Yesterday, al-Sadr's number one man in Najaf was killed by masked men in a drive-by style shooting. Today, al-Sadr issued a statement blaming the U.S. and Iraqi government for the slaying. You would think these people would get a clue, and blame the people who actually pulled the triggers. Maybe point fingers at the faction who were undermining the central government. Or, at the very least, start an investigation to find whoever was really responsible for this. Why would they want to do that? Why cloud the issues with facts? Not when it was so much easier to blame everyone else for their problems, and then do nothing about it. Unfortunately, that seemed to be the normal behavior around here.

What? Give you another example? O.K. A couple of months ago, a news clipping was making its way around the Palace. The story told of a two foot long bull shark that had made its way into an irrigation ditch running through farmlands in the south of Iraq. The shark had been captured in a large section of ditch where the local children swam. When questioned, the locals blamed the U.S. for the shark's presence. America was at fault for putting their children in danger. How could a group of people be so clueless? Really! The U.S. Government had decided to put bull sharks in Iraq's irrigation ditches? To what end? Don't you think, if it had been us, we would have put a fricken laser on the shark's head, or something? I did not know how a whole society could wallow in such ignorance.

And, of course, al-Sadr was still in Iran, living in opulence, giving instructions to his people, living here in the slums, to fight the infidels.

14 April – I had the night off last night! WOOHOO! There was *so* much to do over here.

Earlier today we did have a C-RAM alarm activation on the other side of the compound, about ten minutes before my alarm clock was set to go off. Go figure. There were a couple of booms off in the distance. Even though I was back sleeping in my trailer, they did not sound like anything to get all worked up about.

Since I was already up I did not see any reason why I should not stay up. Tonight was going to be my night off, so I got myself cleaned up, and headed over to the office to make sure my relief got settled in for the night. I was approaching the parking lot, at the front of the camp, when I noticed there was a lot of excitement happening around the gate shack.

Several of the WPPS teams were milling around their vehicles, while a couple more were unloading equipment from theirs. As I got closer I noticed one of the people cleaning out a truck was Lippy, my roommate and dayshift Security Manager at the camp. He was emptying the vehicle we had been given to make supply runs for our guards. I rounded the corner through the gate, passed the guard shack, and was on my way to talk with him when the odor of gasoline combined with burnt explosives hit my nose. Slowing to a stop, I took a closer look around the parking lot, and realized at least one of the booms from earlier today had taken place right here.

This rocket must have been launched from somewhere around Sadr City. The flight path had taken it right over the Hospital, the FOB, the WPPS Camp, and deposited it between two armored Suburbans parked forty feet from the gate shack. Fortunately, the weight and armor of the vehicles had absorbed the majority of the blast and shrapnel, but they had not been able to take all of it. Shards of razor-sharp metal had sliced through several other vehicles puncturing fuel tanks, shattering windshields into thousands of spider webs, and peppering body panels.

If that was not enough, the engine of the rocket had been blown from the tail, and was thrown over the twenty foot high wall separating this part of the WPPS parking lot from the P.X. parking lot. It had landed on the roof of a car, breaking all the windows and crushing the roof down to the top of the headrests on the front seats.

Our vehicle had been parked right next to the bunker, beside the gate, and shrapnel had shredded both front tires, popped a hole in the front of the hood, and put two circular holes the size of dimes in the driver side mirror. Wouldn't you know, the cement barrier right next to our truck only had a little chip taken out of it.

Our truck was dead. The engine would not start, and coolant was leaking from the radiator. It would have to be towed to the garage where, with hope, the mechanics would be able to resurrect it. With nothing more we could do but empty our shot up truck, I helped Lippy carry all the gear to the office, and waited for my relief to arrive. Not much later, he walked into the office, and we went through the routine of getting him settled in for the night. He and I walked posts to make sure he was familiar with them, and their unique idiosyncrasies, made sure he had my phone number, in case anything really weird happened, and headed back to the office to relieve Lippy.

With shift change complete, Lippy and I grabbed a quick bite at the Palace chow hall. Lippy went back to the trailer to drop his work gear, and I stopped off at the Lizard Lounge to wait for him and Finch. The Lizard Lounge was nothing spectacular. It was just a picnic table outside our trailer, next to the bunker in which I had been sheltering instead of sleeping, where some of us gathered to drink a few beers, shoot the breeze, and wind down at the end of the day. Most days I did not have the opportunity to attend any of these gatherings, I would have already been at work, but having the night off I was able to make an appearance.

Like me, Lippy and Finch were both retired military, and were not quite ready to completely give up their commitments to supporting the military, and their country. Ergo, after retirement they had both transitioned into contracting. Both men were of average height, average weight, average build, and unlike me, had been blessed with an everyday look that gave them the ability to blend into a crowd. We called this the ability to become a "grey-man." Not fully in the light, and not completely in darkness, grey-men were able to blend into their surroundings, and not bring attention to themselves.

They were easy-going, and to look at them you would never have guessed Lippy had retired from the Ranger Battalions, and Finch from Special Forces. You would have to get to know them for a while, then it would become apparent. Lippy still retained the discipline and drive of a Ranger, and Finch, well, Finch's sense of humor was not wrapped too tight. Combined with his Special Forces attitude of "it's better to ask forgiveness than permission," Finch tended to make you wonder what he would be up to next.

We sat and talked. We drank a few beers, and told a few stories. All in all, it was nice to just sit and shoot the breeze after all the chaos that had been going on. A few hours later, Lippy and Finch called it a day, since they still had to be at work in the morning. Having the night off, I did not want to hang out in the trailer, while Lippy was trying to sleep, so I grabbed a book and made my way to the Palace.

One of the biggest rooms in the Palace had been turned into, for the lack of a better term, a coffee bar. A small café stand had been brought in to make coffee, tea, and espresso. People could lounge in over-stuffed chairs and sofas while they sipped their brews. A small lending library had been set up as well. Most of the books came from care packages people had received from the States, and when they were done reading, the tomes would be left so others could enjoy them as well. As for the rest of the room the floor was covered in marble, red Italian marble to be exact, over-laid with Persian rugs. White marble columns supported a vaulted roof two stories above, and geometric designs and patterns covered the walls. It was against Islam to draw, paint, or otherwise portray living things. I stayed here for the rest of the night reading and napping, then reading some more. Baghdad nightlife could really wear you out.

I went back to the hooch, my trailer not a bottle of booze, around 0630hrs, and was asleep by 0700hrs. I slept all day. It was great. No booms, no alarms, no nothing. Almost like old times.

15 April – Last night, during shift, there had been a lot of booms across the river. I was not really sure if it had been the result of helicopters targeting launch sites, ground troops destroying launch sites, or insurgent factions bombing each other, but either way it sounded like a lot of somebodies were getting a lot of bad news.

I just could not get to sleep this morning after shift. I guess I was not as comfortable being back in my trailer as I thought I was. I finally fell asleep around 1000hrs, and was jarred awake around 1330hrs by the C-RAM alarm. I hopped out of bed, did not even try for the shower shoes, and scrambled out the door. As I got to the end of the sandbags I realized I had not heard any booms yet, but I paused in anticipation anyway. I also realized the cement pavers that made up the sidewalk, having baked in the spring sun all morning, were getting a little warm under my bare feet. Strike that, those things were down right hot. This was going to be the first, and last time I left the shower shoes in the hooch for a bunker run.

I waited for a second, debating whether or not I should go back for my shoes, before deciding I was close enough to cover I would forgo them this time. Reaching the bunker, I squatted down, dug my toes into the cool dirt under the shade of the cover, and waited. Nothing happened. I sat there for a few more minutes, and still nothing happened. I waited long enough to ensure anything the C-RAM may have been tracking would have landed, or for the P.A. to announce the "All Clear." Since neither of those things happened, I headed back to the trailer. It must have been another one of those "false positives."

With the daily alarm activation out of the way I was able to fall back into bed, and knock right off to sleep. Not an hour later I was jarred awake by the C-RAM alarm screaming next to my trailer again. Kicking off my covers I scooped up my shower shoes, and dashed out the door. At the end of the sandbags I stopped to put my shoes on, and waited for the first bang. Again, nothing. This was not turning out to be a good day.

Not even bothering to leave the sandbags. I waited for a while to make sure the rocket was not taking its lazy time about getting here. Hearing nothing, I went back to the trailer, and flopped back into bed.

Around 1530hrs, I was awakened by a new, and peculiar sound. The sound of tapping, as of someone gently rapping, rapping at my trailer door. Notes had been posted on all of the trailers advising the occupants KBR maintenance crews would be coming around, tomorrow mind you, to do preventive maintenance on the air conditioners. Being a day sleeper, I had written on the paper that I wanted them to come by after 1600hrs, when I would be awake. Not only had they gotten the time wrong, they were a day early as well. Did I think my notes to the maintenance guys were ever going to work? Nevermore.

16 April – So far tonight things had actually gone fairly well at work. With the lead-up to work time yesterday afternoon, I was really doubtful it would.

Time was quickly approaching for some of the other Security Managers to go back to the States on vacation. During the shuffle to get those going on vacation out, and bring those returning from vacation in, some of the remaining Managers were getting shifted around. One change was going to be Finch. He was going to be moved from day shift CACs, and head up to the TOC to be our representative there. It had been suggested I would also move from night shift at the camp, and take over Finch's vacated day shift. I guess that meant I would have to get smart on the access policies for the palace, but until this actually happened, I would soldier on at the camp.

I was still sleeping in the trailer. Well, not so much sleeping as getting a succession of naps. It still took me a little while to get comfortable enough to fall asleep. The alarms were beginning to outnumber the explosions, and many of us were starting to question whether they were real activations or not. I know, I know, why take the chance, right? I too had heard the story of the boy who cried wolf.

This morning I woke gently to the dulcet tones of my alarm clock. Leisurely, I sipped coffee before immersing myself in a warm, comfortable shower. Clean, and freshly shaved, I was ready for work by 1615, way too early to leave. Pouring another cup of coffee, I laid back down to read a book, and pass the extra time.

As 1700hrs approached, I decided I still had enough time for a quick latrine call before heading over to the chow hall for dinner. I was pulling my pants back up when, doesn't it figure, the C-RAM alarm went off at the same time the sound of an explosion thundered through the trailer park. Once again, there I was with my pants in my hand, my pistol belt on the bed, and rockets on the way. Somebody out there had a really warped sense of humor.

Quickly, I fastened my pants, not worrying about tucking my shirt in, grabbed my pistol belt off the bed, and took off for the bunker. Of course, having been in the bathroom the C-RAM alarm had not been all that audible. The explosion had been the dead giveaway. Charging out of my hooch, I made the mad dash all the way to the bunker without stopping. No additional booms followed. One rocket was all we received, and that one had impacted outside Edgewood, detonating on the riverbank. It looked like we were back to getting the 5 o'clock fusillade.

17 April – The morning started with a fairly thick dust storm. Not so much windy, just dusty. In the wee hours of the morning the bright, white light cast by the streetlamps had begun to haze over. By sunup, everything had a deep red/brown tinge to it, and you could not see more than fifty yards.

If you had never been through a dust storm, they were an experience. The worst of them was a phenomenon known as Haboob. If you had ever lived in the Sahara Desert of Africa, the deserts of Arabia, maybe around Phoenix, Arizona, or the American West during the dust bowl years you know exactly what I was talking about. If not, let me tell you about them. Some deserts were primarily sand, but not Iraq. It was primarily dirt. Remember that whole Fertile Crescent Thing?

Sherman, set the way-back machine for a whole lot of years ago, when Iraq used to be lush, and green. Then, for some atmospheric, possibly geologic, reason the rain went away, causing everything to dry out. Big time emphasis on dry. Now that the majority of the country had been turned into one giant dirt lot, along would come this big wind to stir everything up. Even though a lot of the dirt remained in rather large clumps, or was still attached to the ground, some of that dirt, a lot of that dirt really, had been ground down to fine particles. And when I say fine particles, I mean particles as fine as baby powder.

Along would come this wind, and it would pick up all those fine, little particles of dirt. As it drove across the country, accelerating as it went, it would push this dirt ahead and within it, creating a wall of dust up to sixty miles wide, and a few thousand feet high, with winds up to fifty miles per hour. Speeding along, the storm would pound the ground with dust and wind, grinding the top layers of dirt into ever finer particles, and kicking up more and more dust in its path. Atmospheric conditions could cause those winds to run across the open desert in a wall lasting only minutes, or they could sustain them for hours, sometimes days. This was a Haboob, and out in the deep desert you could watch them roll in from miles away.

Being in Baghdad, we did not usually get the strongest of these storms, but we did tend to get the residuals from them. What I mean is, the winds could last for hours, or days, blowing just hard enough to keep the dirt particles airborne for the entire time. Everything got a red/brown tint to it, and enough dust got deposited on every surface, flat or otherwise, to make it look like no one had cleaned for years. During the stronger of these city storms, dust and dirt would blow around and drift like snow, only not as wet, and a whole lot less wonderlandish. If I did not mention it, while you were out in one of these storms, every breath you took sucked a little of this dirt into your mouth, nose, and lungs, and made every bite just a little crunchy.

End of shift came, and I went back to my trailer to go to bed. Soon enough, I fell asleep. Something kept waking me up though. A thud here, a bang there, a thump somewhere else. Unable to stay asleep, I crawled out of bed, and poked my head out the door to find a work gang rebuilding, and reinforcing the sandbag wall in front of my row of trailers. Once I realized what was making all the noise, I was able to get some sleep.

My alarm clock went off at 1500hrs, and I got out of bed to go to the bathroom. As I was standing in front of the toilet, it happened again. Wham! Rockets! They sounded far enough away I was not too worried about any of them being a serious threat to me. Even still. I did not take my time getting out of the trailer, and heading for the bunker. I rounded the corner into the bunker at full speed, and found it had already been completely filled by the work gang who had been slinging sandbags. I almost pulled a couple of muscles trying to keep from plowing over two of them. I also found out the C-RAM was not working right. The rockets had hit, and then the alarm had gone off. Great!

The "All Clear" was called a couple of minutes later, and I figured I would hurry up and get my shower done before they hit us again. Apprehensive, with a generous sprinkling of foreboding was the best way I could describe that shower. The pattern of past attacks suggested I had plenty of time to wash before the next set of rockets were launched, but it was still torture. I forced myself to remain under the spray of water, deafened by the deluge to all but the loudest of outside noises, and confined to the small space of the stall. Rinsing the final remnants of soap from my body, I dove out of the shower into a towel, dried off, and scrambled into my work clothes.

I met the rest of the dinner crew at the chow hall, Lunchmeat from the P.X. Parking lot, Lippy from the Camp, Finch from CACs, Chief from Towers and Grounds, and Manny from the Palace, and we sat down to eat. We were almost finished with our meals when we heard an explosion, felt a rumble, and then the C-RAM alarm went off. The explosion had been fairly distant, the rumble rather faint, and none of us realized we had chosen a table right under a loudspeaker. When the alarm went off, every one of us jumped a full foot out of our chairs.

As all the other diners were throwing themselves on the floor, we abandoned our trays, and started heading for the door. Time to go to work. The rockets at 1500 had hit behind the K.B.R. facility on the south side of the compound, and these rockets sounded like they had struck in the same area. We got the word from the guards everyone was O.K., no one had been injured, and damage had been minimal. Day Shift started making all the required notifications.

Someone, we did not know who, had called the TOC and told them the most recent rockets had landed in the P.X. parking lot, instead of behind the K.B.R. facility. We had all heard the parking lot Supervisor radio Lunchmeat to tell him everything was copacetic out there. But, the R.S.O.'s radios were on a different frequency than ours, so they only got the call from the R.S.O. in the TOC, and had taken off to check it anyway. Since it was Meat's venue, he took off after them.

The clock ticked away the minutes after the strike. As silence returned to the grounds those who had dived under their dinner tables at the bang of the alarm were now beginning to cautiously emerge from the chow hall. Somewhere between ten, and fifteen minutes later the "All Clear" came over the loudspeakers.

One thing to consider at this point was the rockets had been coming fairly regularly for the past three weeks or so, and everyone had become more than a little jumpy. This skittishness resulted in the hind-brain, the more primitive and instinctual part of the brain, registering any sudden, loud noises coming from any loud speaker as an alarm. Automatically, the fight or flight response kicked into high gear, not waiting for the higher functions to determine exactly what the ears had heard. Having been close to fifteen minutes since the initial warning had sounded, when the P.A. finally blasted the "All Clear" it appeared most everyone had forgotten we were still supposed to be under hard cover. Some people obeyed their hindbrain and took off for the bunkers. Some people stopped dead in their tracks while their frontal lobe processed this new information. A few indecisive people could not figure out which one they wanted to do, so they did both.

Lippy and I walked to the office on the Palace grounds where we conducted our shift change briefing, in the company of the other Security Manager, as they conducted theirs. The Camp had been relatively quiet today, and we ended up gabbing more than briefing. By this time, the others had finished with their exchange of information as well, and the official handover from day shift to night shift slowly devolved into a cluster of old soldiers talking shop, making jokes, and generally blowing off steam.

Collectively, the herd migrated outside to gather on the front porch until slowly, the group began to break up, and everyone started off in whatever direction they needed to go. Lippy, Finch, and I were still standing on the porch when, once again, the C-RAM alarm blasted to the accompaniment of two explosions. These detonations sounded much louder than the one we had heard in the chow hall, and I was afraid at least one of them may have landed inside the Camp. Without a smoke plume to identify the impact site I got on my radio, and called my Guard Supervisor for a SITREP (pronounced like "sit" and "rep" together, it was military speak for situation report).

Within seconds he radioed back, and reported everything on the Camp was green. No rockets had impacted on our turf, and my presence was not required. However, he did think the explosions had come from somewhere between the Rhino Staging Area and the North CAC to the Palace grounds. Having been a part of Lunchmeat's Parking Lot venue, not mine, the Rhino staging area was not officially in my A.O.R. (Area of Responsibility), meaning I had no requirement to respond. No requirement, except I had no idea where Lunchmeat was, if his shift change had been complete, or who would be responding. For me, the next decision was not difficult, not in the least. I could either stay in my own lane, not leave the porch, and take the risk that others were suffering and dying because the proper people could not get to them in time. Or, I could cross lanes, and respond. Provide any aid which may be required, and pick up Meat's slack if he was not able to get there quickly enough. Either way, it was a good bet I would be able to get there before he could, and if those rockets had inflicted injuries faster would be better. Lunchmeat would understand.

"Let's go!" sprang from my mouth as Lippy, Finch, and I sprang off the porch, and raced toward the North CAC. As we drew closer, the radio began to light up with more impact and damage reports. I think I had mentioned the bulk of our guard force came from Central and South America. Spanish was the first language for all of them. However, some of them did speak English with varying degrees of fluency. Spanish was their native language, but when they got scared, or excited, I was not sure what language they spoke. We flew through the North CAC, expecting the worse, and got our first sight of the staging area. Nothing was happening. No chaos. No excitement. Nothing. A little anticlimactic, to say the least.

We slowed to a walk. Definitely not because we needed to catch our breath after sprinting from the office, since we were still young, and being former military kept ourselves in great shape. So, definitely NOT because of that. Listening closer to the radio, we paid more attention to the on-going reports. As three native English speakers, with little more than high school level Spanish, it took us a few minutes to translate that the rockets had actually impacted on much the same area as the ones from earlier today, over by the K.B.R. facility, on the opposite side of the compound. Standing outside when those rockets had exploded made the detonations sound much louder than the earlier ones. The echo of the blasts bouncing off stone buildings, cement barriers, and concrete T-walls had caused confusion, and it took everyone a bit of time to pin-point the exact impact points. The fog of war was not just a saying, that stuff really happened. Fortunately, no one had been hurt by the strike, but it certainly looked like the insurgents had the K.B.R. facility pretty well dialed in.

Today in the news, Al Qaeda had hit a funeral procession, outside a village in the Northern Iraq province of Diyala, with a car bomb killing fifty people. Shi'a Kurds who had died while fighting Al Qaeda were being buried when the attack happened. I still did not understand how these people did not learn. They would bunch together for a funeral, thinking they would not get attacked. Let a couple of guys with guns terrorize their villages, and they would not band together to kick them out. Have they not learned? Security. Security. Security.

They would whine and cry all day long about being attacked, but would take no action to protect themselves. They blamed everything that was wrong on the U.S., and our presence in Iraq, instead of taking the responsibility necessary to fix their own country, or even their own neighborhood. I did not get it.

18 April – If it was not one thing, it was another. I got off work this morning, went to breakfast/dinner, and headed off to my hooch. I took a quick shower, set up the coffee pot, and settled down into bed for a little light reading before sleep time. I was just beginning to nod off when, out on the lawn there arose such a clatter, I sprang from by bed to see what was the matter. Away to the door I flew like a flash, and found the Iraqi work gang who had been repairing the sandbag wall yesterday had returned. This time, they were working right next to my trailer. I asked them to try to keep the noise down while they were working, but I was not totally convinced Iraqis knew what an inside voice was, let alone how to use one. Sometime afterwards, I was able to fall asleep. And to all a good night.

Around 1130hrs I was woken up again. This time by someone trying to get into the trailer. The door would open about a foot, and then close again. Cautiously, I got out of bed, and went to see what was going on. It was Lippy. He had been trying to open the door so he could get in, and get his laundry bag for turn-in at the cleaners. The idiots who had been rebuilding the sandbag walls had taken a couple dozen filled sandbags, and stacked them on the porch. Right in front of my door. Unlike the front door to your house, the doors on the trailers opened out. I may have been able to squeeze my way through the opening, if my life depended on it, but there was no way I was getting that door to open any further than that. Still standing on the porch, Lippy said he would take care of this, and he walked off in search of the work crew. I waited until I heard voices outside the room before trying to open the door, and when I did I saw the work gang Foreman yelling at his guys to move the sandbags. Had this been done on purpose because I yelled at them to be quiet? Had they purposefully blocked my door for some reason? Or had they just put them there as part of the process of rebuilding the walls? I had no idea, and since the Foreman was also Iraqi, and handling the situation quite efficiently, I considered the issue dealt with, and went back to bed.

Finally, I got back to sleep. As a matter of fact, I wound up getting about an extra hour of sleep. 1500hrs came way too early, and by the time I stopped punching the snooze alarm it was 1600hrs. Continually hitting the snooze, I had been too tired to realize I was sleeping through the afternoon barrage time. By the time my feet hit the floor I realized what I had done, and scrambled to get out of the trailer as fast as I could. The sandstorm that had blown in yesterday, and tapered off by this morning, was back again, and everything had that reddish hue once more. This was one of the reasons I came back to work in Iraq. Spending time in the States, I had not been getting enough dirt in my diet. Dinner and shift change went off quickly and quietly, and the rest of the night was fairly quiet as well. All the way up to around midnight.

I may have mentioned, once or twice, after we got beyond the 2200ish time frame we were usually good for the rest of the night. Well, not so much tonight. I was sitting in the office, reading a book, when about midnight the C-RAM alarm blared through the speaker right next to the office. I jumped like a startled cat. Looking at the clock, I figured this had to be another false alarm, so I dropped my book on the desk, took my reading glasses off, and strolled out the front door.

Once again, experience having taught me there probably was not enough time to make it to the Main Gate Shack before the rocket came, I walked down the steps, turned right, and headed toward my hiding spot between the cement block and the perimeter wall. This time, when I got there, I found two other guys were squatting there. I guess I was not the only one who thought this was a good spot to hide.

I squatted down next to them, and we waited. Actually, we waited longer than usual. We waited long enough I was about to stand up, and walk back into the trailer, when the rockets finely started to explode. Four of them. Some serious hangtime on those rounds. Four loud detonations erupted in rapid succession. The crack of the blast suggested they had impacted fairly close. Suddenly, that concrete block felt very, very small.

By the time I reached the safety of the front gate, all posts had checked in, and my Guard Supervisor had radioed the thumbs-up. I pulled my cell phone out of my pocket, and dialed my boss to give him the report that we were all good. While we were talking, he confirmed my suspicion about how close the explosions had been by telling me most of the rockets had landed behind the CaSH. The odd thing was there had been an "odd man out," as one of the rockets had landed to the West of me, somewhere around the 14th of July Circle.

Time for a little geography lesson. The street running in front of the Palace was called Haifa Street. It started North of the Green Zone, entered the I.Z. at Check Point 2, and generally ran parallel to the Tigris River. It then continued its Southerly route past the CaSH and FOB Blackhawk (the FOB directly behind the WPPS Camp. I mentioned it before), before sharply curving West, to travel between the Palace and the WPPS Camp. It continued on, between several other secure compounds, before terminating at a traffic circle called "14th of July Circle".

Named to commemorate the revolution that overthrew the Iraqi Monarchy in July 1958, this was one of the major traffic circles in Baghdad. You would have thought someone would have changed the name, since it celebrated the date Saddam's Ba'ath party rose to power. Go figure.

Where Haifa Street entered the circle on the West side, it exited the East side with the name of al-Khindi Street. Named for the 9th Century scientist, mathematician, physician, and calligrapher Abu-Yusuf Ya'qub ibn al-Khindi (a bit of a mouthful, isn't it), Al-Khindi Street continued on to the West, where it passed the New Embassy Compound (the NEC), and several Army FOBs before T-walls bordering the I.Z forced it to merge with another street. It then exited the Green Zone through Check Point 12. There, it became Route Irish.

Entering the circle from the South, and exiting to the North, was the street that bore the same name as the traffic circle, 14th of July Street. This street entered the Green Zone by crossing over the only bridge that gave direct access to the I.Z. (yes, you guessed it, the 14th of July Bridge), and continued North where it was blocked off by T-walls and barriers forming the Northern boundary of the Green Zone in the vicinity of the Iraqi Government buildings in the I.Z., and the Al-Rashid hotel.

19 April – Today was a good day. I got off shift, had some breakfast, and headed back to the hooch. I got the coffee

pot set up, took a quick shower, the shower head having been fixed days ago, and lay down in bed for a beer and a quick read. I did not remember falling asleep.

I woke up around 1130hrs, rolled over, and went back to sleep. The alarm clock went off at 1500hrs, and I did a couple of snooze alarms until 1545hrs. I lay in bed, drank some coffee, and woke up. I got in the shower around 1615hrs, got dressed afterword, and ready for work. All of this without a single boom, or alarm. No rockets. No one slamming sandbags against the side of my trailer. Nothing. It was great!

20 April – No more than one day of quietness. Let me tell you, this was getting really old. Again, about five minutes before my alarm clock was supposed to wake me up the C-RAM woke me up instead. And, of course, the alarm started screaming about the same time the rocket impacted. The good news was the impact was nowhere close to my trailer. The bad news was the impact was over by the Icehouse.

This was another one of those things you did not think about until the convenience was gone. For most of us, ice was only as far away as the freezer. Open the door and scoop out a glassful, or push the button on the door and the glass was filled. Either way the automatic ice machine was taking over, and resigning to antiquity the day when an ice tray would be manually filled and we had to wait while the water froze.

The next thing most people did not think about was the cleanliness of the water from which their ice was made. In the States, our tap water was kept very clean, chlorinated at the water treatment plant, fluoridated, and pumped right to your faucet. Water in third world countries, and war zones, was not quite so clean. Ever hear of Montezuma's revenge? You could catch it just as quickly from using ice made from the very same water you had been warned not to drink.

Keeping things cold at home was also not an issue when the other side of the freezer was a refrigerator. Unfortunately, the whole process was not that simple for us. Small, dorm room style refrigerators were fairly common over here. But, as you college grads know, they did not hold very much. They also required a pesky little nuisance known as electricity for them to work, and to receive that electricity you would need another piece of equipment known as a generator. And that opened up a whole new can of worms.

To make life a little easier, K.B.R. (Kellogg, Brown, and Root. The logistics, maintenance, and service company that conducted the majority of the life support functions over here) had set up an Icehouse across the street from the H.L.Z. Potable water, the official description for drinkable water, was pumped from a water purification unit into an industrial sized ice maker. Once frozen, the cubes were bagged and doled out to those agencies under contract to receive them. With electricity being such a scarce commodity (most of the guard posts were not hooked up), we had to scrounge as many big coolers as we could get our hands on, and spread them around the posts so they could be filled with the ice we got from the Icehouse. When summer temperatures could reach as high as 140° Fahrenheit, ice became a very important commodity.

Well. I was up. So I started the coffee, turned on the lights and the TV, and went back to bed for a snooze alarm while the coffee brewed. As the machine sputtered out its tell-tail gurgling, signaling the coffee was done. I decided to go ahead and get up for the day. Sitting up in bed I sipped coffee, and watched TV while the caffeine cleaned out the cobwebs and kicked my brain into action. Having already received our midafternoon rocket, I was not in a great hurry as I showered, shaved, and got dressed. Even though I was not being rushed these motions played out as a well-choreographed process designed to keep me in a position where, if necessary, I could get out of the trailer as fast as possible.

The soap did not stay on the face and head any longer than necessary. Scrub and rinse. A face full of soap could be such a bother if you had to run to the bunker, especially when you were trying to keep those bubbles out of your eyes. This was another reason I kept my head shaved. Even though shampoos had come a long way in their "no more tears" formulas, I preferred a couple of swipes with a washcloth, as opposed to taking the risk of having to bolt from the shower with a mop full of suds.

Soap on, soap off Danielson. Get wet. Get dry. In. Out. Sleep shorts immediately went on for the walk across the room to the wall locker. In a flash, the shorts were replaced by drawers and pants, with socks and shoes directly following. Shaving and the brushing of teeth were done half dressed. I did not leave the trailer door open while I was in the bathroom anymore, but I did open the window, and turn the volume on the TV off. Just in case.

It was going on 1700 as I was finishing up in the bathroom. We had not received the 5 o'clock fusillade in a while, and as I wiped down the inside of the sink I thought I heard the sound of the C-RAM alarm. I stuck my head into the bedroom, and sure enough, the C-RAM alarm was sounding, off in the distance. It was very faint, but as I listened it started to get louder and louder as the alarms started going off closer and closer. Walking the sound toward me.

I grabbed my shirt from the bed, scooped up my radio and pistol belt, and got out of the hooch. Fast. Stopped at the end of the sandbag wall, I crouched down, put my shirt on, and waited for the explosion. It did not come. Slowly, I stood back up, and looked around to see if I could find an answer to my confusion. Maybe this had been another false positive. It was also possible the rocket may have been dud. Either way, time was marching past the normal alarm to bang interval, and deciding to err on the side of caution, I completed the trek to the bunker. Pistol belt around my waist, radio clipped to my hip, I buttoned my shirt as I walked. I slipped between the edge of the bunker and the end-cap, ducked my head, and crouched under the roof of the shelter as a high order detonation exploded, answering the false positive/dud question. Another rocket with serious hang time.

Hunched over inside the bunker, I could tell by the blast the rocket had not dropped in Edgewood, but the intensity of the detonation told me the point of impact had not been very far away. I switched on my radio, and began scanning frequencies, trying to hear any report of where the rocket may have landed, and listening for the calls that would summon First Responders. Monitoring my radio, I waited in the bunker until the "All Clear" sounded without a single transmission. No damage report, no calls for help, no requests for assistance. Nothing. Although not unheard of, it was very uncommon for the radios to remain this silent after an impact, and I mulled over all the possibilities as I returned to my trailer to finish getting ready for work.

Unable to discern any clear reason for the lack of information, I grabbed up the rest of my gear, and headed off for shift. Walking around the chow hall, I bumped into one of our guards who told me the rocket had landed on the opposite side of the pool, between the laundry service building, and the Palace loading dock. Curious to see if I could discover why no radio calls had been made I skirted the pool, and passed the laundry to discover a mass of people clustered around a bunker, craning their necks. I guess I had found the impact site.

Being taller than most came in handy every now and again, and in this instance it allowed me to look over the crowd of gawkers, and get a good look at the impact site. To be honest with you, as far as destruction went, this one was pretty lame, and I could not figure out what everyone was so fascinated with until someone mentioned that two people had been wounded by the blast. Their wounds were fairly superficial, and both had already walked off to find a medic. Everyone else was just hanging around, talking about what had just happened to them. I did not need my additional height, however, to see that once again, the second-floor balcony was packed with rubber-neckers. All snapping pictures. Newbies and noncombat troops with nothing better to do, and not enough sense to do it somewhere else.

Leaving the impact site, I cut through the Palace on my way to the office. While walking through the large, marble coated rotunda in the center of the palace I noticed a mass of activity. TV cameras, lights, podiums, and a bunch of guys in suits. All talking into their jacket cuffs. This was not my venue, and all of this commotion was none of my concern, so I merely noted the activity and moved on. Lippy was meeting me at the Palace Grounds office, and upon arriving I mentioned what I had seen. He told me all that activity was due to the Secretary of State being in town, and she was currently inside the Palace.

That explained the radio silence. All the reports, and calls for assistance, had gone out over the R.S.O. radios, a secure bandwidth, instead of being broadcast over our radios, not so secure. Our project was equipped with enough internal radios to issue one to each Security Manager, the Guard Supervisors, and one for each post. The frequencies were internal to BESF (remember, this was pronounced bee-sef, and stood for Baghdad Embassy Security Force), and we could talk among ourselves with them. Since the rockets had not hit near any of our posts, there had been no need to talk about them. The R.S.O. radios, on the other hand, came from the State Department's inventory. They gave us a secure line of communication directly to our R.S.O., and the TOC, and were only issued one per venue. The on-duty Security

Manager carried that one, and handed it over at shift change.

Currently, Secretary Rice's motorcade, and all its attendants, were staged at the main entrance in front of the palace. A small portico located below the front balcony where all those people had gathered to photograph the rocket strike. Additional security agents were wandering around on the roof of the building, and several military vehicles had been staged at various gates around the grounds in support of her visit. Standing in front of the office, we could see everyone standing around waiting for her to finish her visit, and subsequent press conference, and walk out to the motorcade. That was when more rockets came. It was like throwing a rock on an ant hill.

At the sound of the C-RAM alarm people ran for bunkers. They ran for vehicles. They ran for anything they could hide in, behind, or under. Lippy and I hunched behind the stone columns supporting the porch roof outside the office. We heard the familiar jet-engine like roar of the rocket engine cut over the top of the alarm as it flew overhead. Over the Palace. Beyond the grounds. And detonate somewhere around the Icehouse, again. Tentatively, heads poked out of bunkers, and around car doors, to see if the coast was clear. Cautiously, people emerged from their cars, and other hard cover, only to scramble again.

Neither the C-RAM alarm, nor the Duck and Cover alarm had gone off to signal this new excitement. Bewildered, Lippy and I exchanged glances in the hopes the other may have the answer. He looked as confused as I felt. Not quite ready to become unsmall, not just yet, we both looked back toward the motorcade, and were instantly provided with our answer. Doors on the limo were being thrown open. Drivers were jumping behind steering wheels. Engines were revving to life. A clutch of people came thundering down the steps from the Palace to mass around the rear door of the limo. And with doors slamming, the motorcade lit out the front gate like a scalded dog.

Boy, what a show. Chuckling lightly to ourselves, Lippy and I relaxed a little, stood up, and took a step away from the columns as the loudspeaker blasted "All Clear." I think my heart skipped a beat.

It was Sunday night at the Palace Chow Hall, and you know what that meant. Prime Rib. And it was excellent. So as not to mislead anyone, let me start by saying eating in the Chow Hall was a little different from going to a restaurant and ordering a steak.

We all can conjure up fond memories of going to a fine steak house, and ordering a nice, thick cut of meat. For me it was rare, swimming in au jus, lightly salted, spiced with garlic and herbs, steaming on a huge plate. Here, it was just a little different. Most restaurants only prepare a finite number of servings for the night, and once they had all been served anyone late to the table had to order something else. Sorry about your bad luck, but we are out of Prime Rib tonight.

This was a Chow Hall, excuse me, the current politically correct name for it was Dining Facility, DFAC (pronounced D-fack) for short, but I was Old Army, so Chow Hall it was. They had to make sure there was enough food for everyone, and since the Palace Chow Hall served easily over one thousand people, that was a lot of Prime Rib. That wonderful garlic and herb rub you have become accustomed to on the outside of your cut of meat, well, we did not get that. Do not ask me why, I did not know, we just didn't.

Additionally, most of the Chow Hall workers were not from the U.S. The Supervisors were, but for the most part, the rest of the staff was not. So, I would be willing to bet most of them had never seen this much beef in one place in their lives. Nor had they ever had to cook this much at one time either.

The meat was all prepared before the Chow Hall opened, so there was no "cooked to order." Once you grabbed your tray and utensils, you walked over to the carving station, and they sliced off a steak when you arrived. It was pretty much hit or miss whether you got a well-done end piece, or a center cut closer to medium rare. That depended on how many hunks they had carved off before you got there. Some people were known to hang around, and only walk up when the slicing had reached the level of doneness they desired. You did get a bit of a say as to how thick a slice you got, so that was nice. As they finished with one chunk-o-meat, they reached into the warmer, and pulled out another.

Your Prime Rib was specially ordered by the restaurant. It came from pampered cows, was fawned over by the head chief, delivered early, stored lovingly, and prepared only after you ordered it. Ours came from cows. Where those cows lived was anyone's guess. It was transported from another country, through a combat zone, in the back of a refrigerated truck. It came only when the convoys got through, arrived when the convoys got here, was stored in a freezer unit until it was time to pull it out to thaw. How long did all that take? A mighty fine question. Wish I could answer it.

Armed with this knowledge, when I tell you the Prime Rib was exceptional tonight, and it was, you have a better understanding of how good it really was. Midnight chow, on the other hand, pretty much sucked. But hey, you cannot have everything, right?

21 April – Not bad today. I got a full day's sleep. I made it over to the P.X., and picked up some more coffee, I was almost out, had dinner, and went to the office. That was when the rockets started for the day.

Around 1800hrs I was sitting on the bench in front of the Palace Office, shooting the breeze with Lippy, Finch, Chief, and Lunchmeat when the C-RAM alarm went off. You could tell this had been getting just a little too routine for all of us because everyone simply stood up, and calmly walked inside the office. Once inside, we were not able to hear where the rockets had landed, but the Towers started calling in reports of impacts right across the river, by the Sheraton Hotel. The same hotel where CNN had been reporting during the invasion.

With the P.O.I. (point of impact) having been identified, we headed back out to the porch to have another sit down. Around 1830hrs the C-RAM alarm went off one more time. Back inside we went, and again were unable to hear the impacts. Again, the Towers called Chief to report these rockets had landed short of the river, falling on the riverbank just over the East wall of the Palace grounds. By looking at the two impact areas, it seemed the insurgents were now launching their rockets from the Southwest side of town. The opposite side of the I.Z. from Sadr City. I guessed they were learning.

Yesterday, al-Sadr had publicly announced he had given the American and Iraqi Governments their last warning to stop harassing his Mahdi Militia, or he would declare an "open war until liberation." Whatever that meant. Of course, we were not going to stop, and it looked like the Iraqis were not going to stop either, so things could get a little interesting around here for the next few days.

Al-Sadr had even gone so far as to compare the elected Iraqi Government with the oppressive dictatorship of Saddam Hussein, and had threatened to respond to it as such if the crackdown on his followers continued. I was definitely not sure what that meant, but since we had been getting a fair number of dust storms over the past few days the air cover had not been able to fly over Sadr City and engage launch sites. I had a bad feeling the Mahdi Militia was starting to figure that out as well.

Lately, I had been filling out the paperwork required to reactivate my security clearance. There was a possibility I could be moving into the TOC some time down the line, and the first step was to have an active clearance prior to being given the job. Today, I made an appointment to have my fingerprints taken, and that should finish things up. I have had my fingerprints taken so many times in the last couple of years you would think someone would have a copy of them just laying around somewhere. I guess not.

22 April – One more on a very short list of quiet days. No I.D.F., no rockets, no booms. A full day's sleep, and I felt pretty good.

Last night I did have two guards decide they wanted to get into a fight though. Drama. Drama. Drama.

I guessed it was part of the Latino mind set. It started with one of the guards talking a lot of smack, and ended with the second guard smacking him, a lot. Tonight, instead of recommending they be fired, I was able to split them up by sending one of the miscreants to work over at FOB Blackhawk. It could have been possible the stress of getting rocketed for almost a full month had started to wear on their nerves. I knew mine had been running a little thin lately.

23 April – Another quiet day today. Lippy had the day off, so he was sleeping in. It was a little strange not having the room to myself after I got off shift, and I did my best not to make too much noise as I downed all my gear, changed, crawled into bed, and tried to get some sleep. (Yes, there were two separate, single beds in the room, so knock off the snickering) We had been leaving the window open a crack, so we could better hear any alarms, and today was no different.

Around 1100, I was woken up by something coming over the Palace loudspeakers. It took me a couple of seconds to realize it was not an alarm, but the muffled and garbled notes of some kind of announcement. They sounded like the adults on an episode of Charley Brown. Thinking nothing of it I rolled over, and went back to sleep. I was just drifting out of consciousness when a huge explosion rocked the trailer. And when I say huge, I mean something close to the blast the 240mm made a couple of weeks ago. Crap, crap, and crap! Here we go again! I climbed down from the ceiling, and made ready to run out the door. Looking over toward Lippy, to make sure I was not going to run into him as we both bolted for the door, I saw he had rolled up against the front wall of the trailer. Since he had moved into the trailer before I had, he had chosen the bed against the wall with the sandbags.

It took me a couple of seconds to realize that in the aftermath of the explosion no alarms were going off. None at all. No C-RAM alarms. No Duck and Cover alarms. Nothing but silence. As I tried to make sense of this, I felt a tapping on the back of my mind. My subconscious turned around, and found my hindbrain pointing at me, laughing its ass off. My brain finally caught up with my reflexes, and replayed the loudspeaker announcement I so recently had ignored.

E.O.D. had been busy little beavers, collecting up all the rockets that had failed to detonate on impact.

Bundling them all up, they had taken them out to a little island in the middle of the river, wrapped them with detonation cord and plastique, and destroyed them in a process they called controlled detonation. Controlled det for short. The announcement had been the one-minute warning. I lay back in bed, and did my best to go back to sleep.

When I got to work tonight, they told me E.O.D. had conducted a total of three shots today. I only remembered hearing two.

24 April – Today was not as quiet as previous days had been. Around 1450, the C-RAM alarm began blaring, and I hopped out of bed, plucked my shower shoes from the floor, and headed out the door on my way to the bunker. By the time I reached the end of the sandbags there had not yet been an explosion, so I slipped my shoes on, and waited. The boom never came. Later I learned the rocket had exploded in the Red Zone. Over-shot. But why had the C-RAM sounded the alarm at the Palace? This was not the first time the C-RAM had initiated an alarm in Edgewood, with the rockets landing a good distance away. I was going to have to think about this.

I waited a few more minutes for all clear to sound before heading back to my room. About ten minutes later the alarm went off again. Up scooped my shoes, out ran my body, and again I waited at the end of the sandbags. One more time I did not hear anything. This one had been an over shot too. I guessed they were still ranging their new launch sites.

After returning to my room I gave up on the idea of going back to sleep, and instead started my usual morning routine. While completing the last few details that would get me ready for work a distant explosion announced that the rockets had not finished falling for the afternoon. The intensity of the blast gave the impression the P.O.I. was not very close, but the resulting concussion had been strong enough to rattle a few things around in the trailer like yesterday's controlled det. Since no warning alarm, or announcement, had been broadcast this must have been another 240mm.

Curiosity getting the better of me, I stepped out onto the front porch to see if I could locate the impact site. I scanned the skyline for anything that would indicate where this round had fallen, and looking off to the west and a little south, I saw a column of thick black smoke rising up in the distance. The source of smoke was far enough away I could tell it was not on the Palace grounds, and the density and volume suggested something very flammable had been hit. Later I learned this round had impacted on one of the compounds by the 14th of July Circle. The rest of the afternoon turned out to be quiet.

Dinner and shift change went off without a hitch, and my initial post checks had been uneventful as well. Heading back to the office to start my paperwork for the night, I ducked into the Chow Hall, and made a quick stop in the latrine. I really did not know what it was about rockets, toilets, and me, but this time their timing was off. They were a little too early. My pistol belt was already on the floor, but I had only just started to unbutton my pants when the alarm had gone off. HAHAHA! Missed me this time!

I grabbed my pistol belt and strapped it around my waist as I walked out of the bathroom. Entering the main dining room, the cooks and kitchen staff were still bustling around the floor and serving line, clueless to the sound of the alarm. I drew a breath to warn them of the alarm, but before I could issue an alert the rattle of pans and the din of clatter abruptly stopped. Frozen in place, in various stages of work, all heads turned to look at the ceiling as the wail of the alarm broke over the silence.

The snap-shot of chow hall activity burst to life. Food containers thudded as they were dropped on the serving line. Silverware and trays crashed to the floor as those who had been holding them dove for cover under anything they hoped was tall enough to hide them.

The Camp Chow Hall was not a hard structure. It did not have over-head cover like the Palace Chow Hall either. If a rocket were to detonate on the roof, it would produce a blast with similar effects as the one that had exploded in the trees by the Logistic Building, spraying shrapnel and debris throughout the Chow Hall shredding pretty much everything in the main dining room. I got the hell out of there.

So far, nothing had exploded yet, and as I ran toward the front gate, I took advantage of anything big enough to hide behind should the missile land before I reached the shack. Still nothing. The alarm continued to blare. I moved by rushing from obstacle to obstacle, expecting to feel the impact at any second. Still nothing. The time lag common to short, snap shots passed, and I began to wonder if this was another rocket with hang time. Still nothing.

The alarm went silent as I sprinted across the open area in front of the gate, and still nothing went boom. We had been getting rocketed fairly steady for the last month, or so, resulting in so many alarms, explosions, false positives, and dud impacts that it had become difficult to keep count of them anymore. One thing was certain, though. We had certainly learned how to deal with them. The hardest part about learning to deal was there was really nothing we could do about them. It was not like we could shoot back at a rocket. Armed with pistols and rifles, we certainly could not shoot at the people who were launching them either. Coming to terms with the realization there was nothing you could do but react to what was happening, with no chance of changing that, was not an easy thing to do.

Some folks had chosen to simply leave, and the nightly Rhino runs to BIAP had been filled to capacity. I guess I should not be too critical of their decisions. Most of them had never been trained for this. A lot of the folks who came here provided what we commonly referred to as "life support" functions. They ran the laundry service, built and outfitted new buildings, serviced and maintained the non-tactical vehicles, cooked the food, and so on. Most of them came from the same civilian jobs, back in the States, and were only here to earn the type of paycheck they could only find in a war zone. They were not here to build a country, or fight an insurgency.

For the rest of us, the feeling of only being able to react was just as frustrating. But coming from military and police backgrounds, we were better equipped to deal with it. Better equipped in no way meant we were impervious to the fear. The frustration. The terror. The angst. It just meant this was not our first rodeo. For most of us it was not our second or third rodeo either.

One thing that differed was the way we perceived it. First, we accepted the fact that rockets were not all that accurate as a weapon. Do not get me wrong, they were quite formidable in the destruction department, and could cause a huge amount of damage. But they were not so much aimed, as they were pointed. Unlike artillery and mortar rounds, there were a lot of factors involved in the correct operation of a rocket, and it only took one small problem for them to malfunction. Artillery and mortar rounds were also shot out of tubes, anchored by vehicles or heavy baseplates, and had highly accurate aiming capabilities. They could be adjusted before, during, and/or after the fire mission for more accuracy. Rockets on the other hand, especially the 107mm ones, were mostly fired from portable sleds, trays, or tripods simply placed on the ground. Artillery and mortars were used for precise, adjustable destruction. Rockets were more harassment, intimidation, and generalized nonspecific destruction.

The next step was to realize getting killed by one of those things was not the worst thing that could happen to you. Getting severely wounded was far worse. I know, at first glance that statement does not make a whole lot of sense. Look at it this way. If you got dead, you were dead. And being dead, you no longer had the capacity to worry about anything. On the other hand, if you got A.F.U.ed (that's All Fouled, or any other F word you cared to use, Up). Well. That was a whole new issue. It could mean losing body parts. It could mean becoming paralyzed. It could mean being reduced to a permanent vegetative state. Kept alive by machines, and fed by tubes. Either way here, as the Bard would say, was the rub; becoming comfortable knowing these things, and accepting them as possibilities when the alarms went off.

This time, nothing happened. No boom. No pops. No bangs. False positive? Dud? I had no idea. Either way, we seemed to be getting more and more of these.

26 April – There were two different schools of thought out there. One school stated al-Sadr had fled to Iran, and from over there was stirring up trouble over here to stage a shadow government with him as the head. If that were true, it would mean there was going to be a lot more trouble from the Mahdi Militia, and probably a lot more attacks.

The second school stated al-Sadr was merely a spoiled child. He screamed every time he did not get his way, and pounded his chest when he felt people did not respect him. I thought a little of both. He was a spoiled child who wanted power, and would expend his followers to get it. I read articles that went both ways, but one thing they all agreed on was the rockets were not going to stop falling for a while longer.

For those unfamiliar with this gentleman, allow me to give you a little background on him. His full name was Sayyid Muqtada al-Sadr, and he was born in Baghdad in 1973. A mid-ranked Shi'a religious leader, he tended to get the majority of his power by being related to a great man, not necessarily by being one. He was the fourth son of the late Grand Ayatollah Mohammad Mohammad Sadeq al-Sader, who had been a very highly respected figure throughout the entire Shi'a Islamic world. Muqtada was also the son-in-law of another Grand Ayatollah by the name of Muhammad Baqir al-Sadr.

His cousin is/was a man by the name of Musa al-Sadr, the founder of a popular, and very successful Islamic political movement in Lebanon. I say is/was because Musa disappeared, under suspicious circumstances, back in 1978 while dealing with the leader of Libya, Muammar al-Gaddafi, and has not been seen since. Oh, and in case I forgot to mention it, Muqtada al-Sadr's Great-Grandfather was a Grand Ayatollah as well.

It appeared al-Sadr did not get much of his power through his position as a cleric. His education level, and degrees were not high enough to allow him to make interpretations of the Koran, or gave him the authority to issue fatwas, religious edicts. The majority of his notoriety came from his father and two older brothers having been killed by a directive from Saddam Hussein, and his Father-in-Law having been executed by the Iraqi authorities in 1980. The fact that he constantly assaulted Americans and the Iraqi Government during his sermons did not seem to hurt his case either. The curious part was he continued to enter into negotiation with the Iraqi Government, and then preached his approval or disapproval of them depending on his success or failure at the negotiating table.

This morning, I was able to get to sleep fairly quickly. Lying in bed, reading a book, and drinking a beer probably did not hurt anything either. Of course, I was woken up by the C-RAM alarm going off. It felt like I had just gotten to sleep. It could not have been 1500hrs already. And it was not, it was only 1030hrs. Damn it! I made it as far as the front porch when the "All Clear" was given. The only time the all clear was given that quickly was when the initial alarm was a false one. Great. Thanks guys.

27 April – Yesterday had been a rather quiet day. Only one alarm, and no explosions. Today, not so much.

I had gotten up early for my appointment to get my fingerprints taken for my background check, so I was up around 1330hrs, and at the fingerprint shop by

1400hrs. Having been an Army Military Policeman for over twenty years, I can tell you I have fingerprinted a legion of people in my career. I can also tell you the guy doing this printing did not have a clue about what he was doing. He was not rolling my fingers far enough. He was pushing my fingers, instead of rolling them. He would stop a finger in mid-roll, then continue, and he would push down on my fingers before picking them up from the paper. I hoped these prints came out O.K.

Lunchmeat showed up when I was about half finished. Coincidently, he had an appointment to get his prints taken right after mine. I was not sure if I wanted to hang around until he had finished, but it would have been rather rude for me to merely tip my cap, and walk away without waiting. During the last quarter of my military career, I had watched as many of the friends I had come up through the ranks with had been promoted to senior N.C.O. ranks in the M.P. Corp Regiment. Some of them had been changed by it. Lunchmeat had retired as an M.P. First Sergeant, and up until now I only had limited contact with him. We worked opposite shifts, so I had no idea if the rank had adversely affected his personality.

I did not know if the massive increase in responsibility was what caused it. Maybe it was because the Regiment was so small, and competition for promotion and assignments was so fierce. Maybe the greater authority had something to do with it. Maybe it was the way junior enlisted soldiers responded to them with increased, projected respect and formality with each promotion. That kind of thing could go to a person's head if they were not careful. I did not know what caused it. I only knew something turned a lot of them into pricks.

I was not talking about the "firm but fair" Sergeant you saw in the movies. Nor was I talking about the tough, hard-driving Drill Sergeant who rode and yelled at their soldiers for the greater purpose of pushing them to accomplish more than they ever thought they could. I mean pricks. The kind who chuckled after berating a soldier for messing up. The kind who swaggered through the company area, not answering soldiers as they gave the greeting of the day. The kind who acted like only George Patton, or Audie Murphy were better soldiers. I did not know if this happened in other branches, or other career fields, but I had seen it too often in the Regiment. Some of the best First Sergeants I had ever worked for had not come from the M.P. Corp.

Checking the Service CAC with him, after that massive attack, he had seemed personable enough. The few times he had joined our group bull sessions, or the couple times he sat down with the dinner crew, nothing indicated he was one of "those" First Sergeants. But that had been a group setting. So, what the hey? Give the guy the benefit of the doubt, right? I hung around until he was done. Then, we headed for the office, shit-shatting in the way old soldiers did, looking for common duty stations, and identifying mutual acquaintances.

"Where did you retire from?" I asked.

"Fort Campbell, 716th M.P. Battalion." He replied.

"716th M.P. Battalion? I used to be assigned to that Battalion, but that was back when it was at Ft. Riley."

"What about you? Where did you retire from?" His turn to ask.

"I retired out of Ft. Hood. 720th M.P. Battalion." And on it went.

"Fort Hood, eh? Do you know Sergeant Major Eric Brently?"

"Sure do." I replied. "I was an Operations Sergeant when he was a First Sergeant."

"Man, what an ass-clown. I had him as my Squad Leader when I first pinned on Sergeant. He wasn't so bad then. Ran into him later when we were both First Sergeants at Campbell. He had turned into the lead clown, and driver of the butt-mobile."

"Oh, for the love of God. Don't get me started on him." Well, how about that? Point, Lunchmeat.

We were cutting through the Palace when the C-RAM alarm went off. HAHAHAHA, missed me again! I was already out of bed! One more time, we did not hear any explosions with this alarm.

Walking down the main corridor, we passed the barber shop. Uncharacteristically, there was no line of people waiting for a trim, so I decided to get my hair cut, and Lunchmeat and I parted ways. A haircut may not sound like much of a big deal, and to most people it probably would not be. But for me it qualified as a rarity, so it was a bit of a deal. Right after 9/11, my unit deployed to Egypt. We had been boots on the ground for a very short time before I realized all the dust and dirt, grit and grime, were playing marry havoc with my scalp.

Normally I kept my hair high and tight, short on the crown and top of my head, shaved all the way around the sides and back, but this time I decided the easiest way to deal with it would be to just shave it all off. So I did, and have been keeping it shaved ever since.

Now I shave my head every couple of days, but since the rockets started falling I had not felt very comfortable engaging in the practice, and the P.X. never seemed to have electric razors for sale. For some reason, I could not get comfortable with the idea of possibly having to run to the bunker with half my head shaved, and the other half still covered in shaving cream. It may have had something to do with my slight aversion to clowns, I did not know. As a result, it had been almost a month since the last time I had taken a razor to my scalp, and the stuff was really starting to bug me. Ever grown your beard out? Remember the point when your new face fur started to itch? Imagine that feeling all over your head. Add the fact that it had been years since the last time I had this much hair, and you begin to get the idea. It felt like bugs were crawling all over my scalp, constantly.

The other part of this little adventure was, inside the Palace they only employed local Iraqis in the barber shop. I did not know what kind of vetting process they put these guys through, but I did notice a couple of things that made me believe room for error had been built into the system, just in case they missed anything. What were those things? Well, for starters, there were no razor blades in evidence anywhere in the shop. Both the observation, and the reason for the answer should be pretty obvious. The more subtle indicator I spotted, after settling into the chair, was that none of the scissors ended in points. They were all rounded at the ends.

Fortunately, mine was a fairly straightforward cut, and the barber grabbed his electric clippers from the counter, pulled off the plastic guard, and got to work removing the offensive growth. Working the clippers like a pro, it was not long before I was left with a head full of stubble that looked quite reminiscent of my first haircut in basic training. At long last, the itchy crawly feeling began to fade. But the Barber did not seem satisfied with leaving me looking like a recruit. With a quick turn, and a short flick of the wrist, he produced an even smaller set of clippers, the ones they used for trimming the fine hairs on the back of your neck, and attacked the remaining stubble. Doubling down, he next grabbed an electric razor (so that's where they all went), and finished putting a smooth shine on my head. It felt good to be bald again.

As was always necessary after any haircut, I wandered back to my room, and jumped in a quick shower to rinse all the clippings off. Showered, and redressed, I headed over to the Palace office to meet with the dinner crew.

Once again, Finch, Lippy, Chief, Lunchmeat, Manny, and I trouped over to the Chow Hall. We did not have to wait long for things to get real interesting. Having filed through the chow line we walked our meals to the closest table, and began eating when the C-RAM alarm went off. The table we had selected was at the front of the Chow Hall this time, and wouldn't you know it, right under a loudspeaker again. As the alarm did its best to make everyone deaf, we heard the deep concussion of five explosions off in the distance. Time to get to the office, get our kit on, and go to work.

Abandoning our trays of uneaten food, we wove our way around the prone figures of the other diners, and ran out of the Chow Hall in the direction of the South doors to the Palace. The alarm had stopped blaring by the time we entered the building, and guards were beginning to send status reports over the radio.

Walking through the Palace the other Security Managers were engaged in intense communication with their Guard Supervisors. Being the only Security Manager not currently on duty, I was the only one who did not have their hands full receiving reports. To help speed the flow of information, and quickly get First Responders to any location they may be needed, I pulled out my cell phone, called the TOC, and started relaying the reports the other Security Manager had been receiving.

Like a huddle of stock traders moving across the exchange floor we negotiated our way down the main hall, out the front doors of the Palace, and began to shuffle our way through the area we had come to call Death Valley. The main drive leading to the front of the Palace entered the grounds to our left, through the Main CAC, and curved toward the doors. It passed under the front balcony, and a high portico directly in front of the entryway, then curved away from the building. The drive originally exited the grounds through a gate right next to the Palace Security Office, originally built as that gate's security building, but the gate had been chained shut and blocked with T-walls. Death Valley was the stretch that ran below the front balcony, between the Main Palace Doors, and the Palace Security Office. Several rockets had already exploded here, beginning with the truck on Easter Sunday. It also happened to be the ground we had no choice but to cross to get to the office.

The Security Managers were receiving reports from their Guard Supervisors. As each report came in, they would pass the information to me. I was on an open phone line to the TOC, and would pass that information directly to the incident coordinator. The reports flooded in, hot and heavy, and information flowed in a steady stream. Everyone was so intent and focused on getting the job done the entire group moved and flowed as if we were one entity. No thought was given to the movement of feet. No thought, that was, until the C-RAM alarm went off again. With a jolt of realization we came to our senses and discovered we were standing outside, in the open, right on the edge of Death Valley. Helmets and vests be damned, we did the only thing we could do. We bum-rushed the door.

The doors to the Palace were set up in a two door system, with a vestibule in between. Also known as a mantrap, or airlock, both sets of doors were heavily armored, and remain closed and magnetically locked when not in use. If someone needed to enter, or exit the Palace one of the doors would be opened, and the person or group entered the airlock. Only after the first door had shut and locked, could the second door be opened, ensuring there was never an open corridor leading all the way into the Palace. The other thing this meant was the doors were controlled by a guard who had to push buttons to disengage the magnetic lock on each set of doors. Leading the pack, I slammed into the outer door, and peered through the ballistic glass. The inner door was still closing, denying us entry, and the safety that lay beyond.

Hitting the door so hard I bounced, Lunchmeat stepped in to fill the gap. The buzzer sounded, signaling the magnetic lock had been disengaged, and like a striking praying mantis Meat stabbed at the handle with both hands. Heaving the massive steal reinforced door open, he pulled it wide, while the rest of us crowded through the opening into the airlock.

Reports about this second barrage were being broadcast by the Guard Supervisors, and everyone fell back to their stations of receiving and passing information. The alarm went quiet, and once again we took our show on the road. Reports came in, and information flowed out. From the guards to supervisors, the supervisors to the managers, the managers to me, from me to the TOC. With our attentions centrally refocused on coordination and information our movements went back on automatic. As one, we ebbed out the door, and began to flow toward the office. We had not quite cleared the overhang of the balcony when the C-RAM alarm went off again. Crap! Bum-rush the door! Again!

This time, Lunchmeat was the last one to reach the door. Already open, he was about to cross the threshold when his Guard Supervisor's voice came shrieking from his radio. The urgency in his voice stopped Meat dead in his tracks, and he stood in the doorway to listen. That is right, full in the doorway. Neither in nor out. With the door wide open.

"Meat!" I cried. "Get in here and close the damn door!" So intent had he been on listening to what his supervisor was telling him, he turned around and walked back outside. Letting the door swing shut behind him.

The alarm was still blasting "Incoming! Incoming! Incoming!" as we looked at each other with a mixture of "Did that really just happen?" and "You have got to be kidding!" Three more explosions rocked the air as I pushed the door open just enough to stick my head out.

"Hey Meat. Anyone ever tell you it's a smart thing to come in out of the rain?"

I had barely finished asking my question when the largest of the explosions erupted in front of the Palace. Dirt and dust were knocked from the underside of the balcony. Mud and grass were thrown over the top of the T-walls protecting the front of the portico, to land at our feet. The chandelier hanging over our heads jumped in its suspension chains. Crystal facets tinkled and chimed as it bounced and swayed. Knocking years of silt loose to waft down around us in a fine reddish cloud.

That last rocket had impacted on the grounds in front of the Palace. Between the fountain and the outer wall. Less than fifty yards beyond the T-walls that stood between us and the blast. Had we still been on our way to the office, that rocket would have landed less than a stone's throw away from where we would have been. The T-walls they had so recently erected were the only things that kept Meat and I from being in a direct line of sight with the explosion. I was quite sure they were the only reason we had been showered with dirt and grass, and not pelted with shrapnel.

I looked at Meat. Meat looked at me. I blinked first. I almost jumped out of my skin when I felt a tap on my shoulder, and heard Meat's voice come from behind me.

"Hey Rooster, you gonna' close that door or what?" For a big guy, he was surprisingly quick.

The alarms had gone silent again, and we were still on the wrong side of Death Valley. Each of us knew we did not have much choice about what needed to be done for us to reach the office. And right now we were batting zero for two. Looking from face to face, eye contact was made one to another. Without having to say a word our resolve was conveyed, and acknowledgment and agreement was passed in a glance. As one we turned toward the outer door, and fell into line. Stacked up on the door, each of us leaned slightly forward, and lightly rested one hand on the shoulder of the man in front of us. The door buzzed, and Meat hit the push-bar. Leaning his shoulder in the weight of the door he threw it open. In single file, like paratroopers from a plane, we burst through the doorway, and sprinted for Death Valley.

Hot on each other's heels, we made the turn outside the door, pointed ourselves toward the office, and picked up speed. Arms pumping. Legs churning. Our feet pounded across the longest hundred yards of asphalt I had ever crossed. Fully exposed, and completely in the open. Anxiety hung thick as we chanted our mantra in unison.

"No rockets! No rockets! No rockets!"

We crossed the last twenty yards gulping down lungsful of air. Feeling like our hundred-yard dash had actually been a mile long, we burst through the office door high on adrenaline. Once inside safety, fear and dread became excitement and relief, and everyone started laughing, poking fun at one another about how foolish we had been, and how stupid we must have looked. The only difference between bravery and stupidity? The benefit of hindsight.

Did I also happen to mention a dust storm had started blowing in about an hour ago, and the air had gotten so thick visibility was not much more than one hundred yards? That may have been one reason for this rocket strike.

As I mentioned, the Palace Office was inside a small, hard building along the front wall. The comfort its cover provided gave us the ability to refocus our attention. Everyone spread out to their workstations, and we began the task of collating the reports from our guards. Initially, the SITREPs had been fairly spotty, and our first concern had been to just pass them along. Now, our concern was to distill all the information, sift through its contents, and make sure we had identified all the usable data. Conducting these additional checks was a way to make sure nothing had been missed, and no impact site went unnoticed. The limited visibility, caused by the dust storm, was causing headaches for everyone at all levels, and we wanted to take one more look at the details. Since, as you know, the devil, he's in 'em.

During times of limited visibility, we had learned to use a variation of an old Forest Ranger trick. The way they pin-pointed forest fires was a process known as intersection. This is how it worked. One Ranger, standing in his tower, would point a compass toward the center of the fire, look at the compass reading, degrees between one and three hundred sixty, and call this reading, also known as an azimuth, to the control center. A second Ranger, standing in a different tower, would do the same thing, and report his azimuth to the same control center.

Someone in the control center would then go to a map of the area, and starting from the first tower draw a long line along the azimuth they had called in. Starting at the second tower, they would then draw a line along the second azimuth. Where the two lines crossed, or intersected, would be the fire.

Even when conditions were good, and we could observe the flash of an explosion, our process still pretty much mirrored that of the Forest Rangers. A tower guard would announce from what tower they were reporting, identify what he was calling in; an explosion, small arms fire, automatic weapons fire, etc., and then give the azimuth. As soon as a second tower called in a report, the Security Manager would plot the intersection, and pass the location up to the TOC with a reasonable degree of accuracy.

When conditions were not so good, and we could not observe a flash, that degree of accuracy tended to widen a bit. If the explosion could not be observed, the only thing the guard had to go on was the direction of the blast. And, as we had seen before, there were a lot of factors that could mess with your ears, and a number of objects that could cause echoes or change the sound.

As directions were being called in, we plotted them on the map in the office. Lines crossed over the CaSH, and a couple of sets crossed over FOB Blackhawk. A good majority of the intersections were over the Palace grounds. But some of the lines never crossed at all. We just had to scratch our heads about those. Calling our findings in the TOC, we discovered we had identified a couple of sites they had not, and they had found one or two we had not plotted. During the next hour, the C-RAM alarm went off three more times to the accompaniment of scattered explosions. And I had not even walked across the parking lot to the WPPS camp yet. Great! Lippy, on the other hand, had taken advantage of one of the breaks between shots to come over from the camp. We conducted the shift change handshake in this office instead.

After a while, there developed a lull in the action, and I took advantage of the opportunity to head over to the camp. I left the office at the Palace, and exited through the North CAC. To walk toward the Main CAC would have meant walking right past the crater caused by the rocket that had sent me and Meat scrambling back inside the airlock, and I was not up to pushing my luck quite that far. The North CAC was located directly across Haifa Street from the Rhino staging area, which sat outside the back gate of the WPPS Camp. This route also contained the most areas of hard cover, with the least amount of distance between the shelters. Considering the number of rockets that had been thrown at us today, I figure this would be the smartest way to get to work.

I arrived at my office, and settled in for the night. I could only hope, since they had been shooting at us pretty steadily all afternoon, they already shot everything they had, and tonight would be relatively quiet. Wrong! Around 2300hrs the C-RAM alarm went off, immediately followed by a couple of explosions. An hour and a half later there were a couple of explosions, immediately followed by the C-RAM alarm. Half an hour after that, we received explosions mixed with alarm activations. In total, I would have guessed, just for today, we had been hit with close to thirty rockets, and it was not even 2230hrs yet. The last explosion, so far, had been a couple of minutes ago, over by the CaSH. The C-RAM alarm did not activate.

There was a whole nighttime culture that worked here after dark. Of course, we security guys had an around-the-clock job, but there were a fair number of other offices that were also staffed twenty-four hours a day. Vampires, night walkers, moles, pariah, whatever anyone chose to call us, our day started when your day ended.

Because there were enough of us, the Chow Hall opened in the middle of the night to serve a fourth meal. The Army called it midnight chow, the Marines called it mid rats (short for midnight rations. Or maybe another name for us night workers, I don't know), but most of us just called it a reason to get out of our offices for a little while, and eat something. I guess there was another group who would simply call it lunch, but they had no imagination. The selection consisted of a mixture of breakfast foods (scrambled eggs, omelets, bacon, stuff like that), short order lunch foods (hamburgers, grilled cheese, french-fries, stuff like that), and leftovers from the dinner meal. Of course, being left over, those were the items nobody wanted to eat for dinner, and they tended to get passed over at mid rats too.

Usually, I walked across the street around 2315hrs. By this time, the WPPS guys were all in their trailers, the guards had settled into their routines, the insurgents had been tucked into bed, and operations had pretty much downshifted into night mode. With all the excitement from this afternoon's rockets, and a dust storm currently blowing across Baghdad, I was running a little late tonight. It was closer to midnight before I could get away.

I walked in the entrance, and washed my hands at the bank of sinks installed in the front anti-chamber. Wash your hands before you eat. Moms had been doling out this sage advice since the invention of Motherhood. Back in the World (that means back in the U.S.A.), this activity tended to fall by the wayside. Remember that dust storm? While it was depositing a fine layer of filth on everything around you, it was also coating you with a fine film of crud.

Something else most people did not realize was salmonella bacteria ran rampant over here. You could even find it in the dirt and grime the dust storms kicked up. Not long after crossing the berm, my unit pushed up to the area around Tikrit. We had not been on station very long before a few of the soldiers in my platoon had begun to suffer from stomach problems, diarrhea, and fever. For the next couple of weeks the symptoms spread throughout the soldiers. As some would get better, others would fall ill. It took Doc a little while to realize the first effects had hit following a right nasty dust storm, and salmonella had been the culprit. Believe it or not, after building a better hand washing station, and revising a couple other basic sanitation procedures, the illness passed and no one else got sick. So, wash your hands.

I selected my food, got something to drink, and sat down to feast. With my first bite of food, that's right, you guessed it, the C-RAM alarm went off. I could not begin to tell you just how tired I had become of that alarm, and just like everyone else in the room I sat stock still, and waited for the rockets. I waited. And I waited. No booms followed. After all the explosions today, I was more than a little confused. Maybe it had been an overshot. Maybe it had been a dud. Maybe it had been another false positive. One thing was for sure, this was much later than these guys had ever shot at us before.

Eating quickly, I finished my food, and walked back to the camp. Around 0200hrs, I left the office to make a check of my posts before making a quick trip to the gym. I was in the middle of walking posts when the C-RAM alarm activated again. Now this was just ridiculous. They never hit us this late. Fighting the urge to ignore the warning I found the closest bit of cover. Nothing happened. False alarm? Dud? Who knew. So tired of these alarms.

Close to 0500hrs the loudspeakers throughout the city wailed the call to prayer. I decided this would be a good time to check the weather, and see what the morning was going to be like. The forecast had predicted a fairly clear day, with a light chance of rockets, and I walked out of the office to find the dust storm was indeed breaking up a little. Even still, visibility was still not all that great. Prayers usually finished a little after five, and we had become convinced that was when the insurgents headed over to their launch sites so they could have rockets in the air by 0530hrs. 0545hrs at the latest.

I was willing to bet yesterday's dust storm had been a major contributing factor for the high number of rockets shot at us. With so much dirt in the air, helicopters did not fly because all those fine, little particles acted like sandpaper on the moving parts. Not to mention visibility was for nothing, and they would not be able see anything to shoot at anyway. Even though the dust storm was winding down, it was still strong enough that it might ground the birds this morning.

It was still early in the timeline of morning rocket events. So, I thought I would get ahead of the power curve, and made a latrine call. I headed over to the Chow Hall, settled in, and had just gotten the seat the proper temperature when… This was no new situation, and I think you can fill in the blanks by now. It was times like these when a person had to make some really tough decisions, and mine was to sit tight. Oh, the irony.

Fortunately, no sooner had the alarm stopped blasting when a voice came over the loudspeaker announcing it had been a false alarm. That was a first. False alarm or not, I was still going to stay right where I was until the paperwork was complete. I still thought they were going to have a Good Morning Baghdad shot this morning, and I planned on not getting caught with my pants down. Again. For the umpteenth time.

CHAPTER 5

Soldiers usually spent a year over here, with time out for R&R. Our rotations only lasted about four months, although we could stay longer if we asked to, and then we got to go home for a month. The downside was when we went home, we were not getting paid. You take the good, you take the bad. Right? The actual rotation usually consisted of the incoming group of Site Managers arriving in Baghdad, receiving their gear, getting their assignments, and then heading out to their venues to learn the ropes. Once the outgoing group passed on all their knowledge, and relevant information to their replacements, they turned in all their issued equipment, and were ready to go home.

2 May – We were currently in the middle of one of those rotations, and a lot of us had been moved around to new venues. Finch had been moved from CACs to be our company liaison in the TOC, and I had been moved from night shift on the WPPS Camp to take over the day shift Finch had vacated. A brand-new Security Manager had

been moved into my position at the camp, and another newbie had been assigned to replace Lippy on the day shift. He was going out on rotation with this cycle.

Tonight, I was making the final transition from night to day shift, and it had not been a lot of fun. I had grown quite used to working all night, and sleeping all day. Well, not so much sleeping as napping and running to the bunker. Then, napping some more. Then, running to the bunker some more. Wash, rinse, repeat. I took the first step in making the change to my new work hours by going directly to bed after shift. Instead of trying to sleep all day, I had taken a power nap this morning, stayed up until after lunch, and had another power nap this afternoon. To help keep me from dozing off between naps, I had walked CACs with Finch, trying to learn my new job.

Over the past week, or so, the rocket attacks had fallen off to once or twice a day. The dust storms, however, had been coming and going fairly regularly. We were beginning to realize when the storms blew in we had about six hours before they started hitting us with rockets. It looked like the insurgents had also learned that UAVs and helicopters did not fly in those conditions, and they could move their ordnance around without retribution.

Lippy was due to head out in the morning, and tomorrow would be my first day on day shift, so he and I were relaxing in the Lizard Lounge. The picnic tables close to our trailer where so many of us had spent time enjoying a couple of beers. The rest of the brew crew had taken off for the night, and we were the last two left. As we were talking, Lippy suddenly became very quiet, and sat straight up. His beer halfway to his mouth. I realized what had caught his attention when I heard something that sounded like a police siren winding down. Relaxing just a little, I let go of the breath I did not even realize I had been holding.

"Relax, that was just a siren." I said as I lifted my beer to take another sip.

Slowly, Lippy lowered his can to the table. "I don't think so."

"No, really, it was just." Kaboom! So much for that idea. Both of us ducked our heads, leapt off the table, and bolted for the bunker.

The rocket had flown over the far side of the Palace, and the explosion sounded like it had landed somewhere around FOB Blackhawk.

Yes, we brought the beers with us to the bunker. No, we had not spilled a drop during the mad rush for cover. We crouched in the bunker, sipping from the frothy, slightly shaken cans, as it quickly filled with others seeking cover. All of us waited to see whether this was going to be a one act performance, or if there was going to be an encore. As our cans gradually grew empty, and the slow minutes passed, we grew more certain there would not be anymore. For now. The bunker slowly emptied, and Lippy and I returned to the picnic table to crack one more beer before calling it a day. A man had to have his priorities.

I have mentioned the CACs before, but since they would now be falling under my responsibility let me expand on them a little more. CAC stood for Controlled Access Center, and everyone had to pass through one of them before they could enter the Palace grounds. There were five CACs spread around the perimeter, and even though they shared many similarities, each one specialized in something different.

The North CAC, directly across Haifa Street from the Rhino Staging area and the WPPS Camp back gate, processed a large number of the local laborers who worked on the grounds. It was also the primary entry point for the military, and others who were going to Camp Travis. Camp Travis butted up against the North side of the Palace compound, and was primarily accessed from here.

Moving to the West, and slightly South along Haifa Street, the Main CAC was just that, the main CAC. Also called the Center CAC, it was the primary entry point for most visitors, VIPs, Motorcades, and folks just coming and going. Directly across the street lay the WPPS camp main gate, and the P.X. complex.

Continuing west, farther along Haifa Street, and a little further to the South, was the South CAC. It was also a general access point for the Palace, and a couple of other adjoining compounds. However, being so far away from the Palace itself, and only a back entrance to those other compounds, it did not get used much.

Turning directly South, and heading toward the river, located in the back corner of the compound, was the Service CAC. This was the other place where local laborers were processed for entry onto the grounds, and was the only CAC with large search pits, and enough personnel to process delivery vehicles, maintenance vehicles, and any other big trucks needing access.

The Mid CAC was the only other CAC I did not mention yet. It was located out on Haifa Street, on the outside of the perimeter wall, between the South and Main CACs. Staffed with explosive sniffing dogs, and mechanical bomb detecting equipment, its only purpose was to search and screen all vehicles wanting to enter through the Main or North CACs.

Working night shift at the WPPS Camp had pretty much been a solitary venture. Lippy and I would meet for shift change at the camp office, or sometimes the Palace grounds office, where we would exchange information needing to be passed on. At the same time, our guards would be conducting their formations, then go about the process of relieving the off-going shift. I only needed to meet up with my Guard Supervisor at the beginning of shift, after that any time as needed, pass any relevant information to him, and he would ensure the guards were briefed.

Since most of the WPPS missions were finished before dinner, all the Window Lickers (World War II bomber crews would have called them waist-gunners. They sat in the back seats of the armored Suburbans, weapons at the ready, facing outward, looking through the windows for any signs of threat. Hence, window lickers), Trunk Monkeys (The same bomber crews would have called them tail gunners. They sat in the back compartment of the last Suburban in the convoy, facing backward, usually behind a mounted crew served machine gun with belts of ammo), Wheel Spinners (drivers), and the like would be back in their trailers by 2100hrs leaving me, and my guards, as the only ones up and around for the rest of the night.

Now I was working day shift, and at the Palace things were a little different. I woke up around 0400hrs to make sure I was up and about, in and out of the shower, dressed, and leaving the trailer before the Good Morning Baghdad rockets started. Two of the other Security Managers met me in the Chow Hall for breakfast, and by 0530hrs we were at the formation area to check on our guards before shift. This was day shift at the Palace, after all, and we needed to make sure everyone was sharp, and looked their best.

For those of you with military background, you know exactly what I mean by First Formation, so you can skip over the next paragraph while I explain it to the civilians.

First formation was, of course, a formation. Ours was held in the parking lot next to the building that housed the guards, right around the corner from the Chow Hall loading docks, and next to the R.S.O. bar, The Lock and Load, that had been rocketed earlier. Each venue formed up in their assigned area. In my formation, the Guard Supervisor for each CAC took roll call of his guards, to make sure everyone had shown up for work, and inspected their guard's uniforms, to make sure they did not need any repairs, or needed to be exchanged. The results were reported to the General Supervisor. The General Supervisor would brief the full CAC formation on any information needing to be passed on for the day, and then return the proceedings back to the CAC Supervisors to post their guards. Most of our guards came from military backgrounds, and those who did not caught on quick, so the whole formation tended to run rather quickly, and smoothly. While all of this was going on, the Security Managers hung around the fringes of their formations, kind of like the Cadre at any service school, just to make sure there were no issues, and should any problems or questions arise were there to promptly handle them.

Every morning the formation area was a buzz of activity as more than a company sized element of guards moved around, and conducted their business. All the guards who worked inside the Palace, controlling the doors, and guarding the other entrances to the building were there. All the guards who manned the towers, along with the guards who patrolled the Palace grounds were also there. All the guards who secured the P.X. parking lot across the street, HLZ Washington, and the entrances to a couple of the other compounds next to the palace were there, as well. And, of course, all my guards from all of the CACs were there too. Well over a hundred guards participated at each formation, and you could guarantee well over one hundred pairs of ears were listening for any indication that a rocket may try to introduce itself to the group.

Once the formation concluded, and all of the guards had headed off to work, the Security Managers headed over to the Palace office so we could get our stuff started. These Security Managers were Lunchmeat, Rak, and me. You already met Lunchmeat. He was in charge of the guards in the parking lot, HLZ, and the adjoining compounds. Like me, he was a retired Military Policeman. Both of us stood well over six feet tall, although I was a little taller, and we both tipped the scales around two hundred fifty pounds, though he was in a bit better shape. Both of us kept our heads clean shaven. Although, whereas I sported a full, dark, luxurious goatee, he preferred to grow a mustache, flecked with grey, all the way down to his jawline, keeping his lower lip and chin clean. Which was probably why his guards called him Hulk Hogan. We were constantly being mistaken as being brothers, and unless you had pretty specific descriptions of which one of us you were looking for, a stranger could easily mistake one of us for the other. That was, of course, until you realized I was much better looking.

Rak (pronounced Rock) was a retired gun bunny, Artilleryman for those of you who don't know. Having been assigned to the 187th Airborne, he took his call sign from the Regiment's nickname, Rakkasan. Considerably shorter than me or Meat, he was a mere five foot nine, Rak had a couple of things going for him neither of us had. The first was a full head of dark hair. I was not sure exactly how that qualified as an asset, although he sure thought it was, but his second attribute certainly was. Having a Hispanic heritage, Rak spoke fluent Spanish. Chief had rolled out on rotation, and Rak was his replacement as the Security Manager in charge of the towers and Palace grounds.

Mornings in the office were fairly routine, and usually drama free. Everyone dropped their gear by their desk, loaded a fresh battery in their radio, and got brought up to speed on any information the night shift needed to pass on. The morning manning reports, also known as The Daily, were the next thing to get filled in, before being emailed to the boss. Once all of those things were completed we left the office, on the move to check posts, supervise business, and basically manage by walking around.

4 May – Yesterday we did not get a single rocket all day, but I did have a small issue at the Main CAC with a young

Staff Sergeant (SSG) trying to sign a visitor onto the compound.

People permanently assigned to the Palace were given a special badge authorizing them to come and go through the CACs with a minimum amount of fuss. Each badge was a plastic card, about the size of a driver's license or ID Card, and had the picture of the person it was assigned to embossed on the front. The background color of the badge denoted what level of access the bearer was allowed, and intensity of search procedures they needed to submit to, if any. At the bottom of the badge were special markings that indicated any additional perks they may be authorized. These perks could include things like being allowed to escort visitors, bring electrical devices like computers or thumb drives in, or whether or not they were allowed to carry a weapon on the grounds, and if so, if it was allowed to be loaded or not.

Visitors to the Palace went through a screening process, similar to those conducted at any airport, before they were eligible to receive a visitor's badge, and enter the grounds. Everything got emptied from their pockets, and run through the "X-ray" machine. Any bags, briefcases, pouches, what-have-you were also run through the machine. Once scanned, they got to keep anything allowed to enter the compound, anything not allowed entry had to remain at the CAC until they left. Once their pockets had been emptied, they walked through a metal detector to make sure they had not forgotten anything. You would be surprised at the stuff people "forgot" to take out of their pockets.

This visitor had emptied his pockets, placed all his stuff in the tray to go through the scanner, walked through the metal detector, and was standing by the processing desk. As his stuff went through the scanner, the display screen showed there were two thumb drives buried in the pile. Visitors, all visitors, were not allowed to bring these into the Palace unless prior coordination had been made, and they had received special permission. Of course, this guy did not have that. As the guard was reaching down to pick up the thumb drives from the conveyor belt, the SSG reached down faster, and scooped them up first.

The guard told the SSG the thumb drives were not allowed to enter the Palace, and asked him to return them. "Oh, that's O.K. Since I'm his escort I'll just hold on to them." The SSG replied as he slipped them into his pocket.

In his best broken English, which really was not all that bad, the guard did his best to explain how that was also against policy, and he would have to leave the drives at the gate as long as they were inside the grounds. The visitor could pick them up on his way out. Of course, the SSG did not like that answer, or maybe he just did not like the fact a guard was telling him no, so he asked for me.

I was in the office when the call came over the radio, and I walked over to the CAC to see what was going on. As I walked in the back door, I called the Supervisor over, and asked him what was happening. Before he could even open his mouth to answer, the SSG strutted over, and cut him off.

"Your guard just tried to take two thumb drives away from my visitor. I'll just hang on to them while he is inside, and everything will be just fine."

O.K., so this was how you wanted to play this. "Sergeant, I do not remember addressing you. I was talking with the Supervisor. Show a little professionalism, and I'll be with you in a minute." Sour lemons was the look I got from the troop, but he did back off, and let the Supervisor finish.

Since the SSG had interrupted, and tried to cut him off, the Supervisor gave me the long version of the story the SSG had tried to bluster at me. It was pretty straight-forward, and eventually I would come to find out a fairly common occurrence. Gathering together my best calm, professional persona, I turned to the SSG, and utilizing the quiet, relaxed voice of authority, explained things to the young go-getter.

"Sergeant. Here's how this is going to playout." I started. "Just like that guard, and this Supervisor have explained to you, the drives will stay here at the CAC. When your visitor leaves, he can pick them up on his way out." Of course, everyone wants to know "why."

I told him the thumb drives had already been identified as belonging to the visitor, and visitors were not allowed to bring them in. This was standard State Department policy. Additionally, we were not authorized to release the drives to the escort, as we would be placing the escort at risk of unintentionally breaking that policy. Most people wanted to be "nice," so they would hand the restricted items back to their visitor once they left the

CAC, breaking the policy. The infraction, no matter how harmless the intent may have been, put the escort in jeopardy of losing their escort privileges. Clear, concise, and how do you do. Who could argue with logic like that? He could, that's who.

"Well, he's American. It's not like he's an Iraqi." The SSG countered. Some people had to argue everything.

"We don't discriminate here." I told him. "All visitors have to leave their devices at the CAC. No matter what country they come from." That really seemed to catch him up short.

Trying not to lose his momentum, the SSG pressed on with a new angle of attack. "But he's a retired Major."

I saw where this was going, and doubled my efforts to keep my frustration in check. "Sergeant," I spat. "Exactly what part of "all visitor" is not clear to you?"

Realizing he was not going to get anywhere down this road, the SSG adjusted, and decide he was going to exchange his argument for a new tactic. "I'm not trying to cause a problem." He started. "I'm just trying to understand why a retired American officer can't get into his own Embassy. That's all."

Seeing this new approach for what it was, another attempt, I realized he was not going to accept anything less than his own way, and no amount of reason or logic was going to stop his arguing. He was going to get his way. Why was it some people just could not accept they could not bully or bluster to get their own way?

"Sergeant," I began. "The fact that you don't even know this is not the Embassy, but an annex, tells me all I need to know. The fact that it's not him that's being denied entry, it's the thumb drives, tells me you have no grasp of this situation. Yes, you are intentionally trying to cause a problem by arguing. No, you are not trying to understand them. You are simply arguing."

Feeling anger starting to rise in my gut, and hearing the first hints of frustration enter my tone of voice I took a deep, cleansing breath, and pressed on before he could interrupt.

"Sergeant," I continued, with greater control. "I am not going to argue State Department policy with you. If you want to go inside, leave the thumb drives. If not, take them, and walk back out the front. Or, if you would rather, I can call an R.S.O. down to take them from you. It'll be his decision what happens to your escort privileges." And, with that, I walked to the other side of the CAC. I think he finally got the point.

I have to give credit to the visitor. The entire time this young SSG had been embarrassing himself, he had been following the guard's instruction by filling out the paperwork necessary for him to enter the grounds without saying a word.

Staring straight at the guard, he slowly reached into his pocket. Never breaking eye contact, he withdrew his closed hand, and moved it over the desk. Now, if this whole exchange had not been enough. When he opened his hand, and placed it on the desk, only one thumb drive was present. Still staring at the guard, he stood there defiant, like he was done. The guard never moved either. Never broke eye contact. I looked at the drive laying on the desk, then looked back at my guard. He was still standing his ground.

It seemed there were people in the world who just wanted to be difficult. Who preferred to spend their time complaining about how life was unfair, bitching how life did not conform to their wishes, and blame others for their woes. Swimming against the current, damning every obstacle, expecting the rocks and boulders to move out of their way instead of learning how to use the stream to their advantage, and allow the current to sweep them past the snag. This SSG was not going to quietly comply, he was going to have his victory.

"Sergeant, I know how many thumb drives there were. You might want to take a second and consider that." At least he had the decency to look slightly abashed as he thrust his hand back into his pocket, and produced the other drive. Everyone here is an important person. Just ask them, they will tell you just how important they think they are.

I went home after work, and sat back on my bed to read the paper, and nurse a beer. As I was lying there, with the window open as usual, I thought I heard the sound of a rocket flying over the far end of the Palace. I got out of bed, and on the way to the door heard an explosion off in the distance. As I stood in the middle of my room listening, I heard another distant explosion immediately followed by the sound of a far-off C-RAM alarm.

Returning to the side of my bed, I slipped into my shower shoes as another C-RAM alarm started blaring, this time a little closer. Opening the door to the trailer, I stepped onto the front porch to hear a third C-RAM start wailing over at Camp Hope, just two hundred meters (that's pretty much like two hundred yards, but with a European accent) away to the West. I walked off the porch, and almost made it to the bunker, when the Duck and Cover alarm in Deadwood, oops, I mean Edgewood, finally went off. Boy, did I feel safe.

6 May – Sponge Bob stopped by the palace this afternoon, and told us what had happened the other night. Another one of the grand old men of the project, Sponge Bob was the Complex Manager in charge of all the Security Managers over at the NEC. Easily six feet tall, with more salt than pepper hair, for a man in his mid-fifties he was in better shape than a lot of thirty-year-olds I knew. Having retired from the Navy, someone thought Sponge Bab would be an appropriate call-sign for him.

Those distant C-RAM alarms and explosions I had heard while lying in bed were the results of rocket strikes on the NEC. The first impact had been right at the base of the loading dock just outside the East Service CAC, on Khindi Street. Two guards were standing out front, on the street, in the pre-screening pit, and had been caught so off guard by the rockets they had just stood there in shock as small pieces of shrapnel zipped by and nicked them.

The second rocket had detonated inside the NEC compound. That was when the alarm had finally activated. Everyone was already running for cover by the time it had gone off. After a couple of minutes the alarm stopped sounding, and everything fell quiet again. Heads were starting to poke around the sides of bunkers as people were trying to get a peek at what had just happened. That was when the last rocket had come in.

This one fell a little short, and found our company camp, Camp Jackson. Butt up against the East side of the NEC, Camp Jackson was where all the guards and Security Managers for the NEC lived. Along with a lot of the company administrative folks. It had hit the trees on the back side of the camp, and detonated over the back parking lot, about fifty feet away from the trailers. Most of the shrapnel had blown back into the parking lot, but some of it had splashed forward, into the trailers.

It was a good thing the Security Manager who lived in the first trailer had been at work at the time. When the shrapnel ripped though, it had torn up the side of his trailer, a bit of the bed, and some of the furniture. The bigger shards passed straight through that trailer, and tore holes in the trailer behind it. Fortunately, one of the company armorers had been assigned to that one. When the rockets first started falling, he had moved into the concrete hard, heavily armored arms room in the NEC, and was not in the trailer at the time. Both of those trailers were right in front of the trailer I used to stay in when I lived on Jackson during my last rotation. Another bullet dodged.

The time lag before the last explosion had been caused by a couple of rockets that had fallen a little short. I had been wrong about those rockets flying over the far end of the Palace. They had flown directly over me. The flight path had been high enough for the sound of the engines to be muffled, and as the first rockets flew over us, on their way to the NEC, one of the follow-ons had fallen short, and landed on FOB Blackhawk, just behind the WPPS Camp.

Two female soldiers had been sitting in their trailer, on the FOB, when the rocket came slamming through their roof. It pierced the ceiling, falling just a couple of feet away from where they were sitting on their beds, and jammed into the floor of the trailer without exploding. The two girls did, though. Right out of their trailer. In hysterics. Could you blame them? They had to be taken over to the CaSH, and sedated before they could calm down. I think, had it been me, with all the near misses and dodged bullets I had weathered, that one would have been just a little too close. I would probably have been asking for my ticket home after that one.

A second, straggler round was found this morning on the HLZ across from the Palace. It had punched through the windshield of an up-armored SUV, and embedded itself in the back of the passenger seat without exploding. E.O.D. had to pull that one out of the truck, cart if off to a sandbag bunker, and blow it up.

After work, we were standing on the grand porch that runs the entire length of the Chow Hall, when the C-RAM alarm went off. We heard the impact while walking into the Chow Hall, and found out later one of the rockets had impacted, and detonated, not too far away, off the Palace grounds though.

Tonight, I was sitting on my bed, putting some thoughts down on paper, when the C-RAM alarm went off yet again. I had just finished shaving my head, and was sitting on my bed, with a beer, when I thought I heard the sound of a distant alarm. I got up to go to the door, to confirm the sound, and had only taken a step when the report of a distant explosion drifted through the open window. Immediately turning back to the bed, I stepped into my shoes, walked across the room, and opened my door as the C-RAM alarm right next to my trailer went off.

I was just about to jump off the porch when I heard the sound of heavy boots, moving fast, coming down the sidewalk. It was a good thing I paused because someone came shooting down the sidewalk so fast I could not get a good look at the freight train that had just flown by on the way to the bunker.

Eventually, I was able to make my way to cover to discover Finch had been the one who almost bowled me over. He had been sitting in his trailer, on the phone with a friend, trying to convince him to come to work in

Baghdad when the alarm had gone off. After the all clear had been given, Finch called his buddy back, and told him it had only been a rocket attack, no big deal. It really was safe to come to work here. Special Forces guys have an odd sense of perspective, don't they?

9 May – It had been an interesting day. Last night, around 0100hrs, I was rudely awakened by the C-RAM alarm. I jumped out of bed, and ran to the door. No sooner had I stepped onto the porch than the alarm stopped screaming. Instead of rushing the rest of the way to the bunker, I crouched down on the porch, leaned up against the sandbags, and waited for a couple of seconds to see if I would hear any explosions. Not hearing any, I went back to bed.

I had laid back down for only a moment when I heard the crackle the loudspeaker made just before an announcement. Thinking it was going to be the All Clear, I dug deeper into my pillows. It was not the All Clear, it was another alarm. I jumped out of bed again, and ran to the porch one more time. Crouched against the sandbags, for a couple of seconds, the alarm stopped. A moment or two later, I heard the faint sound of a Duck and Cover alarm going off in the distance. I could not quite place where the alarm was coming from until I stuck my head back inside the trailer. It was coming from the speaker on my hardline phone.

This did not happen automatically. It took someone in the TOC flipping the switch to make it happen. Since I had not heard any explosions with these alarms, I could only wonder if Finch had gotten bored, working the night shift, and had been fooling around with the switches in the TOC.

Lunchmeat, Rak, and I met for breakfast this morning. Well, that was not quite right. Rak and I met for breakfast this morning. Lunchmeat was nowhere to be seen. Normally, the three of us showed up around the time the Chow Hall opened, had breakfast, then walked around the corner to the formation area. This morning, Rak showed up, but no Lunchmeat. I was not sure why. Soon after arriving on project, he had been given a living space in the Palace by the Marine Guard Force occupying the basement. It was not a fancy space, or a very large space. There was enough room for a cot, a place for him to hang his clothes, but he had to step out into the hall to change his mind. The part we found confusing was the part where he was living in the basement of the Palace. Rockets, alarms, and all that stuff were no longer a bother for him. So, why was he late?

It was not like I had never been late for work before. It happened to all of us, once or twice. So, being the good battle buddy Rak pulled out his phone, and dialed up Meat's cell.

"Hey. You got any plans for coming to work this morning?"

I could not hear the response, but it must have been a good one by the way Rak laughed.

"No worries. See you at formation." And he rang off.

The curious look on my face must have prompted him to explain. "No biggie. He set his alarm last night, then forgot to turn it on." Yah, I had done that before too.

Without the need to wait for Lunchmeat, Rak and I went to breakfast. Yes Mom, we washed our hands. Between bites, I told Rak about my adventures with the alarms last night. I got to the part where the alarm stopped as soon as I stepped onto the porch, and his eyes got real wide.

"Oh, man!" he said "You slept through most of that alarm. I was able to make it all the way to my bunker before it stopped sounding." Oh, that could be a problem.

I was not all that concerned about sleeping through a C-RAM alarm. How could I get upset about something if I did not know it had happened? Equally, I was not all that concerned about sleeping through the rocket that hit my trailer, and killed me. First, I would be asleep, then I would be dead. Not much to worry about there, either. I was a bit worried about sleeping through the alarm that foretold the rocket that hit my trailer, and cost me an arm or leg, or any combination thereof. It would suck to wake up, and be all messed up.

The realization I had come this far was not lost on me. Actually making those connection, and linking them to their ultimate conclusion, was not the part that surprised me either. It was the ease with which I made those conclusions, and my rising level of indifference to their conclusions that did. Had I been here too long?

Relatively speaking, work was pretty quiet today. I had been making my afternoon rounds, and had just walked into the North CAC when the Duck and Cover (D&C) alarm went off. Had it been a couple of minutes earlier, I would have been walking along the front wall of the grounds with no place to go for cover. An explosion immediately followed the alarm, but it sounded like it was over by the Chancery.

I got the green report from the CAC Supervisors, telling me everything was OK, and all personnel were alright. Calling the report up to my boss, we waited for the All Clear to sound so we could open the CACs, and let people out. When alarms went off, we were mandated to keep everyone taking shelter in the CAC inside the CAC until the All Clear had sounded. It was for their own safety. We heard the loudspeaker key up, and figured it was going to be the announcement. No. Once again, it was the D&C alarm, along with more rockets over by the Chancery.

We stayed within the protection of the CAC, and waited for the All Clear. Eventually it came, and everyone took off about their business. Life was good. Two minutes later we heard more explosions from the direction of the Hospital, and the D&C alarm went off again. I guess not all the rounds were impacting around the Chancery.

10 May – Not too much today. I got out, and was able to walk all my CACs. Actually, I was able to get out of the office for most of the day, and enjoy the outdoors.

It had been an early morning this morning, though. Around 0300hrs the C-RAM alarm had gone off. I was sleeping, minding my own business, when the alarm blasted me out of a nice deep sleep. Not a lot of drama with this one. The alarm sounded. I went to the porch. The alarm stopped. I went back to bed. It was more annoying than anything else.

I did not mention the mild dust storm we had to endure for most of the day yesterday. It was not all that strong, but was enough to keep the helicopters grounded, and that tended to make folks a little jumpy around here. When the helicopters were able to fly, the bad guys did not get much of a chance to move their rockets around, or shoot them at us without provoking the wrath of the pilots. When the helicopters and UAVs could not fly, well, that was a problem. Actually, there had been much less fireworks than I had thought we were going to get. But it explained why the Chancery and CaSH had gotten hit yesterday.

Our Complex Manager, Manny, had been getting his butt chewed up rather regularly lately. I mentioned this job position before, but should probably give you some context so you can better understand where they fell in the grand scheme of things.

The easiest way I can explain is to use a military example. It's what I know best. Guards were akin to individual soldiers. Pretty simple. Pretty basic. Everyone should be able to grasp that concept. Individual Site Supervisors, in my case the CAC Supervisors, were like Squad Leaders. But, unlike Squad Leaders, they did not have subordinate leaders like Team Leaders, and the number of guards they supervised was more than a squad in most cases. My General Supervisor, or All CAC Supervisor, was something like a Platoon Sergeant. As a Platoon Sergeant would be responsible for their Squad Leaders, the General Supervisor was responsible for the CAC Supervisors. Again, the numbers did not match as much as the responsibility did. This made me something like a First Sergeant and Operation Sergeant rolled into one. Mission and paperwork, I got to do it all. Now came the Complex Manager. They would be the Sergeants Major of the outfit, both staff and command. They were responsible for several Security Managers, each having their own General Supervisor, who supervised a number of Site Supervisors, who supervised the guards. When they say, "stuff rolls downhill," Complex Managers sat closer to the crest than the rest of us. So when the Complex Manager got his butt kicked so hard it wound up around the top of his head, and he was wearing it like a hat, you knew people were extremely unhappy.

The reason he was being made to wear this "ass hat" was some of the new Security Managers were taking way too long getting up to speed on a number of things. The one thing that kept tripping them up, day after day, was the Daily Report of Guards. Called "The Daily," this report was completed every morning. It listed all the guards assigned to our venues, where they were working, who had the day off, who was in training, and who was providing relief so guards could take breaks. Much of the problem stemmed from the guards being listed in The Daily by their employee number, instead of their last name. You would not believe just how many Vasquez and Garcias we had working here. They were like the Smith and Jones of Latino last names.

The reports really were not all that difficult to fill out, once you got the hang of it, but some folks just could not seem to wrap their brains around the concept. Each number represented an individual guard, and sometimes they had been entered twice at the same venue. Sometimes they had been entered to give the impression the same guard was working more than one venue. Other times they were entered as working, when the guard was on day off. While still other times they showed the guard being off, when they were actually working. To show our support for the paperwork challenge, Lunchmeat and I came up with a twelve-step program to help them with their problem. Of course, before you could fix your Daily, you first had to admit you had a Daily.

11 May – You just could not make this stuff up. I was sitting in the office this afternoon when my radio burst into life. It was Toro, my All CAC Supervisor. "Mr. Rooster, you need to come quick!" came a slightly accented, very excited voice. Speaking English as a second language, Toro had put in a lot of work polishing his vocabulary.

Eyeballing the radio, I pushed the transmit button. "Toro? Calm down. Where are you, and what's going on?"

I had barely released the toggle switch when he immediately responded. "Sir. I am at the Main CAC, and a man is here yelling at the guards."

"On my way."

Clipping the radio to my belt, I pushed away from the desk, and was standing to leave when my boss, Manny, the Complex Manager, stuck his head out of his office, and asked what was going on. I told him what Toro had just told me, adding I was on my way.

"Good." He said. "I'll come with you. Now I can watch you work, and see how you handle this." Great. No pressure.

Approaching the back of the Main CAC, Toro was waiting for me outside the door. He was so upset his hands were shaking, and he was pacing back and forth balling his fingers into tight fists.

"Mr. Rooster. This man, he comes in with a visitor. The visitor has a cell phone with a camera. When we tell him he cannot take this inside, the man, he throws the clipboard across the CAC and yells "Who the fuck are you?" then he calls the guards stupid."

Oh! It was on! There was no reason to abuse these guards. There certainly was no reason to call any of them stupid. My anger meter immediately jumped into the red, and the peg bounced a couple times as it bottomed out at the high end of the scale. Realizing my boss was standing right behind me, I slammed a muzzle on the beast that was my furry, and wrestled the creature down until I could put a leash on it. I was not going to give any guarantees though. If this idiot decided he was going to try to pop off on me, or the guards again, I was not all that sure how strong that leash was going to be, or how tight I would be able to hold it. With my anger simmering barely a degree below the boiling point, I set my mind, and walked into the CAC. Some might even say I made an entrance.

For twenty-three years I had been a Military Policeman. I had also been contracting security in Baghdad for a couple more years. I knew I was ready to handle just about anything the fates were willing to throw at me. I had been shot at, blown up, rocketed, and car bombed. I have had to deal with unruly Officers, and enlisted alike. I had faced the wrath, and borne the brunt, of many a Sergeants Major's ire in the course of my duties. And now I was ready to fix this guy's little red wagon, or light into him with both barrels if need be. Striding through the door, I turned toward the interior of the building, took a step, and there, standing in front of the processing desk was a priest. You could have knocked me over with a feather.

That's right. A Priest. A Catholic Priest, by the look of it. Six and a half feet of black suit with a backward collar. And that was when it hit me. God had a wicked sense of humor. The beastie that had once been my anger cried out a frightened yip, and took off running with its tail between its legs. The leash broke as it fled.

Every knot of wind was knocked from my sails, and slowly, ever so slowly, the flow of time began to pick up speed again. The earth returned to its normal rotation, and I realized I was standing, frozen, just inside the door. From behind me I heard a gasp, and realized Manny was standing in the doorway trying not to choke. The quick ka-chunk of the door closing did not indicate whether or not he had won the struggle, but the lack of his presence told me I had been abandoned. Left standing on the X.

Left to deal with this without backup. And that was when this hit me. Buddy was only half a word.

At this point I think it only fair to let you know I am not Catholic. I consider myself religious, just not Catholic. I did graduate from a Catholic high school however, and armed with this little bit of experience I thought I had a pretty decent idea of how a Catholic priest was supposed to act. This was not it. Feeling the eyes of every single guard in the room pleading for me to fix this, I walked across the room and introduced myself.

"Father, my name is Rooster. What seems to be the problem?

Immediately, he waived his Palace Badge in my face, and started yelling. "I've got M.S., and I can't carry my Bag!" he screamed. "My assistant carries it for me, and all this stuff is mine!" I am no expert on accents, but it sounded to me like there was a bit of an Irish brogue to his speech.

This one little piece of information, the Irish brogue, caused me to do a quick reassessment of his denomination. Seeing as how the Catholic church had pretty much been kicked out of England by Henry VIII, although not completely, and the British controlled the northern part of the Emerald Isle, there was a chance I was not dealing with a Catholic Priest. I may have been dealing with a Vicar from the Church of England. His suit could have gone either way.

"Very good Sir," I said. "Is there any identification in the bag that would identify it, or its contents, as yours?"

"Well…uh…um…ohh…No. There isn't!" he yelled as he crossed his arms over his chest, and turned away from me. "But I can't understand why I can't take my bag inside with all my stuff. I've been doing this for years!"

I was the new Security Manager at the CACs, and it seemed any time I came across someone doing something the rules said they were not supposed to the first thing they told the new guy was they had been doing this for years. Implying the last guy let them get away with it. Usually, this was lie number one.

"Sir. I don't know anything about that. If the Manager before me had been allowing this to happen, he was violating policy. Now, I do know the man identified as the visitor is in possession of the bag, and the bag contains a number of items visitors are not allowed to bring into the Palace. Unless you can prove otherwise, that bag belongs to the visitor, and it will be carried by the visitor."

Pointing to a placard hung over the visitor processing desk, I continued. "According to this sign right here, which is an extract from the State Department police, no visitor is allowed to take any electronic equipment into the Palace, or on its grounds." This brought him up short, and he looked like he was not too sure how to deal with it.

"Well! This is mine, and I'm going to take it inside!" He screamed, digging in his heels.

"Father. First of all, you need to lower your voice. There is no reason to yell at me. We're both adults, and I would appreciate it if you acted like one. Secondly. No, you will not be taking that bag inside. I've already told you that. I've also been told you've been cursing at my guards, and calling them stupid." This completely set the Father off, and you would have thought I had just accused him of committing one of the seven deadly sins.

He started screaming about how he was a priest, and did not use language like that. He also screamed that it was right for him to call the guards stupid because, in his opinion, they were in fact stupid for doing this to him. To emphasize his point, he started waiving his canes around. Did I forget to mention that part? Because of his M.S., he needed canes just to walk around.

So, just to make sure everyone is up to speed. There I was, dealing with an Irish Priest. Possibly Catholic, possibly Church of England. With M.S., yelling and waving his canes around.

"Father," I said, "when I replay the tape from the camera over there," pointing to the camera looking at him from the corner of the room, "what is the playback going to tell me?" The look on his face was priceless. He never saw the camera mounted in the ceiling, up in the corner of the CAC, and had not realized everything he had done was on tape. Immediately, he hid his face, and stared mumbling.

"Sir, is it possible an apology is in order?" I prompted.

About this time an Army Lieutenant Colonel (LTC), a Chaplin, came in the back door, and introduced himself as looking for the priest. His arrival must have emboldened the Father because he straightened his back, and launched into a new tirade.

"Father. I've already asked you to lower the level of your voice. There is no reason for yelling."

"Yes, there is! I'm deaf!" He yelled, promptly reaching into both ears, and pulling out two hearing aids. One from each ear. Crap! I did not see that one coming.

"Father, I haven't raised my voice above a conversational tone, and you've answered everything I've said. Again, you need to lower the level of your voice. I've also asked you to apologize to these guards for calling them stupid. Most of these men can speak two languages, and some of them do it quite well. To me, that's not a sign of stupidity. How many languages do you speak?"

Oh, that got him going again. Launching into a new tirade, he put a little more steel into his spine, straightened up on his canes, took a step toward me, and started yelling at me nose to nose. I stood close to six feet five inches tall, and this guy was a little taller than me, a situation I did not run into very often. I tipped the scales around two-hundred fifty pounds, and this guy was probably pretty close.

With hardly more than a foot of space separating us, if I physically moved him out of my personal space I would be a bully, and would have just beaten up a crippled priest. If I were to move back, I would have been giving ground to him, and shown I was willing to back down. If I raised my voice, I was an unprofessional Neanderthal, and would have just shouted at a man of the cloth. Work brain, work.

What was my brain trying to sort out? Simply this. There I was. Dealing with a Church of England Vicar, possibly a Catholic Priest, with muscular sclerosis, who needed two canes just to walk, had a hearing aid in each ear, who had verbally berated and abused my guards, and was now trying to physically intimidate me. All over a cell phone with a camera that was not allowed in the Embassy Annex. It was incredible where, and over what, people would choose to make their Alamo stand.

Unbeknownst to me, a fairly good sized crowd had started to gather inside the CAC behind me. Both of the Iraqi interpreters who work in the CAC had extracted themselves from the brunt of the altercation, and sought shelter in my wake. The All CAC Supervisor, Toro, had walked in behind me, and was now standing next to the Main CAC supervisor, with the guards crowded around them in mutual support. Manny, my boss, my buddy, had not slunk out the door to keep from choking. He had walked outside to call Rak and Lunchmeat, and tell them to hustle their butts over here so they would not miss the show. And if that was not enough, six or eight people just passing through the CAC had stopped to watch, recognizing good street theater when they saw it.

Pretty well backed up against a wall, with no place to turn, and no other alternatives from which to choose, I checked in with my brain to see what it had come up with. All I received was a mental shrug of the shoulders, and a little voice in the back of my mind saying, "Yah, I got nothing."

A thought suddenly occurred to me. Completely out of the blue, a question coalesced. By comparison, it was not one of the brightest ideas I had ever had, but when floundering in the surf, a drowning man will grasp at anything. Seeing this as my only lifeline, I grabbed hold with both hands. The ride to calmer waters was just about to get a lot rougher before easing up. "Father," I asked. "Do you think this is how Jesus would handle this situation?"

If you have never heard the sound of twenty jaws hitting the floor at the same time, it is something you will not quickly forget. The intake of air, as twenty people gasped in unison, not only robbed the oxygen from half the room, it caused my shirt to ripple as the air sped past me. Suddenly, the CAC fell deathly quiet for the space of two or three heart beats, and you could have heard a mouse piss on cotton. Faintly, somewhere in the distance, I could have sworn I heard a ticket dispenser click out my pass for a seat on the express bus to hell.

The Father stared me straight in the eyes. I could see the wheels spinning in his brain. When what I had just asked him finally input, calculated, collated, and processed I could see the exact second he fully comprehended his actions. His countenance deflated, his raiment became less righteous, and he stepped back away from me without saying a word.

"Father. These guards are all from Peru, and the majority of them are deeply religious. Being rudely treated by a man of the cloth, any cloth would be very unsettling to them. If you would like to take a second to compose yourself, I'm sure they are willing to wait for that apology."

I am sorry to say they did not get one. The LTC had witnessed the end of the drama, and suggested maybe it would be better for him to leave the phone. I figured he was never going to make atonement with the guards, and let the situation de-escalate once the phone had been tagged, and set aside.

The LTC walked the Father onto the grounds, and I turned to exit the CAC as well. I was met by the stare of twenty faces, frozen somewhere between total shock, and total terror. Every eye was open as far as the lids would go. Every eyebrow had risen to meet their hairline. Every mouth hung a-gape, as if their jaw muscles had been cut. Oh well. What could I do, right? You could not make this stuff up.

I did head straight over the S.O.B. office, and give the R.S.O.s a heads up. Surprisingly, they were not shocked. They had dealt with him before, and he had been a handful then. The decision was made. Should he show up with his phone again, let it pass. They would update his badge later.

15 May – It had been a couple of days, and nothing but a lot of routine stuff had been happening. Nothing to write home about. Am I funny, or what?

Yesterday, the Head Shed put us back in full kit for a couple of hours. They never gave a reason, so I was not positive what they thought was going to happen. But even-money said someone was expecting a rocket strike. Imagine that. Just before the order came down to kit up, all the helicopters parked at the H.L.Z. took off, and headed toward Sadr City. Military, and civilian alike. Gunships, transports, little birds, everyone. No one said if there was a corollary between the order and the mass exodus, but we did not get any rockets.

The anxiety I had been feeling began to subside as I put my vest and helmet on. Without even realizing it, I had been walking around strung tight like a guitar string. Maybe I had not been the only one. Maybe that explained some of the tensions that had been happening in the Main CAC. Maybe everyone else was on edge too.

I began to realize the worst part about the last month, since the Easter Sunday rocket strike, had not been all the C-RAM and D&C alarms, and there had been so many. It had not been the actual rockets strikes, though they brought their own terror. It had been the waiting. Knowing that at any time a rocket was going to hit, with or without warning, but it was going to hit. It had been the expectation of its arrival causing my nerves to bundle.

When rockets happened terror, confusion, and panic came with them. But there were things that needed to be done when that happened. Something to focus on. Something with purpose. In between there was nothing to fill the mind. Ease the anticipation. Distract my thoughts. And the longer we went between attacks, I realized, the worse that had become.

Back on active duty, I attended a seminar on Responding to Family Disputes. The instructor told us there were people in abusive relationships who went through something similar. If it had been a while since the last time their partner had been abusive, they would deliberately do something to provoke an outburst. Once over, they would move on to the next phase, the honeymoon phase, and the fear generated by the expectation would go away. At least for a little while. He said these cycles tended to repeat, and increase in intensity. Both with the anticipation and the abuse.

Had this been happening to me? Had my anticipation of the next attack been slowly building? It was not like I could provoke a rocket into attacking early, so we could get beyond anticipating the terror. That was out of the question. Had I been using the confrontations at the CACs as sort of an emotional punching bag to siphon off some of that anxiety? I did not know. All I did know was putting on my helmet and vest had its own calming effect. Its own feeling of comfort.

Four days ago, al-Sadr signed a cease fire agreement with the Iraqi Government that was supposed to last four days. What did these cease fires really mean for us? It just meant we usually received about half the number of rockets we usually got. The last three nights had been pretty nice, though. Not a single alarm all night long. I was thinking this was probably the calm before the storm. Who knew?

16 May – A dust storm had blown in early this morning, and set up camp for the day. One of those low-grade storms that produced a reddish/brown tint, and colored the whole outdoors. Shading everything, it looked like a picture of a Martian landscape. The hue was the result of fine particles of dirt crushed to the consistency of talcum powder, light enough to be picked up on the wind, and remain suspended in the air. On a calm day, after the wind

had stopped blowing, and all the powder had settled on the ground, when you walked through it little clouds of dust would puff up around your boots with each step. We called it moon dust.

May and October made up the bulk of storm season, and out in the deep desert you got dust storms of biblical proportions. With nothing out there to act as a wind break, those storms could whip winds up to speeds between forty and sixty miles per hour, and speed across the open expanse. To give a little comparison, in the States, fifty mile per hour winds constituted a tropical storm, and class one hurricanes started at seventy-five miles per hour. Sometimes the dust storms lasted for minutes, leaving behind a fine layer of grit coating everything. Sometimes they lasted for hours, tearing up anything not seriously nailed down.

The remnants of that last kind of storm were what had settled over the city. As the big ones came stampeding out of the desert to envelope the built-up areas, even the feistiest storms would eventually lose their bluster, and the winds would die down until they were more like breezes. The right atmospheric conditions still remained for the dust to stay suspended, the winds just lost their ferocity, and without the turbulence to keep the storm in motion the residuals could hang around for days.

This was where we were, inside terra firma so to speak, and as a result the helicopters were not flying. With the birds on the ground, we went all day without air cover. Today was also Friday, the first day of the Muslim weekend, and that meant all the insurgents would be sitting around the house, getting bored, knowing we had no one in the sky watching them. What do you think they had been doing? Yah, me too. They had been out moving their rockets and mortars around. Tonight might get a little sporty.

Yesterday, we went the entire twenty-four hours without so much as a single alarm activation. Hurray for the sounds of silence.

19 May – Yesterday broke the silence. We went two whole days without a C-RAM alarm, a Duck and Cover alarm, a rocket, or a mortar. One C-RAM did activate an alarm, but it was not ours. That was the good part. The better part was the serious lack of boom accompaniment.

Yesterday had also been a very busy day for me. Barriers not working, electric gates not working, screeners taking off without being properly relieved. Just a busy day.

I was in bed early last night, around 2000hrs, and of course, now that the silence had been broken, we were getting more alarms. I had not been asleep for long when a dulcet, repetitive tone intruded on my dreams. A heavy, masculine voice, which should have automatically told me something was not right with my dream, was droning out a faint beat. As the melody cleared, I realized he was not singing for me to tuck in my covers (I know, it did not make any sense to me either, but do all of your dreams make sense?), I was being told to duck and cover.

"Duck and cover!" Crap! My eyelids slammed open. My now wide-awake ears strained to pick out any sound other than the air conditioner. Unable to hear clearly through the rumbling of the condenser, I rolled out of bed still not sure if I had dreamt the alarm or not, and plodded over to open the front door. Stepping through the threshold, I stood on the porch, and heard the Duck and Cover alarm going off across the compound.

With a deep sigh of relief at the realization I was not so far gone my mind was dreaming up fake alarms in my sleep, and a slight feeling of annoyance at having been woken up by such a far off alarm, I walked back into my hooch. My mindset was, if the alarm was so far away, the rocket was going to be far away too. Not always a truism, but I thought it anyway. Walking back inside I turned to see I had fallen asleep with the window closed. It was a wonder I had even heard the alarm at all.

I mentioned the Duck and Cover alarm a couple of times, but should probably add a few more things. As you remember, the C-RAM alarm was activated by incoming rounds. When the alarm sounded, it started off with three loud, short blasts of a klaxon-like gong. Immediately followed by the words "In-coming! In-coming! In-coming!" Very loud. Very urgent. The first time you heard this alarm it would certainly get your attention. Hear it a second time, and the adrenaline release it caused would probably make your heart beat hard enough to leave scar tissue on the muscle.

The Duck and Cover alarm was a little different. First off, it was not an automatic alarm, but was activated manually. Both alarms were prerecorded, combining alarm tones with voice alerts. Where the C-RAM alarm let you know you were standing on the bullseye, and should probably get out of the way. The Duck and Cover was a more general alert, and first sounded with a series of high-low tones that sounded a lot like the sirens used by European police. Immediately following the tones were the words "Duck and Cover. Duck and Cover. Move away from the windows."

Being a manually operated alarm, most of the compounds around the I.Z. had one plugged into their P.A. system. If a C-RAM alarm was activated anywhere in the Green Zone, the surrounding FOBs and compounds that were not plugged into that system would activate their Duck and Cover alarms. The idea was to get people under cover just in case one of the rockets went wild. Unfortunately, being a reactive alert, activation of the Duck and Cover alarm usually happened after the explosion.

The sandstorm finally blew itself out last night as well. Today was turning out to be bright and sunny, and it was probably going to end up being hot too. We were entering the time of year when the mercury started to climb over the one-hundred-degree mark. Lots of sunscreen was probably a good idea too.

22 May – Today was another good one. Just before lunch I got a call from our company representative in the TOC. He told me there was a lady in the North Wing who wanted to register a complaint about being harassed by one of the guards. Great. Now What?

The North Wing was the secure area inside the Palace where the State Department bigwigs, and Army Command section were located, along with the operational departments, secret squirrel offices, and the three letter agency guys. Since my security clearance was no longer active, and the paperwork I had completed to reactivate it had not finished processing yet, I had to be escorted in. I was met at the door by our rep, and was told I would be going to the Commanding General's office to take the report from one of his secretaries. Nice heads-up guys.

I had originally been briefed the complaint was centered around the conduct of one of my guards working a gate here at the Palace. Had that been the case, it would have made perfect sense for me to take the report, and fix the problem. The thing confusing me was my guards were very good about contacting me any time there had been a problem, and I had not received any calls. As I listened to her concern, the reason for my confusion became abundantly clear.

She had left the Palace grounds, and gone over to one of the offices by the Iraqi Government Building on the North side of the I.Z. One of the local Iraqis working in her office had to renew the badge that allowed him access to the Green Zone, and she was to be his escort. While they were waiting at one of the checkpoints controlling access to the area, one of the guards had been rude to her. It seemed he bumped into her, and did not apologize for it.

To make matters worse, there had been a large number of Iraqis waiting to get into the same office, to get their I.Z. badges, and she could not believe we (the contracting company providing security for the perimeter checkpoint next to the building, not the building itself) had not constructed some kind of shade for all the people waiting to enter the building. The fact that the building, its grounds, and the badging office located inside were run by a combined group from the Iraqi Government, and the U.S. Army (whom she worked for), and not the guards from my company did not seem to make any difference to her. Our guards were the most obvious, prevalent, and abundant in the area. It was our fault. And, after all, we were just contractors. Got a problem? Just get a new contract security company. We were expendable.

You want shade for these folks? Maybe you should have been talking with the Iraqi Government, seeing as how they did own the property the crowd was congregating on. And, unless I am completely off base when it came to a government, they were supposed to be there for their people.

Just to give you a little idea of how these people actually governed. If any of you have ever read the Constitution of the United States, you know it is a pretty lofty piece of writing. It talks of men's rights, nationhood, the right of self-government by the people, it even explains the duties and responsibilities of each part of government. Basically, it contains a lot of ideals that would be tough for any nation to live up to, even in good times. The Iraqi Constitution was a little different. The U.S. Army issued badges that gave access to the I.Z., with the blue badge having the highest amount of access, and the least amount of restrictions. A bit like the blue badges issued at the Palace. The Iraqi Government had written into their Constitution, into their Constitution mind you, all members of Parliament would be issued Blue I.Z. Badges. Don't set the bar too high guys.

If that did not make you scratch your head, roughly six months ago the Stars and Stripes newspaper ran a story on how the Representatives in Iraqi Government were tired of being treated like, and I'm quoting here, "common citizens" when they entered the I.Z. They were appalled at having their vehicles checked by lowly, unclean animals (bomb dogs), and were tired of having their property searched like they were everyday people. What was good for the goose, apparently, was not good for the gander.

If the Iraqis truly owned this country, and their government truly ran it for the betterment of its people, you would think that maybe, just maybe, it was about time they took control of this place. After all, it had been five years since Saddam had been overthrown, and Parliament had been assembled for almost three years now. Maybe it was time they kicked all of the insurgents out, put a leash on all their warring factions, passed a couple of laws to make killing and murder illegal (yes, revenge killings were still lawful over here. They were tried by the tribal elders, not the government, on the basis of whether or not the revenge was justified, not the killing), and possibly, just possibly, begin representing the people of Iraq, instead of their own personal interests. Sure, these people ran this country. If you pull the other leg, it plays Jingle Bells.

She also felt the guard's level of alertness was way out of proportion with the situation. "They stand there, in their helmets and vests, with their guns in their hands. They're too aggressive."

I thought she may be missing the whole point of this being a war zone kind of thing. To fully appreciate this, you had to understand the guards at that checkpoint were not guarding the Iraqi Government Building (AKA the I.G.B.), they were providing interior security at a gate that provided entry directly from the Red Zone. A gate solely used by Iraqis, and third country nationals (T.C.N.s), the same demographic from which the insurgents, terrorists, suicide bombers, and anyone wishing to cause chaos and destruction in the Green Zone came. A gate which happened to be located right next to the I.G.B. I wonder why they stayed at such a high level of alert. Those guards were strung about as tight as a bunch of long tailed cats in a room full of rocking chairs.

About a year ago, that post had been manned by the Iraqi Army. At that time a suicide bomber had been able to make his way through the checkpoint, enter the I.G.B, walk into the Convention Center, and detonate himself. A lot of people died that day. I could understand why those guards were a little on edge.

This was also the building the insurgents tended to shoot rockets at when they were upset with the Iraqi government. A few months after the suicide attack, a rocket had impacted right in front of the building. Well, that was not entirely accurate. The rocket actually landed, and detonated on, an Iraqi man who had been standing in front of the building. The best we could figure was the rocket took him right between the shoulder blades. The resulting explosion had not left enough of him to put in a cigar box, including the two-foot square-ish piece of skin from his chest we found one-hundred meters down the sidewalk. For whatever reason could those guards be a little apprehensive over there?

She seemed to feel if the guards would treat someone as "obviously American" as she was, surely they must be treating the Iraqis even worse. Obviously American? What did that even mean?

I did not know how much the folks working in the Palace got out, but having already done two combat tours I had walked amongst them quite a bit. I saw Iraqis with red hair and freckles. I also saw Iraqis with blond hair, and blue eyes. Maybe it had slipped the collective mind that the British had occupied this area for quite a while. Or that a lot of Russian and Croation blood had been intermixed in the people here as well. Possibly, most folks did not know a good number of invading armies had been making little detours through this neck of the woods for quite a long time as well. The bottom line was, anyone who thought all Iraqis were dark-haired, dark-eyed, dark-skinned people who dressed in head wraps, and robes needed to get out more. There had been so many different cultures, and nationalities, living in this region since the dawn of time you could pretty much bet that any person sitting next to you right now looked like they could be Iraqi. By the way, if anyone knows what it means to be "obviously American," please let me know.

With this comment I had to reach down ... deep, deep, down ... sort through a treasure chest of illogical reasoning, rummage around a collection of coping mechanism, and bring forth as much understanding as I could humanly muster to rationalize that one. It was either that, or let my head explode.

With all of the rockets that had been shot at us recently, I could see how a person with little, or no military background could get a bit twitchy, covered with a light coat of paranoia by now. Hell, I had over twenty years of military background and experience, and I was getting jumpy at sudden, random loud noises these days. With so many rockets exploding in so many locations, pretty much all over the Green Zone, this war was getting a lot closer to people who had never experienced this kind of danger before. I could understand how a certain amount of perspective could be lost by a person who had never received any training necessary to cope with these experiences, and spent most of their day behind a desk.

Up until Easter, the insurgents, the Mahdi Militia, al Qaida, and anyone else with a complaint had been shooting their rockets and mortars at the Iraqi Government, not the Americans so much. The Iraqi Government in the I.G.B. Remember that place? Good. I am glad to see some of you have been paying attention, and noticed the I.G.B. was right next to our checkpoint. For bonus points, can you guess where the majority of the rockets shot at the I.G.B. and miss land? Correct. Right around our checkpoint.

It would also help to understand the mindset of the culture here. If you pointed a gun at an Iraqi, and did not pull the trigger on them, these people would see you as being weak. I may have mentioned how Iraqis do not discuss anything so much as yell about it. Have I also mentioned that since they did not have a lot over here, other than their pride, the machismo of the average Iraqi male was pretty much equal to, if not greater than, the machismo found in the Latino community? Needless to say, this lady's perception was typical of the attitude people got when they did not get out very much. When they thought a trip across the parking lot, to the P.X., was a trip to the Red Zone. Believe it or not, I am really not trying to be judgmental, I just expected more.

Being the quiet professional, I did not bite back at her with all the information I just shared with you. I sure thought it really loud, but that was all. Instead, I listened to her complaint. I wrote down her information, and all the details she could remember surrounding her inconvenience. Throughout her dissertation I politely nodded my head, and interjected things like "Yes ma'am.

Please go on" and "I understand," with a few sprinkles of "I'll look into that" and a "We'll get that corrected" thrown in for good measure.

In time, she blew herself out. Having listened to her vent her frustrations, I excused myself, and left the room. The Company Rep who had escorted me up was no longer there, and a woman, I had no idea who she was, was sitting next to the door as I walked out. Crossing the room, I heard her scramble to her feet, and as I rounded the corner into the hallway she caught up with me. Drawing parallel to my right shoulder, we fell into step. Well, not so much into step, as she was a lot shorter than I was, but I did slow down so she could keep pace. Still breathing a little hard from her efforts to catch up, she turned her head toward me, and huffed "So! What do you plan on doing about this?"

"Me. Not a thing. I'll send the information up. The Guard Force Commander will decide how to deal with it. My area of responsibility only extends as far as the CACs around the Palace. I have no authority where this happened."

Taking a breath to spit back a retort, she paused instead, and contemplated my answer. A light appeared to flick on. Maybe she realized I had been thrown into the fire like a sacrificial lamb, sent to endure the fury and animosity only a General's Secretary could project. Maybe I had been sent because it was figured, since she worked in the Palace, the incident must have happened at one of my CACs. Maybe I had been sent because, if a head needed to be put on a platter, mine was the most expendable. Maybe I had been sent because I was the best person to handle a General Officer's Secretary. Maybe I was the only one thinking those things, and I was just projecting them onto her. I did not know. All I knew was we walked the rest of the way out of the secure area without saying a word.

26 May – Not a lot had been going on recently. Oh, we had a few "special" people come in. You know the ones who screamed how security applied to everyone else, not them.

Yesterday, we had another one of those famous Baghdad dust storms, and visibility had dropped down to less than one-hundred meters. You had to love air you could chew. We had been expecting rockets all day, because of the storm, but did not get as many as we thought we would. In the afternoon there had been a couple, three booms across the river, but no one could see exactly where they hit due to the dust. The rest of the day had been pretty quiet.

With temps 100°F for the past week, the pool here at the Palace had been a pretty happening place as well. The rockets did put a bit of a damper on the aquatic activities for a while, but the diehard swimmers and sun worshipers were slowly returning. It was a wonderful thing to see bikinis in a combat zone. I could not help but think if this culture could learn to appreciate the bikini, in its entire glorious splendor, there would be a lot fewer men willing to blow themselves up.

28 May – Things seemed to be getting back to normal, fast, but normal. It had been a while since the last time we had anything shot at us, so you knew we were due, and I was walking the long route from the North CAC, around the back of the Palace grounds, along the river wall, making my way to the Service CAC when it came.

It was a bright, sunny, cloudless day, and the morning temperature had not yet risen to the "oh my God it's hot!" level yet. The frequency of rocket strikes had taken a big nose dive over the past few days, and I was restless to get out, and stretch my legs on a long, leisurely stroll. Leaving the back door of the North CAC, I walked down the street that traversed the corridor between the walls of the Palace and Camp Travis, past the North Drop Arm, and continued to the rear of the compound. Arriving at the back wall, the Tigris River just on the other side, I turned right, and began to saunter down the road on the longest leg of my excursion.

As I passed, the guards in their towers came out onto the catwalks, and waved. We exchanged greetings, in Spanish of course, and I practiced some new clips and phrases Rak had taught me. Every now and then, feeling a little dangerous, I would free form a few short sentences, and shoot them up to the guards hoping I had constructed them correctly. Most of them would chuckle or smile, which never really told me whether or not I had gotten it right, and they would respond back with slow, elementary answers that, to my surprise, for the most part I understood. Poco a poco (little by little) my Spanish seemed to be getting better.

I left the base of one tower, and was negotiating the intervening expanse before the next, when my wanderings were interrupted by the shriek of the C-RAM alarm. Great! There I was, out in the open. Again. Looking off to my right, and a little behind me, I spotted the small, one story brick building I had just passed sitting off the side of the road, a little way beyond the base of that last tower, and across the road. An Alaska barrier had conveniently been abandoned next the building, and one end had been pushed up against the wall at a shallow angle. I sprinted for the opening.

Alaska barriers were basically Jersey Curbs on steroids. They stood over six feet tall, about eight feet long, were a whole lot thicker, and sat on a wide, deep base. Scrambling around the corner of the barrier, I hopped up on the two-foot-wide base, and wedged my six and a half foot tall, two hundred-fifty-pound ass as far away from the opening as I could get. Jammed in between the wall and the side of the barrier, I did my best to dismiss the two-foot gap behind me where the width of the base kept the vertical of the barrier from touching the wall. Stuffing a finger in each ear, I began scanning the sky, looking for anything that may be flying my way.

Eyes wide, I peered beyond the top of the barrier, out over the back of the Palace grounds, but never caught as much as a glimpse of what may have caused the alarm. Eventually, I decided I had been in my make-shift cover long enough, and anything the C-RAM may have picked up had already fallen. Even though the All Clear had not yet sounded, I felt sufficient time had passed, and it would be safe enough for me to continue my walk.

I checked the rest of the CACs without drama, and headed back to the office. Walking in the door I noticed Rak was sitting behind his desk doing a little web surfing. He had completed his checks before me, and was taking a bit of a break. We got to talking, and I told him about the alarm, where I had been when the alarm had gone off, and the meager amount of cover available out there. Being the Security Manager for the Towers, he had traveled that route extensively, and knew exactly what I was talking about. He also recognized exactly where I had been when the alarm had sounded, and knew the building next to which I had taken cover. He knew, because he had taken cover there several times.

Additionally, he had received a report from the tower I had passed, as I sprinted toward cover, telling him the rocket responsible for the alarm activation had flown over the open space I had been walking through, before splash-landing in the river without detonating. The fuel in the rocket engine must have burned out, removing the source of the roar that usually announced their arrival. That was something new I needed to think about. Quiet rockets. As if I did not have enough to worry about. The guard also reported the missile had passed so close to the tower he could hear the whistle of its flight over the wail of the alarm. Looking back at it now, I could have gone the rest of the day without knowing that.

Tonight, after work, as per our new routine, I trouped off to the Deli D-FAC with the rest of the day shift Security Managers from the complex for dinner. With the number of rocket attacks dropping off lately, more people were finding the courage to venture out to the big Chow Hall. The addition of this new mass of diners caused the lines to become inconveniently longer, and slower. Being a serve-yourself style of dining, the Deli D-FAC was much faster, and a lot more convenient.

We talked, we ate, we hung out for a while. And, with dinner finished, I headed back to my trailer. I walked in the door, dropped my pistol belt on the bed, and headed into the bathroom so I could open the valve, and vent the pressure the water I had been drinking this afternoon was exerting on my bladder. To be honest with you, I thought we had gotten past this next part. I thought we had evolved beyond waiting for me to go to the bathroom before shooting rockets. I guessed not. P.S.I. had barely dropped from fifty to twenty-five when the C-RAM alarm next to my trailer screamed to life.

Yes, I was able to get my pants zipped without injury before careening out of my trailer. For those of you who have ever had to stop mid-stream, it is a whole lot more difficult, and messier, on the run.

30 May – Once again, the Mahdi Militia was yelling foul. They believed al-Sadr had duped them into surrendering to the U.S. Army. Here was how this one went.

Al-Sadr's cease fire with the Iraqi Government, the one he made back on the eleventh, now stated that after the initial push into the city had taken the ground it was intended to capture, and the U.S. Army had pulled back to the outskirts of town, the U.S. Army was not to enter Sadr City again. However, nothing had been negotiated for the Iraqi Army to leave, and they had stayed in the city. Popular reasoning thought part of the confusion stemmed from the possibility al-Sadr was trying to demean the Iraqi Army by insinuating they were the puppets of the Americans, thereby only mentioning the U.S. Army, echoing the preachings of the local clerics on how all the evils that plagued the country were the fault of the U.S.

Additionally, as part of the cease fire, al-Sader further demanded the homes belonging to his militiamen were not to be searched, nor his men arrested, but it looked like this part of his demand had not been accepted by the Iraqis. With the U.S. Army pulled back to surround the city, the Iraqi Army had been conducting raids on suspected caches, houses, and strongholds for the Mahdi Militia, and surprisingly had done a fairly decent job of cleaning them out.

Here came the sticky part. Having negotiated another cease fire, like he had so many times before, al-Sadr told his men to lay down arms for a while, and they had. This time, however, the Iraqi Government was taking full advantage of the lull to round up the troublemakers, and seize their accoutrements of war. Here was why the militiamen were throwing their conniption fits. Having been told to stop shooting, when the Iraqi Army showed up to arrest them they had to go along quietly, at least as quietly as an Iraqi was capable of going, because to do otherwise would be to disobey the order of their holy man. Therefore, the Militiamen were under the impression al-Sadr had surrendered them to the Iraqi Army, and by proxy to us. It was amazing how those people's minds worked.

The Stars and Stripes newspaper ran a story today saying, due to the perceived betrayal, the Mahdi Militia may start ignoring al-Sadr altogether, and start hitting the Americans again, beginning another round of dodge-rocket.

Tonight, I fell asleep reading. I remembered seeing 2230 on my watch, but not much more. An hour and a half later I was rudely awakened by what? That's right, you guessed it, another C-RAM alarm. It had pretty much gotten to the point I was not even running all the way to the bunker anymore because, lately, the rockets that were not landing somewhere else had either been duds, or the alarms had been false. Yah, I knew this was liable to end up biting me in the butt, but at this point I was getting rather tired of getting shot at, tired of getting jarred awake in the middle of the night for no apparent reason, and tired of running every which way for cover.

Tonight was nothing different, no explosions. An alarm with no boom. Great. Back to bed I went, and off to sleep I got. In the morning, I found out FOB Fernandez, a little base on the West side of the I.Z, next to Checkpoint 12, had gotten hit with two short shots. The rockets came in fast and quick, exploded before the C-RAM could pick them up, and initiate an alarm. Two of the Filipino construction contractors working on the FOB took the hit while they were sleeping in their tailers. One bled out before help could arrive, and the other died on the way to the CaSH.

CHAPTER 6

1 June – It was Sunday, and in Iraq that meant the first day of the week. This brought the sounds of a good-sized explosion, followed by the crack of small arms fire (S.A.F) from the direction of Check Point Two, to the East. A few seconds later, another explosion erupted from the same general direction. This progression of pandemonium was not only an indicator of, but was also consistent with, the sounds and events that played out during a complex attack.

A complex attack usually consisted of two or more attacks striking a single target. Sometimes, this meant a simultaneous assault from multiple directions, but in the case of the checkpoint it usually meant multiple charges at one location. Historically, one suicide bomber driving a car loaded with explosives, known as a vehicle born improvised explosive device or VBIED (pronounce V-bid), would storm the gate. Once he had advanced as far as the barriers would allow, the VBIED would detonate. Ideally, for the attacker that was, this explosion would take place deep inside the checkpoint killing as many guards as possible, and blowing a hole through the obstacles to clear a path for follow-on assaults. Ideally, for the checkpoint guards, this explosion would happen somewhere else, far away somewhere else.

Every now and again, the checkpoint guards would get lucky, and were able to identify the threat before it got to their doorstep. Whether the car started its charge too early, or the driver gave himself away by some other means did not really matter at that point. Once spotted, guns would be brought to bear, and every guard able to do so would lock onto, and engage the bomber in the hopes they could keep him from pushing the button. Best case scenario.

If the bad guys got their way, and the vehicle did energetically disassemble inside the checkpoint, the guards fortunate enough to survive the initial blast tended to engage anything, or anyone who looked like they may be trying to continue the attack. Those were the sounds of Baghdad, and something my guards at the CACs were vigilant to ensure did not happen in our area.

6 June – I had been working the CACs for a little over a month now. The first few weeks were an exercise in

sensory overload as I tried to absorb all the information I could get regarding the operation of the CACs, policies applicable to accessing the Palace, and dealing with the oh so wonderful personalities who came and went every day. I had spent enough time with my guards that I was now able to recognize almost all of them by face, even though a few names still eluded me, and was beginning to learn some of the quirks in their personalities. I had to credit a portion of that last part to Lunchmeat, and give an appreciative nod to Rak.

After taking over for Finch, It had not taken long for the three of us to find where our work patterns overlapped, where resources could be pooled or consolidated, and where the efforts of one of us could enhance the productivity of all of us. It was what solders referred to as a battle rhythm. Food service workers also experienced something like this, in the ebb and flow, as diners packed in during mealtimes, only to thin out in between.

Keeping to the same concept, over the last month I learned when each CAC reached their peak activity for processing workers, visitors, and other mass migrations onto the grounds. They varied a little, day to day, and peaked at separate times, allowing me the ability to be there, or close at hand, in case there were problems. And inevitably, there were. The relationship between Meat's venue, and mine, became apparent when we realized certain activities on the H.L.Z. forewarned traffic increase to and from the Palace, and certain forms of business in the Palace telegraphed future movements to the H.L.Z. Having eyes and ears in the towers, and on the grounds, Rak was able to keep a pretty deft finger on the pulse of the Palace, and we all passed information back and forth. The lack of a language barrier meant Rak was up to date on even the smallest observations of his guards.

And it was thus we operated. Breakfast almost became strategy meetings. Each of us would go over the regular tasks scheduled for the day, and touch on any new or different activities that were supposed to happen. With events aired, we would give each other suggestions on how to tweak particular portions of our plans, or advise on ways they could alter them so one, or both of us could provide cover and/or support. With each passing day we become more streamlined in our operation. Finding new ways to work smarter, not harder.

Conducting formation was nothing new for any of us either, so that bit of the morning came together quickly. Completing our Dailies became less and less of a chore as we became familiar with the particulars of our venues. Meat, having been on his venue longer than me or Rak, was already on top of his. It did not take long before we were all able to bang out the numbers, check the forms for accuracy, and quickly send them off to the boss. Getting the formalities of the morning out of the way.

It was during this next part where we were really starting to come together as a team. Walking posts, supervising activities and inspecting operations, had always been a time-honored tradition of the N.C.O. Corps. It was called management by walking around, and that was what we did. Paperwork complete, the three of us would set out from the office to start our post checks. The Service CAC was the farthest point from the office, and a few of Rak and Meat's posts were on the way, so sometimes we would start there. During the past month we had been out and about so much people had taken to referring to us as the Thundering Herd.

So, the Thundering Herd would head out, cutting through the Palace, appreciating the landscape as we walked (that meant looking at all the beautiful women), meandering around the pool, because it was on the way. No. Seriously. It really was on the way. Arriving at the Service CAC, Rak would usually drop off to check more of his posts. His towers spread out in the opposite direction, along the river. Lunchmeat and I would continue along a different path so we could check a few more of his posts on the way to the South CAC. These walks had given me and Lunchmeat the opportunity to compare notes and trade stories, and the longer I accompanied him the more I was both surprised and impressed. He still retained a great connection with the troops.

Unlike many of the senior M.P. N.C.O.s I have had to endure in the past, his connection actually seemed to come from a position of genuine respect. Do not get me wrong, when he had to drop the hammer, because one of his guards had been acting a fool, he did. I had watched him do it. The thing was, he went about it in such a way his guards responded to him more like a wise Grandfather, giving sage chastisement, than a boss on the worksite fuming over screw-ups and demanding amends. An attribute I had been trying to develop.

For the first time in a long time, I was beginning to think not all senior M.P.s had to turn into dicks. In some small way, after becoming a senior N.C.O. myself, that had been one of the worries I had about being promoted to the next level, Master Sergeant. Master Sergeants and First Sergeants were the same paygrade. The difference was Master Sergeant was an administrative billet, and First Sergeant a troupe leading billet. My worry had been what effect the promotion would have on me, and whether or not I would become a prick like most of them. It would really have helped if I had more First Sergeants like Lunchmeat from which to learn.

In some small way I would like to think I was not the only one who benefitted from this exchange. During our ramblings and roamings, I hoped I had given something in return. Payment in kind for what I had been learning. But, since asking was a bit beyond my comfort level, I was not going to deal with that. But either way, I had not realized how feeling like a part of a team had been something I had been missing for a long time, and Rak and Lunchmeat were returning that to me. True battle buddies are rare. I had only accepted two during my career. One when my unit first deployed for the initial invasion, and one years earlier.

Approaching the South CAC, Lunchmeat would take his leave and pass straight through the building, cross the street to the H.L.Z., and continue on to check the rest of his posts. I would remain, talking with the Supervisor, finding out what was new and important for the CAC as well as the guards. Thanks to Rak, my Spanish was getting a little better every day, and I was increasingly able to talk directly to more of the guards. More importantly, I understood a little more of what they were saying every day. Supervisors were required to be functional in English, and most of them continued developing their skills, with some of them achieving a rather high degree of fluency. The guards, on the other hand, did not have that requirement. However, many of them took advantage of the "English as a Second Language" classes given at our Company Main Camp, on their off time. They worked twelve-hour shifts, just like we did, so you can imagine how important these classes were to them.

Although my Spanish was getting better, I was still thinking in English, and I knew that was slowing me down. You don't quite get it? It's O.K., I didn't at first either. Proficiency in a language comes when you are able to think in that language. Because I was not at that level, I would hear the words in Spanish, translate them to English, formulate my response in English, translate it to Spanish, then speak the words. I was sure the same thing held true for the majority of the guards still floundering with English too. Doing all this conversion in my head also meant some words hit my ears at an odd angle. They would careen toward my brain at a less than optimal trajectory, glance off the atmosphere of my cognition, and spin back off into space. In other words, I did not always pick up on what my guards were saying, even when the words were simple, and I should have known them.

This was the case just the other day. Lunchmeat had hung around the South CAC for a few minutes, joining in the conversation before traveling on. The door was still closing behind him when my ears picked up a slice of conversation two of my guards were having. The words were familiar, but my brain just could not link them together, and the phrase continued to bounce around in my skull. Now translated, the Spanish and English words kept swirling around each other, but I was still unable to mesh them together. Calling it quits, I turned to the guards and asked them to repeat what they had just said.

I think they may have been afraid I was angry about what they were saying. When you spoke your native language all day, in the company of others who spoke the same language, you got used to everyone understanding what was being said, as it was being said. It was easy to forget a person learning your native tongue did not always follow along at the same speed.

Hesitantly, the senior of the two raised an arm to point out the front window.

"Yo dijo, tu hermano de bufalo, si?"

Following the line of his finger, I looked through the glass, and found he was pointing at Lunchmeat. Context brought clarity, and the English translation superimposed itself over the Spanish words. I chuckled. As much at my initial bafflement, and inability to put this simple sentence together, as at what he was saying. As a chuckle grew into a genuine laughter, the guards visibly relaxed, and joined in.

Pointing at Lunchmeat, he had said "He is your buffalo brother, yes?"

Until now, I never realized the guards knew people were calling us the Thundering Herd. Since these guards only saw me and Meat traveling together, they had extended a variation on that theme. Buffalo Brothers. I liked it.

There we were, the Thundering Herd. Playing off each other's strengths. Shoring up each other's weaknesses. Our guards saw our teamwork, and they too were blending their efforts, forming tighter bonds between the venues. Instead of existing as dozens of individual work sites, with their own personalities and agendas, they were developing identities that augmented a larger consciousness. The Army called it "Team Building," and every guard, every Supervisor, every Security Manager working day shift around the Palace was a part of that team.

10 June – According to the Stars and Stripes newspaper, the official count was in. Because they had been reporting on all the rocket attacks in and around the Green Zone, someone in their administrative section had been keeping

a running count of the number of rockets that had been shot at us. According to their tally, in the eight weeks following Easter over one thousand rockets had been shot into the I.Z. We referred to those eight weeks as Rocket Fest.

Let's do a little reverse math on this. First, we round the number off to an even thousand, which translated into five hundred rockets launched each month. Breaking that down even further, we find an average of one hundred twenty-five launched every week, meaning eighteen were launched every day. Yah, that felt right. Some days it sprinkled, others it poured, but I think the math still held. It was surprising, looking at these numbers, that tensions around here were not higher than they were. This must have been what the frog felt like as the water boiled. What? You don't know how to boil a frog? Refill your drink, and I will tell you.

First, get a pot. It does not have to be a big pot, just big enough for your frog to get comfortable. Next, fill the pot with warm water. Do not forget to leave some room for the frog. With the pot full, place it over the heat. Now, here is where I pass on the secret for successfully boiling your frog. Do not wait for the water to boil before dropping it in, he's not pasta. So drastic a change in temperature will cause him to panic, and out he will jump. No boiled frog. Instead, place it in the water as it gets warm. Then, slowly, ever so slowly, turn up the heat. Why? Because frogs are cold blooded. That little hopper will sit in the pot, all cozy and warm, never realizing it is being cooked until it is too late. As a matter of fact, as his body temperature increases with the water temperature, the warmth will entice him to stay right there.

See the similarities to our situation? No? Fine. The pot was the I.Z. The heat was the rockets. The water was our stress level. And we were the frogs. Given enough time people can adapt, even learn to accept and tolerate some pretty stressful situations. PS – Don't go out and start boiling frogs. If they ever learn to shoot .45s they're going to be pissed, and we'll all be dead.

14 June – O.K., someone please tell me how this made any sense. Iraq just finished playing China in the World Cup (that's soccer, folks), and Iraq won. To celebrate their victory, and this was the part I needed help understanding, every Iraqi with a gun, and that was just about every one of them, was shooting their gun in the air.

Over here, the locals called it Allah's Fireworks, and they did this in celebration of pretty much everything. Officially, it was labeled as celebratory fire, but we called it happy fire. Personally, I called it something way different, and thought it was one of the prime reasons explaining why Iraq did not have a space program. Not a lot of rocket scientists around here.

Plus, it would be one thing if there were only a couple of guns going off. But, by the sound of it, you would think major firefights had broken out all around the Green Zone. Both inside, and out. Most of it had been automatic weapons fire too, not just rifle or pistol fire.

I was checking on my guards inside the Main CAC, when three bullets dropped out of the sky, and impacted in front of the building. One round pierced the hood of a truck waiting to go around the Main CAC, on his way to the North CAC, and the other two hit the ground in front of the bumper, not two or three feet away from the guard directing traffic. I walked out of the building to check the scene, and just as soon as I asked the guard if he was O.K., a dozen more bullets thumped and smacked into the pavement around us. We decided to let the traffic fend for itself, and made haste for hard cover.

I think we should line up all our howitzers, tanks, automatic rifles, machine guns, rifles, pistols, sling shots, and water guns around the I.Z. on the 4th of July and have some happy fire of our own. Only this time we point all the guns out.

As you can guess, we had not had too many problems in the month of June. There had been a few C-RAM activations, a couple of rockets had come in on the other side of town, and some huge explosions had been heard close to several of the checkpoints. Pretty much normal business.

I already mentioned the Stars and Striped had published their count of rockets that had been shot at the I.Z. since Easter, a little over one thousand and counting. Having been on the receiving end of a lot of those launches, I could easily believe that number. In my opinion, it was probably even a bit low. In the beginning, almost all of the rockets had worked the way they were designed; launch, fly, impact, explode. As time went on, more and more of them seemed to fail on the last part though. It seemed the 107 mm rocket was a rather finicky beast. I'll explain.

To keep us from finding their caches of rockets, the insurgents tended to use the best camouflage at their disposal to hide them from us. They buried them in the dirt. Big Army had found this out. A good idea in theory, a bit flawed in practice. Here is what happened. You did not want to bury your rocket with the fuse inserted in the nose of the warhead, because that made your rocket live. With a live rocket, enough pressure on the fuse would cause the rocket to go boom, and the simple act of filling in the hole could result in instant bad juju time.

On the other hand, burying your rocket without the fuse inserted meant the cavity the fuse threaded into was empty, and tended to fill with dirt. Unless you packed the area with something that did not bung up the works, when you dug up your rocket you had to clean out the fuse cavity completely. And when I say completely, I mean thoroughly and completely. After recovering and cleaning your buried treasure, chances were fair any remaining dirt would cause your rocket to malfunction during the part you really wanted it to work. The part where it was supposed to make a loud and thunderous noise while energetically spreading itself about. Instead, it would act more like a dart, and less like a rocket.

Here was where the dynamics of the thing changed a bit. Overhead cover was constructed in a way as to cause a rocket to detonate on a hard outer surface, above and separate from the ballistic protection layer. This allowed the ballistics to absorb and distribute the concussion and shrapnel from the explosion. Not all the destructive forces of the explosion though, since that would be impossible. Whan a rocket became a dart, it tended to punch through most everything it hit. Imagine a four-foot long, four inch wide, forty-pound dart hitting something while traveling close to three-hundred-fifty meters per second. For those still not getting the hang of metric conversion change the word meters to yards, and you will be close enough. You could see how they ended up burying themselves pretty deep. Like the man said, with enough velocity I can push a pin through the earth.

Al-Sader had decided to rearrange his Mahdi Militia. Again. This time, he said he would only put guns in the hands of his hard-core followers, and the rest would be given the job of propaganda. The hard-core guys were only supposed to target the "occupier," and leave everyone else alone. I guess that meant us, and not the foreign fighters who came to Iraq to overturn the oppressive government of a dictator, expel the factions destabilizing the region in an attempt to restore order, and establish a governing body elected by the majority vote of the people which is directly representing the opinion of the populace for the good of the nation. Or was that us in the first place?

17 June – We were required to make no less than three checks of all our posts per shift. Not a hard task when we spent most of our time circulating pillar to post for most of the day. The big thing to remember was, if it was not documented, it had not happened. Anyone who ever worked a job like this, providing a service not a product, could vouch for that. Partially for this reason, log books were kept at each position. Entries were made to establish historical evidence when significant events occurred, checks were made, or anything happened that may require additional action. It was in one of those books, at the North CAC, I was logging my visit when Meat walked in the front door, shaking his head.

To change things up a bit, our first check had been random, following no particular path. Sure, it took longer to crisscross the compound than it did to check off the posts in succession, but the variation introduced an element of uncertainty to anyone who may have been observing. It also helped to keep the guards on their toes. Once complete, we immediately launched into a second check, varying the time between checks.

Arriving at the South CAC, Meat went on the check the H.L.Z, the Parking Lot, and the Rhino Staging area, while I cruised the Mid CAC and the Main CAC. Finished with his exterior checks, Meat left the Staging Area, crossed back over Haifa Street, and was now strolling in the North CAC where I was finishing my checks. As usual, the changeups and curveballs we threw this morning, to confound any potential spotter from thinking they were going to catch us in a pattern, had failed to catch our guards by surprise.

Building our posts into teams, and integrating those teams into a larger unit, had certainly increased their cohesion. Although we had intended this unity to provide the basis for a more comprehensive accomplishment of our mission, and establish a greater sphere of protection, layered in defense, a few unforeseen by-products had developed as well. One of the unintended results was our guards realized they could use this new condition to give warning when we were out making checks. It would seem we had been hoisted on our own petard. Somehow, they were spreading the alert, and I was pretty sure they were not using the radios. Most everything broadcasted over our net was work related, and recognizable. Even being hindered by a limited vocabulary. The upside I was going to take away from this was, If we could not catch our guards goofing off, I was pretty sure our boss would not be able to catch them either.

21 June – Last night a VBIED detonated just North of FOB Prosperity, over on the West side of town. Out in the Red Zone. The explosion occurred around 2030hrs, and was loud enough I thought it had actually happened close to my trailer. Making me think the rockets were starting again.

22 June – It got up to 130^0 F in the P.X. parking lot today. We had pretty much been keeping within the 120^0 F range for the past couple of weeks, but today pushed us over. It was not even July yet. This was going to be a hot summer.

Yesterday, we had a C-RAM alarm in the afternoon. Well, not exactly us. I was not positive where the alarm occurred, but it sounded like it may have come from around the British Embassy, West and a little North of us. It had happened before.

Standing outside the Main CAC, I was talking with some of my guards when we all heard the klaxon of a C-RAM alarm activated somewhere in the distance. We had been getting hit often enough, and hard enough, that everyone now reacted to any alarm no matter how faint. Why? Because a far-off alarm did not always stay far away, and our reactions had become as much a matter of reflex, as they were of instinct. The first guard to hear an alarm would yell out "Incoming!" to alert everyone to take cover.

I know, I can hear you out there. It sounded pretty redundant for someone to yell they heard an alarm when the alarm should be loud enough for everyone to hear. And normally, I would agree with you. But some of you seem to have forgotten the Palace was not the only place hooked into the C-RAM system, so some alarms were not as loud and obnoxious as others. I think I also mentioned the presence of all the concrete, asphalt, and stone that had been used for construction around here. Add the effects of their echo producing properties to the sound absorbing abilities of the multitude of sandbag walls so recently reinforced, not to mention the occasional dust storm, and acoustics could change dramatically in the space of a few feet producing audible dead spots. I would also forgive the fact that most of you have not experienced two full months of continuous rocket attacks, something I will even admit to being a little envious of you for, and are not subject to the jitters produced by the ordeal. But, I am beginning to rant, and starting to stray a tad off topic.

Anyone who ever played sports has heard the coach say "you play like you practice." Practice. Practice. Practice. Until it becomes second nature. This was along the same lines. Because rockets were not as predictable, or accurate, as mortar rounds, they tended to go where ever they took a mind to. The insurgents had also been known to launch more than one strike, on more than one target, and an alarm you heard in the distance could be a precursor for an alarm in your area. This was why the first guard to hear an alarm yelled a warning to everyone else. It also worked when the alarm failed to sound, and the first warning we got was the sound of the rockets flying in, or their impacts.

Born out of sheer repetition, everyone responded to the alert by repeating the call, and all exterior guards headed to the nearest bunker or hard cover. Once inside, the guards put their armor and helmets on and hunkered down to ride out the attack, or wait for the all clear to be given. Fortunately for us, that was the only alarm to activate that day, and there was no explosive accompaniment. It could have been a false positive, or possibly a dud.

Today there would be another soccer game for the Iraqis. We would have to see how it went. If they won, it was going to be happy fire all over again. I thought I would stay under hard cover after the game was over, long over. The last time was close enough.

23 June – Today had been Mad, Mad, and did I mention the word Mad, Monday. This afternoon, a bomb sniffing dog at the Service CAC had shown a great deal of interest in a truck parked in the search pit. The official description for this increased interest was called "change of behavior" and occurred when a dog showed more than average enthusiasm regarding a specific area they had been inspecting, but not enough to go all the way to a final

response. A final response was when a bomb dog smelled a sent strong enough to indicate an explosive was most likely present. When they smelled that the dog would sit, and point their nose at the area.

Standard practice with a change of behavior was to then have another dog go over the area, so we brought the dog team from the second search pit over, and had them check out the truck too. This time, nothing. Next, a few visual checks, along with a couple of mechanical checks, were conducted by the guards. Coming up with nothing, the truck was declared clean, and processed to enter. Big sigh of relief.

Walking away from this incident, I received a radio call from the Supervisor at the South CAC. An Iraqi man had just put a big garbage bag, filled with something bulky, inside the bunker across the street. A bunker that just so happened to sit on the corner of one of the busiest intersections in the Green Zone. Why so busy? Because it was one of the two roads that crossed the I.Z. Anyone going to the P.X., H.L.Z., the Fuel Point (gas station), the vehicle maintenance facility, The Ice House, pretty much all of the life support activities for the Green Zone had to pass through this intersection. It was also right across the street from the South CAC, and cattie-corner to the entrance to the vehicle lane for vehicles going to the Mid, Main, and North CACs. Basically, all the front entrances to the Palace. If that was not enough, it also sat ten feet away from the H.L.Z. perimeter wall, right under the helicopter approach/departure glide path, and we had a Tier One (very high level) motorcade heading for the H.L.Z. soon.

Lunchmeat had stopped by the Service CAC to watch the dog show. No, he did not bring a pony. He was still there when the suspicious package call came in. Being the Security Manager for both the H.L.Z. and the P.X. parking lot, he would have been called to come play anyway.

I radioed my All CAC Supervisor, Torro, to meet us at the South CAC, and Meat called for his General Supervisor to meet us there too. Having gotten the ball rolling, we rolled out too.

Toro arrived at the CAC before we did, and as we walked in the back door it looked like we had just walked in on an exhibit at Sea World. All of the guards, including Toro, the CAC Supervisor, and the Parking Lot Supervisor were crowded around the front window with their hands and faces pressed up again the ballistic glass like they were trying to peer into an aquarium. Time to get things moving.

The H.L.Z. and P.X. parking lot were not State Department venues, they belonged to the Army. Lunchmeat called his Point of Contact in the BDOC, the Base Defense Operations Center (pronounced B-Doc), to let them know what was about to happen. With very little yet known the call was quick. Once complete, Meat sent his Supervisor sprinting back to the parking lot with a warning for the guards to be ready to shut down the parking lot and H.L.Z.

I had Toro call the Mid, Main, and North CACs, on the hardline phone, not the unsecure radio, brief the CAC Supervisors up, and have the CACs shut down. I also did not want him to use the radio just in case whatever was in the bunker might have been rigged with a radio-controlled detonator. Sure, the chance it had been, and the chance it was on the same frequency as our radios was small. But nothing was impossible, some things were just less probable. The South CAC Supervisor was tasked with sending guards down Haifa Street, at least one-hundred meters away from the bunker, so they could stop traffic from entering the area.

Prior to leaving the safety of the building, and venturing across the street to get better eyes on the package in question, I made a call to the S.O.B. Just in case this thing went sideways, got all noisy and boomy, or generally turned pear shaped I wanted to make sure someone knew why. I was also hoping to get him to make the call to the TOC, and break the news we were about to shut down the busiest intersection in the I.Z. He had a lot more juice than I did, and they would be much less inclined to ask him obvious and time-consuming questions to which he did not yet have answers.

The second call I made was to Manny, my boss, the Complex Manager, so I could give him the same briefing I had just given the R.S.O. Prior to walking out the door, I told Toro to remain inside the hard CAC building, and keep an eye on us. Just in case something went kaboom, he could call all the King's horses and all the King's men to come clean us up, and try to put us back together again.

Determining whether an act is brave or stupid can only be made with the benefit of hindsight. With that in mind, Lunchmeat and I left the safety of the hard covered, ballistic building. Intent on approaching the bunker, to check out the bundle, and see if we could get a better idea of what we were dealing with, Meat and I set into motion actions that would keep us as safe as possible. And in doing so, I was about to put my life in his hands, and possibly hold his in mine. Surprisingly, I did not feel anxious about that at all.

In a situation like this, initial contact was always the scariest part, and took the greatest toll on the nerves and senses. Our eyes were trying to watch everything at once. The bunker, the road, the parking lot, the surrounding buildings. Everything. Looking for any visual indicator we may be walking into an ambush. Our ears strained to filter out the ambient noises of the environment, listing for any audible warning of a threat. Our noses were trying to pick apart a myriad of scents, sniffing for any out of place odor, or an aroma that just did not fit. The whole time our brains were trying to process all the little bits of information our senses had captured, at the same time trying to assess their meanings. Trying to determine their intent.

Were the bad guys conducting a dry run? Observing our response? Looking for holes they could exploit to increase the chance of success for the real thing? Had we missed the dry run, and this was the actual attack? If there was a device, would it be set on a timer, or had it been rigged so a spotter could detonate it on command. Like when we walked up. Could it just be a harmless bag? Had someone simply not been thinking, and threw a bag of trash in the bunker because they were too lazy to look for a trash can? There were a million things to consider, and as many different possibilities to sort through.

Whatever you called them: terrorists, criminals, bad guys, or just plain whack-jobs, the worst thing anyone could do was underestimate them. Successfully planting a bomb, and more importantly getting away with it, was not something that just happened. There was a certain amount of planning and preparation necessary. Yes, the bad guys may have been warped and demented, but that did not mean they were not motivated or sneaky. It certainly did not mean they were stupid or careless. If we wanted to stay alive, we could not be stupid or careless either.

Even though the bunker was on the other side of Haifa Street, across from the CAC, this was still pretty much my venue. I would take the lead on this one. Meaning Meat was covering my right. Side by side, we walked out in front of the CAC, and signaled for the guards to stop all traffic from approaching the area. My guards ran off to our left and set up their roadblock a safe, comfortable distance to the West. On our right, East, the road was already blocked from approaching traffic due to being blocked off beyond the North CAC. Those guards had also been instructed to stop all vehicles from exiting the Palace, since they would have to drive past us to get out. Meat's guards were directing all vehicles exiting the H.L.Z. and P.X. parking lot to the north, away from the area, and stopped any other vehicles from entering.

Once we had verified the area inside our cordon had been cleared of people, and everyone had been moved back to a reasonable safe distance, we began the long walk across the street. Still not knowing if we were actually dealing with an explosive device, we cautiously made our way. Walking side by side, I scanned the area to our left looking for anyone who appeared to be taking just a little too much interest in what we were doing. Covering my right, Meat was doing the same thing in his direction.

For this to work, trust had to be complete. If any doubt in your partner existed, you may be tempted to take your eyes off your area of responsibility, leaving the team vulnerable and exposed in that direction. We were watching for anyone who looked like they may be studying our response. Trying to learn from our procedures. Or in the worst case, watching our progress so they could remotely detonate the device when we got to it. As we walked my confidence never wavered. The apprehension I once had for simply meeting the man now guarding my right was gone. Replaced by a feeling, a knowledge, that my back was covered.

After what seemed like hours, we made it across the street, and sidled up to the edge of the bunker. For the first time since stepping off I looked at Meat to give him the All Clear, telling him I had not seen anything, or anyone, suspicious during our approach. The right side had been equally uneventful, and Meat gave me the all clear as well. So far so good.

Announcing "crossing over," I left him standing on the near side of the bunker, and walked around the end-cap, to the other side, to begin the last scan of the area before checking inside. With me peering over the top of the bunker, and Meat standing with his back against it, we rescanned our areas long and slow. Again, we were looking for any possible hiding place that could contain an observer. Any sign someone was putting crosshairs on us. Being almost a full head taller than any bunker did have its advantages, but this was the only one I could think of. Anyone trying to keep this area under surveillance would have to be in direct line of sight, and we should have been able to spot them, from the area being observed, by looking back up that same line. Hindsight being 20/20, I wished I had brought a pair of binoculars with me.

"I got nothing." Meat said. His side was clear.

"Yah, I'm coming up empty too." I replied. Time to finish up our perimeter scan, and get on to inspecting the bunker.

"Cross-check." I called.

Having scanned our own areas of responsibility twice, once during the approach and once upon arrival, I called for a cross-check just to make sure. Here is the philosophy. When scanning an area the brain could decide certain areas did not present a threat, or presented such a low possibility of a threat it directed the eyes to skim across those features without really looking at them. Choosing, instead, to move on to areas that presented a greater possibility of threat. Regardless of how many times you scanned your A.O.R (that's Area Of Responsibility) the brain had already cataloged those "no threat" locations, and skimmed over them. By calling for a cross-check I was telling Meat I wanted him to check the area I had been scanning, and I would check the area he had been scanning. A fresh set of eyes gave new perspective kind of thing.

"Looks like we're in the clear." I said, as I completed my scan of, what now, was my left side.

"Nothing on this side, either." Meat confirmed.

"Here we go. I'm going to take a look, and see what we've got. Watch my back."

I knew I did not need to tell him that last part. I guess some habits still died hard. As I was about to peak around the corner of the bunker, to get the first glimpse of the object, Meat picked up a scan of the entire area. This accomplished two things. First, it kept a pair of eyes watching our surroundings, looking for any warning signs something bad might be getting ready to happen. Second, if something bad did happen, only one of us was fully exposed to the badness.

Slowly, I moved into position so I could peer into the bunker. Squatting straight down, not wanting to give away what I was about to do, I placed my palms flat against the cement side for support. Side-stepping to the left, using as much of the bunker as I could to shield my movements from anyone down the street, I moved toward the opening. Left foot. Right foot. Reaching the end, I moved my left foot out, to widen my stance, and noticed I had inadvertently slid it beyond the opening of the bunker. Exposing my foot and lower leg. Quickly, I jerked it back to where I should have placed it the first time, behind the concrete. Now in proper position, I shifted my weight, and leaned to the left. My head gradually reached the end of the side. First my left eye cleared the corner. Then my right. Fully exposing my face, I got my first look at the bundle.

This was what had caused us to close down the main intersection in front of the Palace. This was why we had diverted all traffic from the primary entrances to the Palace, the P.X., and the helipad. The package that had been the cause of my racing pulse. The reason Meat and I had become so centrally focused on staying alive. On keeping each other alive. Peering into the bunker, I was now face to face with a trash bag. A black plastic trash bag to be exact. I started breathing again.

The longer I looked at this trash bag, the more it just did not look right to me. I could not tell you why. It just did not.

"Meat. I've got a black, plastic trash bag here. It's up against your side of the bunker, and looks like it's been filled with something. The base is pretty flat, and whatever's inside looks like it doesn't have much in the way of a defined shape to it. The sides are kind of rounded and bulgy, and the whole thing sits, oh, say, about a foot and a half, maybe two feet tall. From this angle, I can't see through the side of the bag, or into the top. It looks like the top's been twisted closed. I can't tell what's inside it."

I pulled my head out of the bunker, and took a couple of deep breaths.

"Meat. I'm clear. Give me a second to get set, and see what you can see from your side." He acknowledged.

I dropped my right knee to the ground for balance. After a few more deep breaths, slowly, just a bit shakily (not because being crouched that long had been rough on these old, abused knees. Not because of that), I levered myself back up. Peering back over the top, I told Meat I was set, and he disappeared as he crouched for his look. Intently, I scanned the area as Meat stuck his head around his corner of the bunker to get a different perspective.

"Pretty much the same thing from this side." Meat said. "I'm pretty much staring straight down on top of the sack. I can't really tell the structure of what's inside, but it definitely looks like it's got some kind of form, and heft to it. The top has been tied off with something, so I can't get a look inside either. I think we need to get the dogs over here, and see what they say about it."

"Sounds good to me."

Meat extracted himself from the bunker, and took a couple of seconds to recompose himself. Once he was ready, we walked back across the street, to the CAC, the same we had walked to the bunker. Side by side, scanning our A.O.Rs. Since we still were not sure exactly what we were dealing with, neither of us was ready to completely relax just yet. But as we went, I could feel a tangible decrease in the amount of stress I had been feeling. Like I was wearing a backpack, and with every step a brick was being removed. By the time we arrived under cover, we had drawn quite the crowd.

Most of the traffic stopped by the roadblock had turned around to look for another route to their destination. However, some of the drivers had decided to stay and watch. Some sat in their vehicles, others leaned up against them. Several of the people who had been stopped on the sidewalk had also made the choice to stay, and check out the show.

The CAC building was loaded with people too. Since walking out of the building would have put them smack-dab in the danger zone, they had not been allowed to pass through. Instead of heading back onto the compound, they had decided to stay. It would seem this was becoming the best show in town, at least for the price. People over in the P.X. parking lot were even beginning to drift over so they could see what was happening. Had there actually been anyone observing our actions for the bad guys, we were never going to be able to pick them out of the crowd that was gathering.

Manny and one of our R.S.O.s, call-sign Tick (if you have ever seen the TV show, he looked a whole lot like The Tick), had also shown up, and were waiting for us inside the CAC looking for an update.

Bringing them up to speed was not much of a problem since we still did not know much about what we were dealing with. A problem we were just about to fix. Just as soon as Meat called one of his dog teams to come over from the parking lot search pit, and give us the first real indication whether we were dealing with a device, or not. We hoped. The four of us left the CAC, and took a long, circuitous route around the bunker, along the Palace wall, to meet the team across the street on the P.X. side of the intersection, and give the handler a quick briefing, a description of the package needing to be searched, and its location in the bunker.

Our briefing took place roughly thirty meters away from the bunker, and the dog team headed out. As they drew nearer and nearer to their objective the K9 (his name was Buster, by the way) started to take more and more interest in where he was going. Nose to the ground, nose in the air, Buster excitedly look back and forth from his handler to the bunker. By the time they got there, it was all the handler could do to keep Buster from running straight inside.

The handler (her name was Erica) walked Buster around the outside of the bunker several times to settle him down a little. When she was finally satisfied he was ready, she walked him through the opening. If they were inside for more than five seconds I would be surprised. Both dog and handler sprang from the bunker, and began speed walking back to where we were standing. Buster was jumping around like a little kid on Christmas morning, and Erica looked like she was too afraid to unwrap the presents.

"Something's in there." She said. "He sat."

Oh crap.

Instantly, we all dug into our pockets, and pulled out our phones. Calls to inform those who needed to be informed, contact those who needed to be contacted, and request the presence of those who needed to be present were made. My call went to the TOC to let them know there was a distinct possibility we were dealing with a device. Having blocked off the three front entrances to the Palace, they would have to direct all in-bound, as well as out-bound traffic, convoys, motorcades, and all other vehicle movements to the only remaining CAC, the service CAC. That Tier One motorcade we had been expecting would have to find a different way to get to the helipad.

Meat contacted the BDOC. They would need to dispatch the I.Z. Police. We had closed down the roads at the beginning of the incident to establish a safety cordon around the site, but the roads ultimately fell under the responsibility of the military, not the State Department. To keep them closed required the blessing of the BDOC, and the assistance of the I.Z. Police. The BDOC also controlled operations at the H.L.Z, and with the incident scene sitting right under the glide path, flights in and out would need to be diverted to the opposite side. If they did not shut it down entirely, at least until this situation was resolved, that Tier One motorcade may not be going anywhere after all.

Manny contacted the Explosive Dog Detector Team (E.D.D.T. for short) Leader to ask him to send a second dog team to confirm the results of the first dog. And last, but not least, Tick was contacting the E.O.D. guys. If this thing really turned out to be something that goes boom, or as E.O.D. says "something that comes from together," we were going to need them to safely take it away. You can bet your butt I was not going back in there to pick it up.

The first to arrive were the I.Z. Police patrols. Air Force Security Policeman, they replaced the guards around the perimeter of the cordon, and kept everyone at a safe distance. Next to arrive was the E.D.D.T. Supervisor, with his dog. It was standard procedure for a second dog team to verify the reading of the first team, especially when the first dog indicated an explosive could be present. Just like we had done earlier at the Service CAC. This time the Supervisor was going to conduct the second search. To ensure a clean, unbiased search the Supervisor only asked for the location to be searched. No information about the package. No information about the response of the first dog. Going in cold like that would ensure he was not influencing his dog in any way.

We pointed out the bunker for the team to search, and they headed off in that direction. At a normal walking pace, the dog and handler approached the area to be searched. With his nose in the air, the dog strained at the leash. Tracking back and forth, left to right, he sampled the air as they drew nearer. Once at the bunker, the dog's nose dropped straight to the ground, and he began to show interest in the air flowing from the bunker. Tail wagging and ears perked up, he – the dog, not the handler – excitedly sniffed around both ends of the end-cap. He trotted in, he trotted out. He looked at the bundle, he looked at the handler. But he would not give a final response. It looked like he really wanted to, but he just would not sit.

Deciding he had done everything possible, the Supervisor pulled his dog away from the bunker, and walked back to us. With one dog saying there were explosives present, and one dog showing an obvious change in behavior, there was only one more thing we could do. It was time to send in the robot.

E.O.D. had a cool little robot, and it certainly was no WALL-E. Tank treads, a camera, mechanical arms, what it lacked in charm it made up in lethality. About three feet wide, and four feet long, it was equipped so the E.O.D. Technician could get a close up look at any device without having to be close. Operated on a long tether cord, the controls remained in a separate box so the operator could stay back a safe distance while the robot rolled forward. Before any Technician made an approach to any suspicious package, the robot went in first.

Like a master gamer, the Tech worked the controls to roll the machine right up to the opening between the bunker and the end cap. Rolling on treads instead of wheels, it easily negotiated both curbs to cross the street, and approach the gap. That was when we realized there was going to be another problem. The end cap had been placed just a little too close to the bunker, and the opening was not wide enough to allow the robot to get through. To add to our dilemma, the robot's video camera was mounted on its body, not on the arm. We were not going to get a clear, remote view of the trash bag. If it was not one thing, it was another. Right?

While E.O.D. was working with their go-go gadget, the guards in the parking lot had been busy looking for the owner of the trash bag. The Supervisor from the North CAC had passed the description of the man his guards saw placing the bag in the bunker to the Supervisor of the Parking Lot Guards. While we had been dealing with the bunker, the Parking Lot guards had been observing a group of Iraqi men who were cleaning the parking lot, under the supervision of a K.B.R. employee.

A few of the guards had noticed one of the workers looked like the description they had been given, and was paying a little too much attention to the goings on around the bunker. Notifying their supervisor of what they had observed, the Supervisor had called Lunchmeat. We walked over to talk with the work gang, and see if we could get the lowdown on the local national.

Fortunately for us the I.Z. Police had Iraqi interpreters riding with them, and as one was being called over to translate the interview a small crowd gathered around our suspect. Looking back at it, I guess I could see how this guy may have been feeling a little nervous. Around him stood two armed security contractors who both stood well over six feet tall, with a combined weight over five hundred pounds. A Six foot R.S.O. The Complex Manager, a former Miami cop and drug enforcement agent. An Air Force Police Sergeant, and his interpreter. Two dog handlers. And two E.O.D. Techs. I did not check for any partridges, and there were no pear trees.

Although visibly shaken by all the attention he was receiving, he stayed pretty consistent with his story. He insisted, over and over again, the bag only contained food and trinkets. Working with the cleaning gang he would find stuff people had thrown away, but he thought were worth keeping, and would put them in his bag. He said he put the garbage bag in the duck and cover bunker with the idea he could leave it there while he was working, and no one would steal it. This was his story, and he was sticking to it.

The major problem with his story was the dog handlers were having some trouble believing the food part. For anyone with pets, you know your dog acts differently around different things. Explosive detection dogs are the same way. Their reaction to food was different from their reaction to explosives, and you can guess what reaction they were showing toward the bag.

Unbeknownst to us, during our interview with the bag owner, Tick had decided to slip away and take a stroll over to the bunker to have a look for himself. We only realized he was gone when we heard the sound of pounding feet quickly approaching. Turning to look, there was The Tick, chugging away from the bunker at full tilt boogie. Legs churning, arms pumping, he tore across the street. As he got close enough to realize we were all staring at him he slowed to a nonchalant stroll.

"Hey guys," he casually noted as he sauntered up, trying hard not to look like he was out of breath. "The Package? Yah, it's beeping now."

You would have thought he had just had a near-death experience, and for all intents and purposes, he had. We found out later, with curiosity eating him up, he had leaned his head inside the bunker to have a peak, and no sooner had he laid eyes on the bag when it had started beeping. I was glad curiosity worked out better for him than it had for the cat.

With our nerves as tight as they had been all afternoon, a tiny safety valve was opened, and no one was able to contain their laughter. After realizing he had safely made it away from the bunker, even Tick was able to see the humor in his escapade. Having brought the tension level down a couple of notches, we put our heads together with the E.O.D. Techs to try and decipher the meaning of the beeping, and develop our next course of action.

The Techs all agreed they had never heard of any device in theatre that beeped before exploding, and no intelligence bulletins had been posted anywhere about beeping devices either. Having quickly worked through the beeping issue, we were about to move on to our next course of action when my ears picked up on a familiar sound.

After Meat and I had completed the initial eyeballing of the suspicious object I stopped paying a lot of attention to the noises around us. They were something I was used to hearing all the time, and judging they no longer played a major role in this problem my brain went back to registering them as din. But, for some odd reason, my ears were now keyed on something not quite right.

Looking around, my eyes tried to lend support, and pick up on what my ears were trying to figure out. Four helicopters came into sight, rolling in off the river, banking into the approach path for a landing at the H.L.Z. My eyes and ears worked together to try and figure out why this was significant, but without having yet asked the brain for help they were still drawing a blank.

Elbowing Lunchmeat in the ribs, I pointed at the birds as they flared their rotors on final approach. Joining forces, eyes and ears began pounding away at grey matter for attention. My brain must have stepped away from the desk. I did not know if it had wandered off to the water cooler, gone for coffee, or what. It took the choppers flying right over the top of the bunker, the bunker with the suspicious package inside, for understanding to arrive. Finally, all three senses got on the same sheet of music. And I think to myself. "Why does that ball keep getting bigger?" Then it hits me. Why had this approach to the H.L.Z. not been shut down?

"Meat?" I asked. "You want to take care of that one."

Rolling his eyes, Lunchmeat walked off to call the BDOC.

By this time, E.O.D. had already walked away. They were on the way back to their truck to make preparations for dealing with this situation their way. It had been decided they would blow up the sack in place. Not quite as exciting as it may sound. Blowing up a suspected device with an explosive charge did not always mean packing it with explosives, and blowing it up. No. It sometimes meant shooting the device with a high pressure forced stream of water created by a small, controlled detonation. It was called a water shot. I did not fully understand the whole physics of the thing, but they told me with a little bit of C-4 explosive and an ordinary plastic water bottle, containing a little bit of water, they could safely render a device harmless.

The water shot was given to the robot, and driven up to the side of the bunker. Even though the main body of the robot was unable to get inside the bunker, enough of the bag could be seen to effectively place the shot. The shot itself had been mounted on the extendable arm so it could be placed against the side of the sack.

"Fire in the hole! Fire in the hole! Fire in the hole!" Came the warning from the E.O.D Tech, and the water shot was detonated. For a "little bit" of C-4, the explosion was loud enough to make me twitch. And I knew this one was coming.

"Think you used enough dynamite there Butch?"

The confused look I got from the Tech said he was too young to know that movie.

The robot was brought back to the control panel, and we all walked forward to see what the shot had revealed. Lunchmeat and I, the E.O.D. Techs, Tick, Manny, the Dog Handlers, the Security Police Sergeant, the Interpreter, and last but not least the guy who owned the garbage bag we had just blown up. All of us crowded around the entrance to the bunker.

When the Techs told me they only use a little bit of C-4, and not a lot of water to create the water shot, I think they may have been exaggerating about the water too. Small drops of water dripped from the ceiling of the bunker, and fragments of black plastic bag were scattered all over the inside. As we sifted through the debris we found little bags of candy, like you would give out for Halloween. Buried in the sundry bits of candy bags, and a boat load of other unidentifiable crap, were several empty D.V.D. cases, a play station controller, a game boy, and a tiny little etch-a-sketch. All blown to pieces. Despite the wreckage, and candy carnage strewn around the inside of the bunker, there were no explosives. No pieces of any device to be found.

All this activity. All this coordination. All this response. Just to blow the hell out of a ten-pound bag filled with candy, games, and junk. Ain't that a bitch? Yes, we were confused. The Dog handlers most of all. A final response. A just noticeable difference. But no device. With no explanation. Frustration and anger also made guest appearances. Mostly directed at the Iraqi who had thought leaving a bag unattended, across from a Palace CAC, next to the H.L.Z. was a smart thing to do. So many questions. And no answers.

The only thing I could do was keep telling myself we had done the right thing. In this instance our response may have been over-kill, but all it took was for one person to slip one devise past us, and someone's son, husband, daughter, or wife might not be going home. Nothing about this incident had happened without an audience. People had watched it unfold, and would talk about what they had seen. Maybe they would talk about the speed of our response. Maybe our thoroughness. Maybe our actions. Maybe the word would get out, and be enough to convince any bad guys out there it was too risky to try the real thing around here.

25 June – Rocket strikes had fallen off drastically in the month of June. Envoys in their motorcades had been venturing out into the Red Zone to conduct nation building missions and reconstruction meetings with their counterparts in the Iraqi government.

Yesterday, while enroute to one of these projects the procession was attacked, and a Department of State employee had been killed. It was the first time, in a very long time, someone from DoS had been killed in Iraq. Up until now, it had mostly been military personnel and contractors who had been doing the dying. We would see how this affected the DoS folks. Two soldiers, and a contractor were also killed in the attack.

Today was relatively quiet around the CACs, with nothing overly exceptional happening. I had already finished my last set of checks for the day, and was sitting at my desk, closing out paperwork. Lunchmeat, Rak, and I were just about to walk out the door, and head over to the chow hall when I got a frantic call over the radio.

"Mr. Rooster. Come to North CAC! One car, he broke the gate!" Good grief.

Everyone else went on to dinner while I broke from the pack, and made my way to the North CAC to see what had happened. As I walked the sidewalk between the wrought iron Palace grounds outer fence and the T-walls lining the gutter next to the street, a brown suburban came into view. Half in and half out of the gate. The front corner, on the passenger side, was dipped down. The top of the tire was shoved into the wheel well, and canted at an odd angle not normally seen with a tire.

The truck had been driving through the open gate when the ball joint on the front right wheel had given out. As a result, the wheel snapped off the axle, causing the truck to slide along on the exposed metal for a few more feet. The weight of the vehicle dug a deep furrow in the cement before the driver could bring the whole mess to a stop. More good grief.

The axle had dug along the roadway, coming to rest against the leading edge of the pop-up-barrier. Ironically, the pop-up-barrier was designed to stop vehicles, just not from the down position. The ball joint was dug in deep enough the vehicle could not be dragged forward without seriously damaging the barrier housing. Nor could it be dragged back through the gate without destroying the runners on which the gate wheels roll. In the words of Charlie Brown, AAAAARRRRRRGGGGGHHHHH!

The only gate that gave direct access to the north side of the Palace and Camp Travis had just been rendered useless, plugged up by a thoroughly broken vehicle, and we were quickly approaching the time convoys and motorcades would be returning, and needing to enter through this gate. I had no way of lifting, pulling, or pushing this vehicle out of the way.

First order of business, keep the traffic flowing. I dug out my cell phone and called the TOC. Finch had gone on vacation at the beginning of the month, and his replacement's call sign was Cherry. His last name was Garcia.

"Cherry, I got an issue," I said. "I've got a vehicle broken down in the middle of the gate at the North CAC. One of the wheels has broken off, and I'll need a wrecker to come get it out."

"You can't get your guys to push it out of the gate?" He asked.

I turned to face the grill of the truck in the hope that, while my back had been turned, the situation had gotten better. No such luck. "Wish I could. The passenger side wheel has broken completely off the ball joint, and the thing is resting on bare axle."

"Look, you've got to find a way to get that gate cleared. I have three high level diplomatic motorcades scheduled to roll out that gate within the next couple of minutes, and two General Officer convoys scheduled to come in right after that."

No pressure, right? "Unless you can miracle a wrecker down here, this CAC is going to be shut down for a while. The vehicle has to be lifted before it can be moved anywhere. I'll do what I can to get a wrecker moving as fast as possible, but since he's going to have to lift the front of the vehicle, if he isn't already on the compound it's going to take him a while to get here. You might want to contact those convoys and divert them over to the South CAC or the Service CAC. This one's a no-go."

I hung up with the TOC, and started searching through my speed dial folder for the direct number to the wrecker driver. One thing working the CACs was that I had to deal with the wrecker, and other recovery vehicles, quit a lot. It was not uncommon for vehicles sitting in one of the search pits to break down, stall, or otherwise stop working once they had been turned off so the dogs could sniff them. I called the recovery vehicle so many times I had become a K.B.R. Valued Customer.

"Boss! Boss!" One of my traffic control guards yelled. "Hay el camion de auxillio!"

My Spanish was not all that great at the best of times, and when I looked at him, with sheer confusion written all over my face, he pretty much figured that out. Instead of trying to rephrase his sentence, or worse trying it in English – he was a new guard, and his English was worse than my Spanish – he raised an arm to point down the road behind me. I turned, looked in the direction he was pointing, and immediately understood what he was trying to say. The wrecker was driving up the road toward us. I guess miracles really did happen.

Earlier, he had been called to Camp Travis to pick up a dead vehicle, and tow it to the shop. Once there, he found the vehicle had gotten a jump from someone else, and driven away before his arrival. Now on his way back to the shop, he just happened to stumble onto our situation, and was more than happy to give us a hand. Within minutes, the vehicle was racked, lifted, and loaded on the flatbed back of the truck. The broken wheel had been thrown in the back seat.

Now that the gate was cleared, and opened back up for business, I started off for the chow wall with the feeling of a job well done. I reached into my pocket, retrieved my cell phone, and was just about to pass the good news to the TOC when I received a radio call from another CAC. Trading my cell for my radio, the Main CAC Supervisor told me there was an Iraqi national there, asking for a visitor pass, but refusing to get searched. This was nothing new.

Everyone, and I do mean everyone, got searched if they were coming to the palace as a visitor. American, Iraqi, everyone, and there was always one person who felt they were the exception to the rule. A follow-on call reported the escort had arrived at the CAC, and was trying tell the guards the man was a V.I.P., and was not to be searched. Here we go again. Everyone thought they, and by extension their visitors, were special. I changed direction and headed for the Main CAC, much to the dismay of my stomach. One step, two step, ring went my phone. It was the TOC calling.

"Dude, we caught a break. The North CAC is open." I reported.

"Great. Now, you have a blue badge your guards are trying to search at the Main CAC." Nothing like trying to make a mountain out of a molehill. I talked about Blue Badgers before, but let me add a little more information about them. To hold a Blue Embassy Badge meant you held a security clearance, and were working in a position requiring that clearance to be active. A Blue Embassy Badge was the highest level badge issued at the Palace, and gave the greatest level of access with the least amount of restrictions. Although most Blue Badgers truly were important, and worked highly sensitive jobs, there still existed a small handful who would wave their blue badge in your face with an attitude that said if you did not have a blue badge, you were a minion. The TOC was attempting to imply this type of badge was what was waiting for me at the CAC.

"Not so much." I replied, failing to take the bait. "It may be a blue badge, but it's a blue I.Z. Badge, not an Embassy Badge. I'm leaving the North CAC right now to check it out. I'll give you a call once I've gotten a handle on it."

I hung up the phone, and continued to walk. Unlike the Embassy Badges, I.Z. badges were not recognized as proper entry credentials, and in and of themselves did not grant their bearer access to the Palace or any other DoS (pronounced like the computer operating system) property. Not being small, the distance not me, it took more than several minutes to walk across the Palace grounds, or walk from CAC to CAC. It had not been much longer than that when I put my hand on the doorknob to open the back door to the Main CAC. Just as my phone rang again.

"Hey, what's going on?" Cherry asked.

"How should I know? You barely gave me enough time to get here, let alone find out what's going on."

"I have the Duty R.S.O. blowing me up, wanting to know what is going on."

"You have got to give the Boots on the Ground time to do our jobs." I replied. "Simply tell him I'm still getting a handle on it. Believe me, once I've got something I'll let you know." Again, I hung up.

Walking into the Main CAC, I found our Company Rep from the BDOC standing inside. "Hey Baldo, what's the deal?"

Looking quite confused, and a little surprised, he looked around the CAC. "I'm not sure. I got a call there was a visitor here being harassed, and denied entry to the Palace.

We both surveyed the processing area inside the CAC, but the only people there were my guards, and the screener/interpreters. No visitors. No escort. Nobody. I glanced through the front window of the building, and noticed two soldiers and a civilian standing out front with the Main CAC Supervisor.

"This looks suspicious." I muttered to Baldo, motioning at the window. Walking toward the front door, I attempted to get a better vantage point to see if I could determine whether or not this was the disturbance everyone was so upset about. Still not sure of the significance of this huddle I opened the door, and walked out of the building. "Gentlemen, may I be of assistance?"

One of the soldiers, a full-bird Colonel, slowly turned, and patiently looked at me. He gave me the once-over, place his hands on his hips, squared his shoulders, and let out a breath like I was just another annoyance in his life. "And who might you be?" He drawled.

"I'm the Security Manager for this CAC. Is there something I can help you with?"

And the Colonel let loose. "This man," he growled, pointing at the civilian, "is a V.I.P with the Iraqi government. He has an appointment with General Barnakey, and your guards won't let him in." Yah, I love that movie too, and it took every ounce of self-control for me not to crack wise.

Knowing full well there was more to the story than this, I decided to go along with the Colonel's rendition. I mean, why cloud the issue with facts, right?

"Sir, that's too easy. Since I imagine you'll be the gentleman's escort, all we need to do is have the both of you go through that door right there. We'll run him and his equipment through the scanner real quick, issue him a visitor's badge, and the both of you will be on your way."

"Didn't you hear me the first time?" The Colonel sneered. "He's a V.I.P. He is not going to be searched" like common folk. The Colonel never actually said that last part, but the condescension in his tone certainly implied it.

Now we were starting to get to the heart of the problem. "Sir. My apologies for the misunderstanding. Since I have not been given notice by the R.S.O.s to expect any V.I.P.s that would mean you already have his V.I.P. badge."

I understood the pressure and stress placed on a Colonel working directly for a General. I also understood a Colonel was used to having his order followed, and had this been a straight out DoD venue, they would have been. But it was not, so I could not. State was responsible for the grounds, and the R.S.O.s set the policies to which I had to abide. Were I to deviate from them, it could easily have cost me my job.

The Colonel paused. For just a brief second a flash of recognition raced across his face, as if he finally understood something was lacking, and we were going to have to insert a missing step into the process of getting his visitor through the CAC. Relieved by the feeling he was beginning to understand we were only enforcing policy, and not just trying to be difficult, I transitioned back into the familiar roll of being an N.C.O. Advising and informing an Officer toward the path to success.

"Sir." I said in a low voice so only he could hear. "All it takes is for you to call the Protocol office. They have V.I.P badges for just this sort of thing, along with the authorization to issue them." I gave him a second to digest that information before telling him I would wait inside the CAC.

As I entered the doorway, I found Baldo still standing inside the processing area, craning his head toward the front window, trying to see what was happening without drawing attention to himself. Thinking I could kill two birds with one stone I motioned for him to join me, and pulled out my cell phone to call the TOC. Wouldn't you know it, as soon as the phone cleared my pocket the damned thing started to ring. I'll give you three guesses as to who was calling me, and the first two don't count. Of course, it was Cherry. It was almost like he was watching the camera in the Main CAC. I guess some folks just do not have patience.

With the BDOC Rep standing next to me, and the TOC Rep on the phone, I gave them both a quick rundown on what had happened. The long and the short of the problem was no one from the General's staff had coordinated with Protocol, or the R.S.O. office, for a V.I.P. badge for this visitor. Whether they did not know, or just did not care, that they needed one was not all that important at this point since the Colonel was now in possession of the proper information to correct the problem. Both Operation Center representatives were satisfied with the outcome, and with everyone on the same sheet of music the situation appeared to be heading down a smooth road to resolution. But, as everyone knows, appearances can be deceiving.

I did not know if he had been called, or if he had just grown impatient, but within a minute after ringing off with the TOC the proverbial fly in the ointment walked in the back door wearing stars. With a bit more time, the Colonel would have been able to complete coordinating for a V.I.P. badge, and everything would have been fine. His mission of getting the V.I.P. through the CAC would have been complete. From the safety of the General's office he could have played the delay off as a language barrier with the guards, or problems with the procedures, or, and this one tended to be everyone's favorite, the damn contractor in charge of the CAC. But now that his boss was standing right here, he did not have much of a chance to save face.

The General breezed through the CAC without acknowledging our existence, and strode right up to the Colonel. Watching through the front window it was not too difficult to figure out what was going on, despite not being able to hear any of the conversation. The General walked up behind the Colonel, stopped, and stood there for several seconds. The Colonel, talking on his cell phone, must have realized the General was standing there because he quickly straightened up to the position of attention, and gradually lowered the phone from his ear. Slowly turning, he faced the General.

The sun had already started to set, and it was growing dark outside. The General was standing with his back toward us, but with the lights of the processing area shining through the window we could see over his left shoulder the Colonel was not doing a lot of the talking in this conversation. The exchange took less than a minute, and ended with the one single gesture that not only ensured this situation was not going to be resolved in an amicable manner, but I was going to have to take another stab at trying to keep it from blowing up in my face. The Colonel snapped his right arm up, level with his shoulder, parallel to the ground, and with his right hand balled into a fist, index finger extended and straight, he pointed directly into the CAC. Right at me.

Both heads turned at the same time to stare directly at me through the glass. There was not much I could do but stand my ground as the General swung away from the Colonel to bear down on the CAC. Being a contractor for the State Department, not the Department of Defense, as the General approached the building I turned to look for Baldo, since he was the DoD representative. Wouldn't you know it. While all of us had been watching the General and the Colonel, Baldo had snuck around the back side of the processing table. To the other side of the room. Leaving me standing all by myself. Thanks buddy. Still only half a word.

The General did not so much storm into the CAC as he simply filled it with his presence. A picture of restrained fury. A force manifest. Right in front of me. I have mentioned I am not a short person, and the fact I did not have to look down to look the General in the eyes was not lost on me. The fact I did not have to look up to look him in the eyes seemed not to be lost on the General either. "What seems to be the problem here?" He asked.

"No problem, Sir. We're just waiting for the V.I.P. badge to be brought for the visitor."

"There's no need for that. He's my visitor, and he's a V.I.P."

"Sir, with all due respect, and as I have already explained to the Colonel, regular visitor passes get searched, only V.I.P. visitor passes don't, and we keep being told he isn't going to be searched. The access policies to the Palace have been established by the State Department, not the Defense Department, and those are the policies I have to follow. A simple phone call to the R.S.O., or the Protocol office to arrange for a V.I.P. visitor badge would have alleviated this entire situation. I believe that's what the Colonel was doing when you came down."

I looked at the Colonel standing outside to emphasize my point, and noticed he was standing all by himself, looking for all his rank like a recently chastised child. The Iraqi had left. The General looked outside, saw the same thing, and started mumbling under his breath as he turned on his heels and stormed out the back door. Department of Defense, Department of State, why can't we all just get along?

26 June – At the end of a fairly slow, uneventful day, a nice change of pace, we were all sitting in the office, catching up on paperwork, when a voice from the H.L.Z. came across Meat's radio with a transmission of gibberish. I looked at Meat, Meat looked at Rak, and Rak looked at me. All with the same "what the hell was that?" look on our face. It was clear the guards were excited about something. Which meant their English had gone straight in the crapper, and none of us could figure out exactly what they were saying.

"Rak, you habla the Espanol. What was that all about?" Meat asked.

Having returned his attention to his computer screen, "Not too sure, but it sounds like you might have a fire on the H.L.Z." He said off handedly.

If you have never had to deal with a fire on a flight line, do not be in a big hurry to put it on your list of things to do. Helicopters filled with fuel, parked petrol trucks with tanks full of aviation grade fuel, munitions standing by on hot skids or loaded on launch racks, fuel blivits with full bladders, and a whole myriad of other flammable materials assembled here and there lent itself to a huge possibility for things to go catastrophically wrong with a quickness.

With that in mind, each of us picked up our radio, and started out of the office. We had barely made it through the front door when one of the guards finally came over the radio yelling "Fire! Fire! Fire!" Actually, it was more like "Fuego! Fuego! Fuego!" I just did the translation for you. Yah, Meat got himself a fire.

Changing stride, we picked up the pace, and thundered straight though the Main CAC without slowing down. As we lumbered out the door, and across the street into the P.X. parking lot, we gazed across the open expanse to get our first unobstructed view over the top of the T-Walls surrounding the H.L.Z. The first thing to grab our attention was the distinct lack of fire or smoke wafting over their tops. This was a very good sign, a very confusing sign, but a good sign none the less. Continuing to cut straight across the lot, we got to the entrance of the H.L.Z. at about the same time as the Fire Department from the Rhino Staging Area.

By the time we arrived on the scene all the excitement was over. A Humvee engine had caught on fire, the electrical harness, and started to smoke like a chimney. The fire department stationed on the H.L.Z. had responded but, in the time it had taken them to drive across the flight line, the soldiers had already put most of the fire out with the fire extinguishers from their truck.

For once, in a long time, all the fun was over before we got there. I was expecting Meat was going to have a bit of a conversation with his guards about the level of excitement they exuded when broadcasting over the radio.

27 June – We were still watching the thermometer. It had cooled off to a balmy 118°F .

CHAPTER 7

1 July – Every day was new drama, or so it seemed. Wherever we checked vehicles we used dogs as part of the checking process. Walking around the vehicle being inspected, the dogs were an integral part of a series of steps we took to detect explosives, or VBIEDs, before they could get inside any compound, or any other controlled, heavily populated area, and do some real damage.

Not wanting to overstate the obvious, have I mentioned how summers tended to get a little on the hot side over here? Add the knowledge that most of our vehicle search pits were located in parking lots, or the middle of a road somewhere, and the equation balanced with the realization of how the pavement tended to get a bit toasty as will. When the ambient temperature was around 130^0 F, it was possible for the pavement in direct sunlight to heat up another twenty or thirty degrees. Now, take off your shoes and socks and walk around on that for a while. This was what the dogs had to do. To alleviated the possibility of a hot foot, or four hot foots (poached paws?) in the case of the dogs, we found carpets and carpet remnants from here or there, and laid them out on the pavement for them to walk on while they worked.

Today, a little old Iraqi lady who worked for the Department of Justice's Counter Corruption Task Force (now there was a job that was not making a lot of headway over here) walked into the P.X. parking lot. Meat and I were shooting the breeze, standing under the shade of a gazebo tent just off the side of the pit, when he suddenly went very quiet, and nodded his head in her direction. I turned to look at what had caught his attention, and saw this woman staring intently into the search pit. She cocked her head from side to side a couple of times, stared a little more, and then put her hands on her hips as if she had made up her mind. You could almost see her nod to herself the second before she turned, and walked directly over to where we were standing.

We watched her progress as she bore down on us with a determined step in her gait. Striding with a purpose reminiscent of any Drill Sergeant, she stalked right up, and stopped squarely in front of Meat, set her feet in a shoulder-width stance, dug her fists into her hips, and looked him directly in the face. Well, that is not entirely accurate. When I said she was a "little old lady" I was not exaggerating on the little part. Without tilting her chin up she would have been staring him directly in the belly button, but the height difference certainly did not seem to slow her down the least bit.

"Excuse me young sir," she piped, "but did you know those rugs over there belong in the Palace? I used to visit there as a little girl, and saw them hanging there once, a long time ago. They're worth tens of thousands of dollars apiece." The rugs she was referring to were two twenty by twenty-five-foot Persian rugs that had been sitting in the P.X. parking lot search pit for almost two years, and someone was just now figuring this out?

A couple of years ago all the "I'm so important" people in the North Wing of the Palace decided to redecorate. Well, that may not necessarily be fair since there were a lot of them, and workspace in the Palace was becoming extremely scarce. The North Wing used to house the ballroom of the Palace. Deep marble floors, alabaster statues, huge tapestries, crystal chandeliers, handcrafted wooden balconies, galleries, and mezzanines. The works. I had seen pictures of what it looked like when the State Department first took over the Palace, and this room was what words like palatial, astonishing, and breathtaking were invented to describe.

To make way for the renovation much of the decorations and adornments had been moved around, or just thrown out, to create room for all the offices and cubicles needing to be constructed to house the alphabet soup kids (You know, DIA, FBI, LMNOP). Now complete, this maze of offices within offices, cross connected corridors, and winding passageways had come to be affectionately known as the Honeycomb Hideout.

The R.S.O.s at the time told us, "Sure, you can have any of the carpets you want out of the trash for the dogs to walk on. Have at it." Needless to say, we were not all that worried about what these carpets looked like, they were in the trash after all, just that they did the job a rug was supposed to do. So, out of the garbage they were grabbed, into the parking lot they were carried, onto the ground they were laid, and over them the dogs they did walk, and vehicles they did drive. Dropping all the normal and natural things dogs and vehicles drop, wherever they tended to drop them.

"Ma'am, I don't know anything about that." Meat replied. "This is the equipment I have to work with as provided by the R.S.O.s."

Although she did not seem too happy with the answer, she did not press the issue any further either. However, a debate looked to be raging in her mind. Within a couple of seconds, apparently having won her own argument, she expelled an exasperated breath, turned on her heel, and walked off toward the P.X.

Meat and I exchanged a confused look. Still trying to wrap our brains around what had just happened, he and I left the shade of the pavilion, walked over to the search pit, and looked at the rugs she had pointed out. Two vehicles, parked bumper to bumper, were currently being sniffed by the dog, but even through this distraction we began to see the rugs in a new light. Filthy from the years they had spent laying out, spanning the length of the search pit, exposed to the elements, they really did not look like they may have been important.

Each pattern had been stitched in a classic Persian style with floral and geometric shapes interwoven throughout the body of the rug. The contrasting blues and reds had been weathered by time and abuse until their colors and hues had become muted into dark splotches. Faint gold and green highlight lines and accents, now matted down by the constant flow of heavily armored vehicles, had been ground into the surrounding pile until they almost disappeared.

It looked like the front and tail edges had borne the brunt of the abuse and the fringe had been compressed flat and frayed, with the pile along the border becoming a crushed matte. Two long, dark, evenly spaced smudge trails tracked the length of both carpets. Remnants of the tire grime from the thousands of vehicles driven over them. Walking around these rugs, examining them with this new information, it was hard to believe they had once hung as fine tapestries in a grand palace. It looked more like they had spent their entire lives lining the bottom of a bird cage. A really big bird cage, filled with thousands of birds, all on a high fiber diet.

Meat pulled out his cell phone, and called the BDOC. Even though the lady said she worked for a Department of Justice task force, part of the State Department, and the carpets had been given to the parking lot by the R.S.O.s office, also a part of the State

Department, the parking lot was still under the authority of the Department of Defense, and they needed to know.

Since I was just standing around with nothing else to do while the BDOC was getting briefed, I decided this would be a good time to call the R.S.O. office, and give them a heads-up as well. Knowing he would not want to be left out, I pulled my phone from my pocket, and gave The Tick a call. He always loved getting phone calls from me, and let me know every time I called him. "Hey Rooster. What is it this time?" Can't you feel the love.

I gave him a quick rundown on the little old lady, and what she had told us. I also let him know the BDOC was being notified, as well. The response was nothing close to what I was expecting to hear, and by that I mean there was silence, not even breathing. I waited for a couple of seconds before asking the obvious question. "Tick, did you get all that?"

"Really, how do you come up with these? Only you, right? I'll be down in a minute; I have got to see these rugs." And he rang off.

I stared at my phone for a second, not really knowing how to interpret that call. "It looks like we're going to have a little company on this one." I said to Meat as I punched up Manny's phone number. Neither one of us would ever hear the end of it if Manny did not get an invitation, too.

"Yah, we are. The Battle Captain isn't too sure how to handle this one either. He's on his way to look at the rugs, too." Great! Break out the bubbly, we are going to have a party.

We were waiting for them to show up when a large panel van arrived through the gate. Turning toward the search pit it stopped just short, right in front of the rugs, and a very proper older gentleman stepped out of the passenger side door to amble around the front of the truck. Not very tall, he was dressed in slacks and a jacket, a tapered shirt with honest-to-god cuff-links and a bow tie. A narrow brimmed straw sun hat capped a head of perfectly tended salt and pepper hair and he peered at us through what can only be described as spectacles.

He did not so much walk up to us as he strode up to us, his posture being old-world military correct. The only way he could have been more quintessential would have been if he spoke with a fine British accent. For the life of me all I could picture, as he approached, was

Higgins screaming "Magnum! How could you?" But, alas, much to my disappointment, he was American.

He stopped a stately distance in front of us and politely nodded his head. "Gentlemen, I am from the Counter Corruption Task Force. I have come to claim those tapestries." And with that, he turned toward the driver of the van and nonchalantly waved for him to get to work.

Lunchmeat and I both turned toward the search pit and began walking, the Gentleman walking with us. "Sir," Lunchmeat said, "I can't allow you to take the rugs until the Battle Captain arrives."

"Not to worry, young man." The Gentleman dismissed in proper diction, with a slight wave of his hand. "Those... "rugs"... as you call them, are the property of the State Department. I am merely reclaiming them."

"Oh well, if that's the case," I chimed in, "an R.S.O. is currently on his way." By this time we were standing directly on top of the first rug, and if anyone was going to try to roll it up they were going to have to roll us up in it. The Gentleman did not appear to be amused.

He also looked like he was not used to being thwarted. With finely constrained frustration, the Gentleman doffed his cap, and dabbed his brow with a sharply folded, blindingly white, handkerchief before replacing his cover and returning the handkerchief to his jacket's breast pocket. "You truly have no idea what you have here, do you?"

Oh Buddy, you have no idea. Not only does your question make a very accurate statement, as well as an assessment, but by doing this kind of work in a place like this, it had also become a very normal way of life.

Looking at Lunchmeat, he continued, "This is a handmade Persian carpet. It was originally commissioned even before Saddam Hussein came to power, and has hung as a tapestry in the palace for decades." Well, there's a thing for you.

I was not completely sure about Meat, but I was certainly confused by the sudden attention these pieces were generating, and the vigor with which they were being pursued. Fortunately, the time we had been spending patrolling, watching each other's backs, providing complement to the others actions, a bond had developed between us. Forged deep enough, meat was able to give voice to my bafflement before I could find the words.

"Sir, you do realize this carpet has been out here, in the parking lot, for years. Wind, rain, dust, dirt, dogs, and people have been walking all over it, not to mention the thousands of vehicles that have been driven across it. God only knows what's been mashed, stomped, ground and pounded into it. The things have got to be ruined by now."

"My, my. Dear boy," he chortled, "didn't you know? That's how you break in one of these. They should just be reaching their full potential about now."

Huh, who knew? Meat and I exchanged dumbfounded looks and, for the life of us, could not think of another thing to say. Fortunately, we did not have to as the Battle Captain and Tick both meandered up. Introductions were made all around and the three of them wandered off to discuss the problem, leaving me and Lunchmeat as tacks on the carpet.

To make a long story short, in the end it was decided The Tick would call GSO (Government Services Office, pretty self-explanatory] to come out with another truck, a couple of wooden crates, and pack up the rugs so they could be put in a warehouse until someone could figure out what to do with them. Picture the final scene from Raiders of the Lost Ark. You get the idea.

When they finally came to collect the rugs, they brought replacement carpet with them. Some puke green, indoor-outdoor, carpet pieces that looked and smelled like they had recently been removed from some long over used bar room floor.

4 July – The one day when the rocket's red glare, bombs bursting in air would be appropriate, not necessarily appreciated, but appropriate, and we got nothing. Nada, nyet, null, nix, nein, porcupine. Maybe the insurgents actually did understand irony.

7 July - We had been implementing new Random Anti-terrorism Measures (RAMS- pronounced just like the football team). These procedures were designed to add one, or more, additional security measures, at random times, in order to discourage any ne'er-do-well from attempting a nefarious act.

For security reasons, I am not going to go into the particulars regarding most of these, but one of them was pretty straight forward, the CAC card reader. In this instance CAC stood for Common Access Card. The basic idea was this. On the back of the I.D. cards and access cards was a magnetic strip, much like the strip on the back of your credit card, and all the information on the front and back of the card was coded onto this strip. When swiped through the card reader, the magnetic strip was read, the information was displayed on a screen, and by checking the readout with the actual information on the card, we could tell if it was real or fake.

From time to time, the R.S.O.s had given their readers to Rak, so he could have his guards run them at the chow hall. I also put them into operation at the CACs. DoD had operational responsibility over the P.X., and its parking lot, so the BDOC had Lunchmeat running their reader over there quite a bit lately, too.

Today, I was standing inside the Main CAC when a young Staff Sergeant, new to the BDOC, came in with one of the card reader cases in his hand. "Hey, there you are!" He said, walking over to me. "I'm glad I ran into you, here you go." And he placed the large plastic container on the counter, turned, and walked toward the door.

"Whoa, hey, hold on a minute. What's this?" I asked, walking around the corner of the counter.

Stopping with his hand on the door knob, he turned his head to reply, "What does it look like? It's the CAC card reader."

"Well, yah, I kind of figured that." This being a State Department venue, it was both curious and odd for a soldier to bring a card reader to the CAC, and just put it down. "Are you sure you just want to leave that here?"

A little confused, and growing a bit defensive, the SSG turned to fully face me. "Of course, I was told to bring this to you so you could do RAMs this afternoon."

Curiouser and curiouser. "You were?"

"Yah, I was." I could tell that his confusion was beginning to turn to anger, and that anger was starting to shovel coal into his furnace of defensiveness. Once again, what was a contractor doing questioning a soldier?

My gut was telling me something was not quite right about this, but I just could not put my finger on the problem. "OK, who told you to bring this down here?"

"The Battle Captain did." He said, defiantly.

"You do realize the CACs are DoS, not DoD, right?" Confusion made one more appearance on his face, and it looked like he did not understand what I was asking, or know what I was trying to tell him. The nagging in my gut started to gain a little focus and began tapping my hind-brain on the shoulder. "Who were you told to give this reader to?" I pressed.

A little less sure of himself now, the SSG slightly cocked his head to one side and furrowed his eyebrows. "I was told to give it to you."

Not exactly the epiphany I was going for, I rephrased my question. "What is the name of the person you were told to give this to?"

"Lunchmeat."

Bingo! He had been told to take the reader from the BDOC, and give it to Lunchmeat so he could conduct RAMs in the parking lot. Being new, he probably had not met Meat yet, and was only going on the description someone in the BDOC had given him. I am sure I mentioned how Lunchmeat and I resemble each other enough that people had asked if he was my uglier brother, haven't I?

"Well, that answers that question, doesn't it?" Now, I understood exactly where the problem was and told him, with great relief, this was only a case of mistaken identity. "I'm not Lunchmeat." I said. "I am Rooster, the other white meat."

Looking a bit embarrassed, the Staff Sergeant collected up the card reader case and walked out of the CAC in the direction of the parking lot. I dialed up my cell phone and gave Lunchmeat a quick heads-up that the card reader was on the way to him.

10 July - Meat and I were finished with our second set of checks. Taking a reverse route, we finished at the Service CAC this time. Lunch was already over (the meal, that is) and we took our time meandering back to the office.

In case I had not mentioned it, summers in Iraq got hot, very hot. We were barely into July, and temperatures had already climbed over 120^0 F more than a couple of times. The first few weeks in August would determine the high for the year. The only upside to this extreme heat was Iraq was mostly desert. Arid, extra dry, the climate did not lend itself much in the way for humidity, and yes, that did make a difference. Humidity, the kind August brought to Florida, could really beat a person down. The sweat never evaporated from your skin, and you not only felt wet, you also felt sticky, and your clothes clung to you like hot, damp, limp rags. It was air you could wear.

Dry heat, on the other hand, did not allow the sweat to remain on your skin. With no moisture in the air, perspiration instantly evaporated the second it left the pores, and with it took more of the heat away from your skin. (Hint; wearing a t-shirt under your main shirt helped to keep you cool. The T-shirt remained moist with your sweat, keeping you cooler, while whatever dampness transferred to the outer shirt evaporated, taking some of the heat away.) The trick during dry heat was to remain hydrated. Spending as much time outside as we did, I tended to drink between four and six liter sized bottles of water a day, and still rarely peed. (Again, for the metrically challenged, a liter is basically a quart. Four quarts/liters equal a gallon.)

Another effect this evaporate climate had was, it caused clouds to disappear for months at a time. No moisture in the air meant there was nothing for them to collect to form their nebulas mass. The last wisps of clouds would scoot across the sky in the beginning of April, leaving clear, blue skies until their return around the end of October. That is right, blue skies and sunshine, uninterrupted, for almost seven whole months. Sunscreen should be applied like spackle.

Under this clear, blue sky we strolled away from the Service CAC, retelling stories already told more than once; and still chuckling at them. BOB shone down, bathing us in his bright, warm countenance (BOB, Big Orange Ball. It's the sun, all right?). Meat tended to burn, not tan, so he carried a bottle of sunscreen in his cargo pocket everywhere he went. Me, on the other hand, I must have gotten lucky. Somewhere in my lineage I had Native American blood in my background. This was the only reason I could come up with to explain why I did not burn that much, mostly I tanned; a deep rust color, but I digress.

Months of sunshine had already burnished my dome, and the rays now beating down on me had little effect. Liberal applications of sunblock had left Meat's melon unscathed, and the contrast in hues only left one way to describe it, chrome dome.

Rounding the corner through the South drop arm, the barrier guarding the South end of the road traveling behind the Palace, we passed the chow hall. Unconsciously, we were taking the long way back to the office. A route that would take us through the swimming pool (all right, I lied to you earlier. The pool isn't really on the way between the office and the Service CAC, but, with all this sun and heat can you really blame us for taking the detour?)

A light breeze had picked up sometime during the course of our excursion, but was doing little more than pushing the heat and dust around. I remembered being back in the states, even during some of the hottest days, when any wind, any gust, no matter how slight, would always seem to take a bit of the edge off and cool me, even if only a little. I did not know if the weather in Iraq was an example of relativity, or if it was just that hot, but there was nothing cooling about a summer breeze in this place. Crank up the heat in your house to the mid one-twenties, and instead of using ceiling fans to move the air around, turn on your hair dryer for circulation. I was beginning to understand what a Thanksgiving turkey felt like sitting in a convection oven.

Stepping out of the street, onto the sidewalk, we passed the entrance to the chow hall, and were about to enter an opening in the T-walls lining the boundary to the pool when a fragment of conversation drifted by our ears.

"I think they're brothers. I've never seen one without the other, and they're always out, walking around."

The words did not register with me as much as the tone, and I searched for the source of this wonderfully feminine voice.

Meat must have heard it too. Stopping in his tracks, slightly ahead of me, he was slowly turning, eyes scanning. Our gaze came to rest on two women crossing the street behind us.

Looking toward each other they seemed intent, lost in their own conversation. Neither one was exceptionally tall, but when you are my size no one was, and as they walked a breeze brushed their hair over their shoulders to slightly mask their faces. Deep dark hair, almost black, drifted across the cheek of the girl in front of me, cascading well past her chin and nose, to flutter in the wind. To her left her partner, and source of the statement that originally caught our attention, bore light blond locks. Stirred by the gust, her hair danced around her face, finally coming to rest over the front of her shoulder to lie on her chest as it subsided. As if on cue, both reached up to capture her own diversion, brushing palms past their temples, trapping stray strands between fingers, casually tucking them behind their ear.

Still unaware of our curiosity, they continued talking with each other as they drew closer. Their stride suggested they were soldiers. It never failed, when two or more people with military training started walking, especially side by side, training subconsciously kicked in and they fall into step within a few strides. Their posture suggested they were N.C.O.s, quite possibly senior N.C.O.s. Used to being in front of troops, knowing they were being watched more as an example than being listened to as an instructor, N.C.O.s tended to project a sense of bearing. A steel in their spine and purpose in their gestures younger troops were still trying to develop. Once you knew what it was, it was not difficult to spot. Senior N.C.O.s, the good ones, projected an additional element of confidence in this bearing. They had it.

Hourglass waists accentuating smooth, round hips, and longer than average legs were covered by billowing towels, wrapped around their tiny stomachs, draping to brush the top of their sandaled feet. Only slightly smaller than mildly conservative bikini tops had been entrusted to cover the remaining exposed skin.

Being athletically built, neither one was challenging their suit to accomplish a cumbersome task, nor were they simply relying on the garment to provide basic cover. With each step, the fabric merely applied gentle resistance, barely needing to confine the slightest of motion caused by the action, emphasizing they were not being worn for support either.

Chestnut tanned, the gentle caress of the sun's rays had softly polished their skin to a radiant, bronze luster. As they glided across the street, drawing ever nearer, light would play off their complexion, shading the furrows between muscles and cleavage, gleaming from the ridges and peaks. How I loved this job.

Stepping onto the sidewalk the brunette gasped, noticing for the first time us noticing them. With a start, her left hand leapt out and grabbed her friend by the arm, breaking the spell.

"Whoa, hey, sorry," I blurted at the sudden action, raising my palms in a slight gesture of surrender. " I didn't mean to scare you."

Both chuckled a little, as their surprise faded, and they seemed to relax a little.

"We couldn't help but overhear a bit of your conversation, and were wondering if you were referring to us." Meat interjected, wiggling his index finger to point at the two of us.

"Yah, we pretty much were, I guess." The blonde offered. "We see you guys all over the place walking around, you must have a pretty great job. I have to ask, though, are you two brothers?" (Told ya'. We get this a fair amount.)

What surprised me about this time was Meat's answer to the question. "Brothers from another mother. We're the buffalo brothers, I'm Duck he's Cover." That produced a laugh from all of us.

"That's good, I like that. I'm Kayla," the blonde offered, "and this is Angel." She said, jerking a thumb in the direction of her friend.

Not wanting to be left out of the joke, Angel looked at me and giggled. "So, since you're cover, the next time the rockets hit I should come looking for you?"

"Nice," was about all I could come up with. Way to go, dumb-ass.

Smiling, I tried to rebound. "We've seen the two of you here, at the pool, a few times before. Are you State or military?" Not my best recovery, but it would have to do.

"Military." Kayla responded.

"We're with the Civil Affairs unit over on Camp Travis." Angel added.

Being a little quicker on the draw, Meat pounced on this new information first. "Civil Affairs, does that mean you're friendly about extracurricular activity, or am I getting that one wrong?" A bit of a stretch, I thought, but both girls seemed to find it funny, and exchanging a glance they chuckled a little.

Back and forth we chatted as we ambled on toward the pool. During our stroll Lunchmeat and I tried to explain about our call-signs, being The Buffalo Brothers, and the duck and cover thing. Being military, both were Sergeants First Class, (Senior N.C.O.s), they picked up on all of it right away. Having been here for rocket fest, they quickly got the duck and cover joke. For simplicity's sake though, and after much poking and questioning, we finally gave them our real names too (You already have mine, but I'm not giving you Lunchmeat's).

Walking onto the deck surrounding the water, we found several unoccupied lounge chairs laying in direct sunlight, and our little group meandered in their direction. On the way, the girls (I guess calling them girls isn't quite right being as how both of them were grown women, easily in their mid-thirties, and making it look good) selected the perfect spot for their afternoon sun worship. Arriving, they placed their bags filled with the implements required for the service on the cement next to their chosen chaise. Nonchalantly, they slipped out of their sandals as the conversation continued. Casually, they unwrapped the towels from their waists while we talked, shook them out, bent toward the lounges, and spread them across the mesh seating.

Fortunately, for both Meat and I, they were slightly turned away from us when they did this, and could not see the mesmerization in our eyes as their slow, fluid motions hypnotized us. You cannot convince me women do not know exactly what they are doing at a time like this, and the small grin that appeared on their lips when they turned around, catching us before we could tear our eyes away from the fascination, wrapped in total silence, only helped to confirm it.

Once reclined, Angel peered up to look me in the face. Raising her right hand, she hooked the end of her index finger over the top of her sunglasses, and slowly drew them down the bridge of her nose to reveal two bright, almond colored pools that were her eyes. Vertigo almost overtook me, and I just about lost my balance gazing into their depths.

"Are you just going to stand there, or are you going to sit down?" She asked, brushing her hand along the armrest of the chair next to her as she brought it back to her side. "You're a bit too tall for me to keep staring up at you."

Dumb-ass! You did it again. Quit standing here with your teeth in your mouth! Get a grip man!

Smiling warmly, at least I hope it was warmly, and not dopey like it must have been earlier, I walked my way between the lounge chairs, trying to regain my composure, and sat down next to her. After tripping over my own two feet and tongue a few more times, and fumbling the conversation a few more times, Angel and I fell into a very casual, very relaxed conversation. Nothing too deep or personal, we just talked about this and that.

Glancing over from time to time, I noticed Kayla and Lunchmeat were carrying on famously. Chuckling easily, the low rumble of Meat's laugh was a balancing contrast to the pitch of her giggles. From time to time she would lightly rest the tips of her fingers on top of one of his knees while she made a point, and he would softly lay his palm on her arm, draping his fingers and thumb over its curve to emphasize some part of a sentence. I was right on the verge of envy when a realization occurred to me. Angel and I had been doing the same thing the whole time we had been talking. How about that?

Her personality was disarming, her demeanor enticing. Normally, I take a while to open up to new people, yet here I sat with someone I had just met, feeling quite comfortable in her company. Sneaking a glance at my watch, "Holy Crap" were the words that jumped into my mind. I would have sworn on a stack of bibles I had only been here for a few minutes, talking, but my watch said we had been here for well over an hour, carrying on like we had known each other for a good long while, and I felt good about it.

Kayla was the one to interrupt my epiphany as she dropped her beach bag back on the deck and swore, drawing our immediate attention. "Damn it. I forgot to put my sunscreen in the bag."

One smooth motion was all it took for Meat to thrust his hand into his cargo pocket, scoop out the ubiquitous bottle of sunblock he kept there, and proffer it like a fine bottle of wine for her approval. "Here, take mine." was all he said. The smooth bastard, I will never make fun of that bottle again.

Both girls stared in disbelief before bursting out in laughter, and buoyed by their delight, Meat and I joined in. As the moment passed, and our amusement died down a little, Angel turned back to me, placed her hand on my knee, and softly said. "That's a pretty good friend you have there." Yes, he is.

Becoming slightly emboldened by this little act of approval, I thought now would be a good time to try and take the next step forward. "Angel, tomorrow's Friday. After dinner, they set up a karaoke machine out here by the pool, and people get together to sing and dance a little. Would both of you be interested in meeting us here?"

And there is was. Even though this had not been an outright, one to one, formal invitation, I was still able to push the words past my lips. It had been quite a while since the last time I asked anyone to go out on anything even resembling a date. During my time on active duty I had been married, twice. A third had been developing, but was derailed for the same reason the first two had failed. The Army could be very hard on relationships. Two deployments, starting with the invasion of Iraq, including redeployment, recovery, refit, train-up, and prep to deploy again had also taken a lot of time away from socializing.

Combined with contracting for the last couple of years, working twelve hour shifts, and I had not been in possession of a lot of free time over the last five years. Additionally, the aversion I had developed toward other people, and keeping company with them, had made it increasingly easy for me to spend what little time I did get in other, quieter, pursuits. However, spending as much time as I had with Lunchmeat, I was beginning to think I should reevaluate my apathetic feeling toward others. How much could it hurt?

The silence I got was killing me. She did grin, however, just a little, before turning her head to look at Kayla. Having drawn her attention by my question, she was already looking at me. I could not believe I actually felt my heart racing in anticipation as the seconds stretched into, what felt like, hours as they exchanged that telepathy thing girls do at times like this. They looked at each other for a couple of seconds; then held that look for just one more. I think they do that to just to make us guys feel a little more anxious. Then, Angel turned back, and looked at me.

"I don't think we can," she said, absentmindedly looking down at her toes as they wiggled a little. Raising her face to meet mine again, she took a deep breath as slowly, methodically she reached her left hand up to pull her sunglasses from her face. Staring at me through those gorgeous, naked orbs, a flash of regret seemed to race through them, or it could just have been my imagination. "We have a mission tomorrow and don't know how long it's going to last. It sounds like fun, but maybe some other time."

"No worries." I replied, dropping my eyes, unable to sustain the intensity of her gaze. "Sure, maybe some other time." My heart ceased fluttering, my blood slowed in my veins, and my fingertips actually felt a little chilly.

Catching onto the fact I was beginning to flounder, Meat threw a lifeline. "Ladies, it's been great meeting you, but we've been here too long already, and need to get back to the office. I do hope we get a chance to do this again. You two take care on your mission tomorrow, and be safe. I would hate to miss an opportunity to take you up on the offer for some other time." And we stood.

Waves were exchanged, and hopes of getting to see each other later were passed around as Meat and I walked away.

"Nice try back there." Meat commented as we rounded a duck and cover bunker, walking out of view from the girls.

"Yah, well, we'll see," was all I could muster. "Thanks, brother."

13 July – General Petraeus issued an order to have the entire Palace given back to the Iraqis by 9 November, yes that meant this year. The Marine security force responsible for being the Quick Reaction Force (Q.R.F.), and guarding an exterior point in front of the Mid CAC also received their orders to leave by the 31st of July. Everything else not immediately tied to the NEC was scheduled to be given back in conjunction with the Palace

as well. This meant a lot of people had a lot to do, and not much time to get it done.

Again, it was rotation time for many of the military and civilians stationed around the I.Z. We seemed to be getting a lot of new contractors too. I say this because we had been running our butts off responding to mistakes being made by a bunch of F.N.G.s (that's Freaking New Guys for you civilian types) that wanted to learn the rules the hard way. John Wayne once said life is hard, it's a lot harder when you are stupid. Boy, did he get that one right.

Lunchmeat was writing up to ten incident reports per day due to stupid stuff going on in the parking lot. Most of the folks involved were P.S.D. teams, and a few military, thinking they could leave their weapons laying in plain view inside their vehicles. Not such a good idea.

Most of them seemed to believe a misguided theory. Just because the vehicle was armored no one could break into it. Not so much. Everyone seemed to forget about the slim-jim. Just because your vehicle was armored did not mean there was a burglar bar running over the top of the locking mechanism inside the door protecting the workings from someone with a coat hanger, or other such devise. As a matter of fact, when aftermarket armor was added to a vehicle the burglar bar was usually removed from the door to make room so the armor could fit inside.

In the past two weeks he had confiscated fifty weapons. Some of them were really nice too. AKs with all the bells, short barrel M4s with all the whistles, 1911s, Sig Sauers, you name it and he probably had taken one. Too bad we were not allowed to keep any of them. Once Meat, or his guards, found a vehicle with weapons laying in plain sight they would call the I.Z. Police; read that as Air Force Security Police (they used to be called Security Police, SPs, but now call themselves Security Forces, SF. Either way you say it, it still meant security). Once on scene they would pop the locks, and confiscate the weapons. They filled out paperwork and everything. It was very official. Aim High.

What I had to keep dealing with was photographers. Now that Senators Obama and McCain were supposed to show up on their campaign trail, yippee skippee, all the news agencies were showing up with cameras galore. Oh, I guessed they were also showing up because the word was out that we would be returning the Palace to the Iraqis. I guess that was news, too.

The biggest problem I had to overcome was who was authorized to bring the cameras onto the grounds, and who was allowed to escort them. Normally, cameras were not allowed on the grounds without special authorization from the R.S.O. office. The process was pretty straight forward, fill out the request, get it signed, and you were good. I guess no one wanted to take the time. Another form was required if you actually wanted to take pictures in, of, or around the Palace, and this process also seemed to be getting overlooked.

I had yet to run into anyone trying to do anything sneaky. The problem just came from no one taking the time to do it right. Every time a camera crew showed up I had to go to the CAC, find out who they were, and coordinate with one of our R.S.O.s so they could enter the grounds. Not difficult, but very time consuming, and completely avoidable. Inevitably, one or two people in the group would lose their cool, and that just made the process longer, and more frustrating for everyone. Again, the issue boiled down to everyone was special. Well, at least they felt they were more special than us lowly, little security types just doing our best to fix their self-induced problems. Everyone had an ego.

15 July – I had not seen Angel or Kayla since the day we ran into them at the pool. Lunchmeat and I cut through the pool area two or three times day, at different times, in the hope we would run into them. So far, no luck. Even though the distractions who were actually there were pleasant enough, we seemed to keep missing the girls. It was kind of curious. I remembered seeing them laying out a number of times before ever meeting them, it was difficult not to notice them. Maybe the opportunity just presented itself too late. I did not know. I hoped nothing bad happened on that mission they were going on.

17 July – So much for having a quiet month. I got to work this morning to find out we had already received a rocket. That was not really an accurate statement. We had not gotten one, al-Khindi Street actually did, right between the NEC and FOB Union III.

Around 0530hrs, one of the R.S.O.s had been leaving the NEC, on his way to the Palace, when he heard a tremendous bang as he turned onto the main road. While straightening his turn, entering the eastbound lane, he looked over the top of the hood and saw the tips of rocket tail fins sticking out of the road, barely over the center line in the westbound lane. It was not like tips were barely protruding from the roadway, he was just that close to the impact. The tips were all he could see as the momentum of the turn caused them to disappear from view below the edge of the hood, only to reappear alongside his truck as he straightened out in the lane. Caught as a snapshot in his mind's eye dust was wafting from the divot in the asphalt, smoke still drifted through the apertures of the spent engine, and bits of debris had not yet stopped skittering across the pavement.

The R.S.O. was The Tick, and after his little adventure with the suspicious package earlier he said this was the second time in his life he nearly shat himself. Down-shifting, jamming his foot down on the accelerator, he said he prayed to God the truck would not stall, or he would not lose control of it as he popped the clutch, lifting the front end of the little truck several inches as it leapt away. He told me the effect of the sudden acceleration caused him to lose sight of the rocket as he sped off. It was not until he passed through the al-Khindi Checkpoint, a quarter mile away, he was able to coax his foot off the gas, slowing the vehicle to a more reasonable speed. His biggest fear had been running over the rocket body in his flight to escape, causing the warhead to detonate. Fortunately, the round never exploded. The bang had been the sound of it hitting the asphalt, and digging in.

The down side was the C-RAM alarm at the NEC, and the FOB, never went off. It looked like if we were going to get more steel rain in the near future, the weatherman was not going to announce it before it hit.

18 July – We got our answer today. After lunch, Meat and I walked over to Camp Travis to see if we could find the reason we had not seen the girls since the day we talked to them. The simple answer was they were no longer in Baghdad.

Walking around the camp we found where the Civil Affairs unit was located, the building they worked from at least. Stepping into the operations office, we stumbled across a group of soldiers painting a big, open wall at the back of the room, covering a unit mascot and motto already there with fresh coats of white paint. Immediately, we knew what that meant, having gone through the same routine a couple times in the past ourselves. Talking with a few of the Sergeants working there, they confirmed what we already suspected. They were the new unit, and had just completed RIPing (RIP, pronounced like a synonym for torn, is Relief in Place, the handoff between companies) the outgoing unit. This past rotation had been the end of the girl's deployment, and their unit was on the way home, back to The World. This must have been the mission they told us about.

I guess I probably should not have been too disappointed. Talking with them had been fun. During the little bit of time we had they seemed genuine, laughing in all the right places, even giggling at things I was sure they should not find all that funny. Their questions appeared to come from a true interest, and their answers felt natural. Like they were truly being themselves. And they had been easy on the eyes. Oh yes, very easy on the eyes.

I just wish they had been honest about leaving too. I could not come up with a single reason for them not to. This was a deployment after all. People came and went all the time. I did not get it. Very rarely do people surprise me. Quite often, though, they disappoint me.

20 July – Things had been getting interesting in the P.X. parking lot lately. Many of the contract companies providing V.I.P. and convoy security used this as their rally point when they came to the I.Z. Why not? In addition to the P.X. store they had Burger King, Subway, Boston's Best Coffee, all the little comfort food stations from home. The problem came when people got junk food focused, drawn by the idea of eating something that was not an M.R.E. (Meal, Ready to Eat. They replaced the old Army C-rations. We used to say M.R.E. really stood for mystery [Mr. E]) or chow hall, and decided everyone could leave the vehicle, posting no guards. The private security companies tended to believe that since there S.U.V.s were armored, or set up with after-market armor kits, they could lock their weapons in the trucks and walk away. Not so much. Would it have been too much to ask for them to at least cover them with something?

As I have said before, the armor did protect the vehicles from bullets and what not, but did not do too much good against theft. With a slim-jim, and a couple of minutes, anyone could get into one of these vehicle, and make off with its contents. I had watched the S.P.s do it several dozen times. Big, armored vehicles, the ones specifically designed to resist or repel an armed attack, and were built that way from the ground up, were pretty solid and presented a different story.

Again, it was the S.U.V.'s and armored sedans that produced the majority of our workload. Operations over here had grown incredibly, both in scope and scale. Due to the sheer number of companies, diplomatic missions, and anyone else requiring the use of one, preproduction armored vehicles were now a premium commodity, and it was getting harder for anyone to purchase a new one. Scarcity of these hard cars had resulted in a new niche appearing in the sales market, and postproduction refitting and installation of armor and armored panels had become a more common solution to their lack of availability.

Most of them were actually quite well made, and a casual glance by an innocent observer, especially if you did not know what you were looking at, would not be enough to identify these modifications. Unfortunately, all of this ballistic protection did not directly translate to theft protection, and every time we found weapons left in one of these vehicles, with no one there to guard them, we had to do paperwork on them. It was called an Incident Report.

It would have been one thing if we were only finding civilian contractors leaving their weapons unsecure, but we found military doing it as well. This I could not understand. If you had ever been in the military for more than a minute, you knew it was a cardinal sin to leave your weapon unattended. Duh! The next problem arose when we ran into the military from a coalition country doing this.

Already, we had found the Czechs had left their weapons like this, as well as the Romanians, and the Georgians. The sticking point came when the I.Z. Police had to confiscate them as part of their case. This was all fine and dandy when the offender spoke English, and were willing to surrender their weapons without incident, but when they were from another country, and did not speak English (or at least claimed they did not), well, then it was not so easy.

Yesterday, the Czechs left their weapons in their trucks again. I was killing time in the parking lot, chatting with Lunchmeat, waiting on the time we were going to start our second set of checks, when his guards reported finding a cache of weapons in two up-armored, post production armored, S.U.V.s parked side by side with an empty slot in between them. While strolling over to see for ourselves, Meat hooked his phone from his pocket, contacted the BDOC, and requested they dispatch the I.Z. Police to the scene.

Here is another one that will make you scratch your head. The I.Z. Police Station was located inside the P.X. complex. Not in the same building, but still inside the walls of the complex. Standing next to these S.U.V.s I could almost throw a rock, and hit their front door. Well, that was a bit of an exaggeration. I really would have to be able to throw a rock farther than a football field, but I could still see their front door through the compound's front gate. Even still, it took almost half an hour for any unit to respond to our call. Long enough for the Czechs to return to their vehicles. Long enough for them to start arguing the situation, and certainly long enough for tempers and frustrations to become agitated.

There we stood. Dealing with a stalemate caused by an easily avoidable situation. The Czech solders were spread out standing next to their vehicles. Each by their own door. The I.Z. Police had shown up, two patrol cars worth, along with a supervisor. The Patrolman had taken up station around the Czechs, positioning themselves so they could keep them all under observation. A few more of Meat's guards also responded to the scene, and were fanned out behind me and Lunchmeat. He and I were standing a bit of a way off the front of the vehicles, still relatively centered between the two, having backed away at the arrival of the police (once they get on scene, they take over jurisdiction), and we were all keeping wary, watchful eyes on each other.

The I.Z. Police Supervisor, a Technical Sergeant (Tech Sergeant for short. The rank is equivalent to an Army Staff Sergeant), and the Czech Team Leader were standing between, and well in front of, the two vehicles. The Tech Sergeant was really doing his best to explain the situation to the Team Leader, and defuse the tensions produced by his returned arguments. I did not envy the Tech the position he was in. Each time he explained what procedure required of him the Team Leader would only dig in deeper, add more aggression to his response, and with increasing adamancy refuse to comply.

As these things always did, it started out with a little talking. "We need to confiscate your weapons as part of our case."

"No! You won't! These weapons belong to the Czech Republic, and you can't have them." This would have been a whole lot worse had the Team Leader not spoken English.

"Sir. Procedure requires us to take them, and document them. Once we've done that, they will be returned to you. This directive comes straight from the Commander, Multi-National Forces, Iraq."

If I spoke Czech, or anything remotely related, I would tell you what response the Team Leader had to this. Since I did not, I could only speculate from the tone of voice he used. It did not sound nice. Not very nice at all.

Kudos to the Tech. He never so much as batted an eyelash in response to the growl. I did think, however, he had done this before as he smoothly transitioned to another approach.

"O.K. May I have your I.D. card, please, so I can get your information for my report then?"

The switch in tactic seemed to throw the Team Leader off guard for a second, and the amicable way the question was asked seemed to chill his ire by more than a few degrees. Mulling over the request, it looked like he was unable to formulate any protest, and eventually reached for the lanyard around his neck to which his I.D. card and I.Z. badge were clipped.

"O.K." He responded as he handed them over.

I did not know if the Tech Sergeant had spotted the I.Z. badge hanging from the same cord with the I.D. card or not, but once he had them in his hand he reversed his roll, snap turned back on his original attack angle, and reacquired missile-lock.

"Now, if you want your I.Z. badge back, you know the one that allows you to come and go in the I.Z., and go to the P.X., you'll hand over your weapons. You'll get everything back as soon as we process them."

Instantly, the Team Leader knew he had been had. His body trembled to contain the force of his rage as his anger spiked back into the red. His fists clenched and relaxed. His head shook slightly back and forth as his face grew redder. His lips opened and closed around voiceless words.

The Tech Sergeant stood stock still, a blank slate. He projected no emotion. No sense of accomplishment.

No look of satisfaction. Nothing but professionalism. He simply waited for the Team Leader's compliance. This guy was good.

Up until now their exchange had been rather loud, and fairly animated. Most of this from the Team Leader's side. Even I found it difficult to ignore their carrying on, and remain focused on the bigger picture. Our surroundings. The more activity they generated, the more attention they drew. At the onset no one wanted to stare at the two. In the beginning I had been observing the area. Watching the rest of the Czech team. Standing around their vehicles, they avoided directly staring at the exchange, but would steal quick peeks. As the back-and-forth played out those little ganders had turned into longer stares. And now this last gambit held everyone's attention.

From the corner of my eye I caught a slight bit of motion from the Czech soldier standing next to the front passenger door of the vehicle on my right. Moving only my eyes, I shifted my gaze to see what he was up to. Catching him in mid-motion, I saw the slow deliberate movement of his right arm. Just before hearing the distinct, metallic click of a magazine full of bullets being locked into the magazine well of his pistol. Shit.

"Meat? This is quickly heading down a really bad road. Know what I mean?" I whispered, not even wanting to move my lips for fear any sudden movement on my part might trigger the soldier to act.

"Yah, I saw it, too." He whispered back.

Security Managers were authorized to carry their pistols in what was called red status, magazine lock in the well, and a round in the chamber. It was indicated on our Palace Badges. Both Meat and I carried this way, but I could not vouch for the I.Z. Police. Having just inserted a magazine, I hoped when the soldier first cleared his weapon upon entering the I.Z., placing it in that green status I told you about before, he had done so properly. If he had, after taking the magazine out of the well, he would have ejected the round in the chamber. Completely emptying the weapon. If he had done this, he would now have to work the slide again to put a bullet back under the hammer, fully loading it, before it would fire. Should this thing actually go completely pear shaped, that would at least give us a small edge, but too many ifs existed for that to be relied on.

Cautiously, I adjusted my stance a little to the right so I would be in a better position to face threats from my side head-on. Training my focus on the right hand vehicle I lost sight of the soldiers gathered around the left one, but with Meat on my left they were in his field of vision, his responsibility. Now was my time to cover his right. To engage any threats on his blind side, to watch his back.

Making a quick assessment of possible targets, identifying blind spots, and trying to anticipate what these soldiers' actions may be I realized we had not made the most tactically advantageous decision of our lives. We were standing in the middle of a parking lot, wide open, without a single parked car or bunker to take cover behind. I whispered one more time.

"You know we have absolutely no cover out here if this thing goes south, right?

From over my left shoulder I heard Meat say, "Yah, well, you're the one who keeps saying you don't run for cover, you are cover."

Jokes? He wants to make jokes? "That's different." I insisted.

"I know, more than once, you've passed me on the way to a bunker in the middle of a strike, and I know good and well I was running at the time."

A chorus of metallic clicks popped from around the Czech's vehicles, derailing the rest of that train of thought as we realized the rest of their soldiers were following the lead of the first.

Yanked from their absorption in the Tech Sergeant's drama, the patrolmen adjusted their attention back to the soldiers. They widened their stance just a little, and slowly allowed their hands to drop to their belt buckles. Behind us, our guards had already been grasping their rifles as part of their normal carrying position. Slung over the shoulder of their firing hand, the strap caused the weapon to drape across their body. The rustle of cloth, and the creaking of the hand guards indicated they were readjusting their grip.

Meat and I had been standing with our hands crossed, hanging loose in front of us like a reverse "at ease." Gradually, ever so tenderly, we brought them up to hover just over our stomachs. The Czech soldiers just stood there staring back at us, arms hanging at their sides.

Hands next to their pistols. Fingers lightly splayed. Eyes darting from person to person.

At the sound of the first magazine being seated in its well the Tech Sergeant and Team Leader had become instantly silent, and still. As more magazines clicked home, each locked eyes with the other. The intensity of the hush spread. How the next few seconds would unfold hinged entirely on them as they attempted to stare the other into submission. I could not tell how the Tech Sergeant was holding up, his back was to me, but quick glances showed the Team Leader was intent, drilling holes through him with the force of his gaze. Neither one moved.

Noise from the parking lot faded to an empty void. Vehicle and pedestrian traffic dissolved away. I felt like space and time hesitated, poised, waiting for the next move from one of these two men. Birds in the trees even seemed to stop singing, wanting to focus on what was playing out below them. It felt like the future of the world depended on what happened next. I can guarantee you one thing. If this situation rolled the wrong way, even by the smallest fraction, and fell off the side of the cliff more than one of our futures were going to be adversely affected.

A voice boomed, and the future was set. Off to my left, one word thundered. I almost jumped out of my skin at its suddenness. As if linked to a single string, every Czech soldier's head jerked, snapped in the direction of the sound. I had no idea what language the word had been barked in, but I did know the voice of authority when I heard it, and it was all I could do to resist it. To keep my eyes on the possible threats in my area. To give it my full attention.

At a slightly less dominating level, yet losing none of its power, the same baritone voice that had just shatter the silence like a claymore rifled off a fast, staccato sentence. Again, I had no idea what was said, but the Czechs did. As one the soldiers immediately relaxed their stances, and slipped their arms behind their back to stand at something resembling a loose "parade rest." The Team Leader unlocked his gaze, after quickly glancing at the source of the order (because that was all it could have been) slightly lowered his eyes from those of the Tech Sergeant, and took a small step back.

Something jumped in my chest, and I realized my heart was suddenly beating again. Welcome back buddy. The blood flowed, and my lungs drank deep. The adrenaline that had been stacked up at the gates, waiting for them to be thrown wide for the fight portion, not even considering the flight option, backed away. The attitude being projected by the Czechs convinced the endorphins neither response would be required this time.

Convinced the soldiers in front of me no longer presented an immediate threat, I gave in to the part of my brain that felt compelled to snap-to at the sound of the order. Turning to my left, I gazed past Meat to try and identify the source of The Voice. Looking across the open parking lot, in the direction from which the thunder had originated, I saw nothing. No one. Well, that was not entirely true either. A good forty yards away I spotted a short, squat, little man walking in our direction.

Maybe five foot five, with a balding head, he appeared to be dressed well in a dark suit and tie. When I say he was balding, it was not in the same way I was bald. He did not so much have a forehead as he had a sixhead. A forehead that extended across the length of the top of his head to fall beyond the crown. Baldness also ringed the bottom of his scalp leaving a distinct line of demarcation between skin and hair no less than an inch above his ears, and traveling the circumference of his head.

Stately would be a good way to describe his weight. In another age, he might even have been regarded as portly. Yet, despite his girth, he walked easily, as if it took little effort. There was no huff and puff his size would suggest he should have, and no sheen of sweat glistened off his head and round face. How could this little, chubby, cherubic fellow been the source of the voice I heard containing so much command and authority. Meat must have had the same confusion. As he looked back at me it appeared he too was unable to make heads or tails of this.

As the man drew closer, small details I had initially been unable to see began to take shape. He was not just wearing a dark suit, he was wearing a dark, finely tailored, crafted suit. The bald of his head was smooth, containing no rogue, stray strands of hair, and what hair he did have circled his temples like a halo were finely tended and expertly cut. He did not so much walk as he moved. It was almost like where we were standing was being drawn closer to him, and his motion was simply causing the intervening space to evaporate.

I have worked in the halls of power many times, and have had multiple opportunities to observe powerful men and women while working there. One thing I have deduced from these observations was this; those who wielded true power and authority tended to do so with restrained fury. They did not shout. They did not need to. Rarely did they raise their voice in an aggressive tone. They did not have to. Being that powerful, having that much authority, they need only say a few words to the proper people, and the person causing their frustration was removed to other parts (usually to whatever place that represented their equivalent of a weather station at the South Pole). The few times I have heard one of these people raise their voice, it thundered and rolled much in the same way this voice had.

As the gentleman approached us, the little nuances that belie possession of that kind of authority became obvious. The Czech solders, and their Team Leader, had immediately recognized this guy for who he was, and now we were beginning to catch up. There was no way to deny it, he really was the cause of the cannonade of booming commands that had changed our future.

Having finished dispelling the distance between us, he guided the flow so he would stop to the side, and centered on the Tech and the Team Leader. Easily a full head shorter than both of them, and they were pretty evenly matched, he stood like a referee between two team captains ready for the coin toss. Both arms circled the length of his girth until their hands grasped each other behind his back. In a patient, grandfatherly sort of way, he looked up to gaze upon the face of the Team Leader.

Instantly, the Team Leader rattled off in machine gun fast Czech. Picking up speed as he went his body started to animate, and he slammed the back of one hand into the open palm of the other in staccato counterpoint to each word. He was not finished giving voice to his second breath when the gentleman unwound his right hand from behind his back, deliberately brought it back around to the front, and lifted his extended index finger in front of his face, slowly wiggling it back and forth.

Staring at the finger, the strings pulling his animation were cut, and the Team Leader returned his arms behind his back. A bit more composed now, he seemed to regain some of his bearing, and began to act more like a professional Noncommissioned Officer. Straightening up to a position just short of "parade rest," his body facing the Tech Sergeant, he turned his head and eyes to look slightly over the gentleman's head and began his tale again.

This time the gentleman listened, and the story ended quickly. Appearing to be satisfied, he turned his attention to the Tech Sergeant. His voice was low, and it rumbled. Had Lunchmeat and I not taken a few steps closer we would never had heard a word he said. In a heavily accented voice, reminding me of the accent Russian Officers had when I was stationed in West Berlin and interacted with them on a regular basis, he asked, "What is the problem here?"

The Tech Sergeant related the entire story, glossing over the part where the soldiers put magazines in their weapons, but other than that telling it pretty spot on.

"Yes. I see." Was all the gentleman had to say.

After a few seconds of contemplation, rubbing his chin with his right hand while he thought, the gentleman asked the Team Leader a few, curt questions. Receiving only one or two word answers in response. Continuing to stroke his jawline, between finger and thumb, he took a few more seconds to ponder the information in those answers, and having come to a conclusion returned the hand behind his back.

Looking up, into the face of the Tech Sergeant, the gentleman spoke again. "Do you know who I am?" He asked.

"No Sir." The Tech Sergeant replied. "I don't."

"I am the Ambassador for the Czech Republic to Iraq." Holy crap, we were now officially in the middle of an international incident.

"These men are part of the security at my Embassy." Here it comes. He was about to stomp a mud hole in this Tech Sergeant's chest, and there would not be a thing any of us would be able to do about it.

"I would like for you to follow your procedure, and confiscate their weapons. They do not need them to drive back to the Embassy. Please contact my Military Liaison when you are ready to release them, and he will come pick them up. I wish for you to put in your report everything that happened here, just as it happened. I know what you told me left out a few details, and I would very much like to read about them." And with that, he was done with the Tech Sergeant, and we were left to collect ourselves from the shock of our surprise.

Turning to fully face the Team Leader, the Ambassador launched into a set of instructions, both quiet and forceful, that left no room for doubt over whether or not they were going to be obeyed.

At the sound of the first word, the Team Leader popped to the position of attention so fast I thought the force of his arms slamming against his body, and his heels being jammed together, would cause him to grow an extra inch. Ramrod straight, he remained silent through the entire lecture, making no movement, uttering no sound, until his instructions were complete. Barking out, in Czech, what I could only guess was a resounding "Yes Sir!", he executed a parade field quality about face to stare at his soldiers, and snap out his instructions to the rest of the team.

I knew the Team Leader spoke very passable English, so I was pretty sure he understood what the Tech Sergeant was saying when he glossed over the magazine part of the incident. The Ambassador had also not allowed him enough time to fully recount his side of the story either, nor had his questions and the subsequent answers been long enough to provide him with additional information. How could he have known there was more? Did he guess? Had he been watching the incident unfold, only stepping in when needed? Had he thrown out an ambiguous statement, giving the impression he knew more that he did, or was this team a bit on the rogue side, and needed to be reined in from time to time?

Snapping out of my reverie, I gained the presence of mind to try and find the answers to my questions. Turning to where the Ambassador had been standing, I found he was already gone. Finished with this issue, he had done that thing they do, and re-expanded time and space. He was already on the other side of the parking lot walking away.

After that, this incident became down right easy. The Czech troops loaded their weapons in the trunk of the Tech Sergeant's vehicle, there were so many of them a couple of the machine guns had to be loaded in the back seat, and everyone willingly surrendered their I.Z. badges and I.D. cards so their information could be copied.

Having already been properly chastised, once the task was complete each soldier walked to their vehicle, silently got in, and quietly drove off. As if it were possible, even the vehicles looked slightly humbled.

21 July – Senators Obama and McCain came to town today. Time to comb out the dogs, and brush off the ponies. We received our briefing, and got our marching orders for the event yesterday, but I had never worked one of these where the itinerary did not change at the last minute, kept changing throughout the event, and I was not disappointed by this one either.

Their entire group, strap hangers included, were scheduled to fly by helicopter into the H.L.Z. just like any other flight. I positioned myself with Toro at the Main CAC, the midway point, so we could keep an eye on both the entrance to the H.L.Z. and the front doors to the Palace (the same set of doors Lunchmeat and I had been standing in during the rocket strike). Everyone in the Palace and the H.L.Z. were running around like ants on a mission, and as the time for the delegation to arrive got closer, the activity became even more frantic.

We watched helicopters land, we watched helicopters take off. We watched vehicles drive into the H.L.Z., we watched vehicles drive out of the H.L.Z. A whole lot of activity, but from my vantage point, the dignitaries were nowhere in sight. A little after 1300 hrs I finally got the word from Lunchmeat, the convoy was getting ready to move. The dignitaries had been piece-mealed in on all those choppers, and I was not able to see them through the T-walls as they arrived.

Because there were so many vehicles involved in the convoy we decided to call this Operation Night Train. Not only because there were going to be huge train of vehicles, but that also used to be the call sign for the MP Station in Darmstadt, Germany, way back in the day, and since Meat and I had both been MPs we thought it appropriate. In case I have not mentioned it yet, our radios broadcasted over unsecure, non-encrypted frequencies, and we figured the railroad motif provided us with the most amount of code-words that could be applied to the varying amount of vehicles.

All the passengers boarded the train. The engineers finally arrived (that would be the Senators), and the conductor (the Team Leader for the WPPS team) called all aboard. The train left the station (the H.L.Z.) with four engines (armored support trucks. Picture Brinks truck goes to war), fourteen box cars (armored sedans), and eight caboose (cabooses, caboose, caboosei? What's the plural on that one? Either way, those were the up-armored, machine gun mounted Humvees in the rear). As the lead engine entered the switch yard (the Palace), the first of the cabooses (I looked it up) was still on the H.L.Z. waiting to leave. A whole lot of vehicles and armor just to take two Presidential candidates, and 2 other senators, four hundred meters.

The limousines drove through the Main CAC, pulled under the portico at the center of the Palace, and stopped at the front doors. The Dignitaries were ushered from their vehicles, escorted through the airlock, and conveyed directly into the rotunda at the center of the Palace. All the proper hands were shook, all the proper babies were kissed, and all the proper pleasantries were exchanged. I kept forgetting, this was the kind of thing State Department lived for.

Once their charges had been escorted inside, the remaining WPPS guys were left to reposition the vehicles for the next leg of the trip. After lunch the group was supposed to take a tour of the Green Zone. After all the vehicles had been sorted Lunchmeat, Rak, and I went inside to see if we could help with anything on that end of the mission. The Complex Manager was not only responsible for everything that happened within the complex, he was also the Security Manager for all the guards manning the Palace proper. With all the possibilities for something to go wrong we were there to back him up.

Things went pretty smoothly until, yes, you guessed it, the C-RAM alarm went off. Bad juju time. We ran outside, under the portico, so we could clearly receive the radio calls from our guards. Everyone checked in, and all seemed to be good. There had been an explosion, beyond the Palace, in the Red Zone, and was so far across the river we were not too concerned about it. As all our posts were calling in we began to see the WPPS operators running out of the Palace, and positioning themselves by their cars. The realization of what was happening instantly occurred to us. I looked at Meat, and Meat looked at me. I looked at Rak, and Rak looked at me. Meat looked at Rak, and Rak looked at Meat. Simultaneously, we all lifted our radios back to our mouths, and started fast talking into them. The motorcade was getting ready to move a lot earlier than originally planned.

I took off for the Main CAC to get everyone prepared to expedite the convoy out. No sooner had I gotten there than the advance party showed up at the barriers wanting out. We dropped barriers, blocked all inbound traffic, and rolled the ADVON (Advanced Operational Node. They scout the roads ahead of the motorcade) through the gate with the main body right behind them. I guess the rocket was all it took for them to decide to get out of the Palace.

The convoy returned around 1800hrs that night. We got them inside without too much fuss, and handed everything off to the night shift. The Security Manager in charge of the guards inside the Palace was going to have his hands full that night, so Lunchmeat, Rak, and I decided to hang around to see if he needed a hand with any of the night's activities. Good thing we did.

You have to remember that I stood around six feet, five inches tall and weighed-out close to two hundred fifty pounds. Lunchmeat stood around six feet, three inches, and also went around two hundred fifty pounds. Together, we made up the Buffalo Brothers, also known as two thirds of the thundering herd. We were broad enough at the shoulders that we were not able to walk side-by-side down the halls in the Palace. It was not that we did not fit, but when we did there was not a lot of room for people to pass us in either direction. Needless to say, we blocked up the hallways pretty well.

He and I wound up getting tagged to help the Secret Service with crowd control while the Gentlemen walked the halls of the Palace. Tick took us to meet with the Secret Service Agent who would be our point of contact. In case I had not mentioned it yet, Tick was also a few inches over six feet tall, but his 250lb/260lb upper body looked more like a V, whereas Meat and I looked more like an H. Tick introduced us as former Military Police, and handshakes were made all around. Stepping back the Agent sized us up and down, and turned toward The Tick.

"Do you pay these guys by the inch, or by the pound?" He asked. "They should do fine."

Our roll was not glamorous. They just needed us to block the hallway so the Senators, and their entourage, had a clear path from the Main Entrance to the large, central room where they would be addressing the crowd. The same room with the coffee bar where I spent my night off. Taking up station on the far side of the double door entrance, Meat and I stood side by side. At the signal from the Secret Service Agent, we stopped people from walking down the hallway. Slowly, a crowd started to gather in front of us, and within a few minutes the advance team of agents turned from the hallway into the auditorium.

Soon, the people in front of us started getting excited, which suggested the Senators were approaching. I was only guessing because I did not want to turn and look, and take my eyes off my area of responsibility. The crowd moved forward, toward us, and Meat and I swung our arms away from our bodies to create a visible and physical barrier for them not to cross. Cell phones and cameras appeared, telling me the group was getting closer. I was willing to bet, most of the people who tried to take pictures of the Senators wound up getting pictures of me and Meat instead.

A tiny woman had worked her way to the front of the crowd, a bit in front of me, and a little to my left. She was waiving a picture in the air, and trying to get Senator Obama's attention. She wanted the Senator to sign the picture. With my gaze still front, I saw her thrust the picture over the shoulder of the person standing in front of her at the same time something hit me from behind. I had just been body-checked. Hit on my left side, I had to take a couple quick steps forward in order to keep my balance, and keep from chest bumping the person on front of me. By the time I was able to regain my balance, step back into position, and take stock of the situation to my front the whole thing was over. The lady was staring longingly at her picture, and the procession had moved on. I did not know who slammed into me. A Secret Service Agent? The Senator? An Aide? I was watching my A.O.R., which was not behind me. The one thing I did know was I never heard an "excuse me" or "sorry" or anything.

The rest of the evening ended up being long and fairly uneventful, which was not a bad thing in a combat zone. The Senators walked around a lot, made all the normal promises politicians make, and gave a couple of interviews before going off to bed. Thankfully, the crowd we had been dealing with consisted mostly of military and State Department folks, so there had been a bit more discipline exercised by those we had to corral then there would have been if we were dealing with straight-out civilians. I loved working with professionals.

22 July – It had been a couple of days. Lunchmeat and I were walking down the main hall inside the Palace today following several suits walking in front of us. We watched as they walked up to a few other suits, traded handshakes, and exchanged greetings. As we walked by this group my ears forced my feet to stop walking, for fear I might hurt myself, because my eyes suddenly tracked in the direction my ears were pointing, instead of looking where I was going.

Slowly, I shifted my focus toward the suits. One of them was energetically working his handshake with both hands. His face was beaming with excitement, and in the most enthusiastic voice I had ever heard, on or off the battlefield, he stated, "That was the greatest meeting! Dude! I have to get a copy of that Power Point presentation from you!"

I could die now. I had heard it all. This guy even made it sound like it was the best compliment he could ever give anyone. Suits should not go to war.

Earlier today, for some odd reason, they decided to fly Obama's part of the group out on V-22 Ospreys. I was not really sure why they made this decision, especially since these things did not have the greatest flying history. They used to fall out of the sky, from time to time, on takeoff and landing. I had been told, however, that the problem had been corrected. The H.L.Z. on the other hand, although quite big for helicopters, was not all that large for airplanes – even ones that could take off and land vertically.

The word must have gotten out that Ospreys, not helicopters, would be landing to pick up the delegation, as great throngs of people were assembled around the P.X. parking lot and South CAC to watch the event. Whether they wanted to be a part of the spectacle that had been the visit of the Senators, or they wanted to witness unique aircraft that had never landed in Baghdad before, I could not say. For those of us that have brains, and know how to use them, the Ospreys were the big thing we wanted to see. A pretty impressive sight, really.

If you are not familiar with this aircraft, it was designed for use by the Marines and Air Force. It is a bit bigger than a city bus, intended for use as a transport aircraft, and through the use of a tiltrotor was built to get into some rather tight places. During normal flight it looked and operated like any other propeller driven airplane. The wings were a little shorter, though, and the rotors were positioned on the ends instead of in the middle. It was only when the time came for this airplane to land that its unique design really set it apart from other planes. When presented with a short runway, or no runway at all, the tiltrotor came into play, and provided the aircraft with what was known as V/STAL (pronounced V-Stahl, this acronym stands for Vertical/Short Takeoff And Landing).

Flying through the air, in airplane mode, the pilot will slow the forward momentum of the aircraft by tilting the rotors (hence, tiltrotor) upward. This changes the aerodynamics of the craft from being an airplane to being a helicopter. Pretty cool, right? That was why the propellers were at the ends of the wings and not in the middle. With the props facing up, the pilot was able to land, or takeoff, with no roll-out; just like a helicopter.

Standing across the street from the South CAC, between the intersection and the bunker we had found the suspicious garbage bag in, I watched as two Ospreys banked away from the Tigris and started their approach to the H.L.Z. Engines pointing straight up, propellers churning, they flew one behind the other, a little off-set, slowly descending along the glide-path to the pad. For being as big as they were, I was surprised the engines and rotors did not sound much louder than any of the other helicopters that normally land here. What did catch me off guard was the tornado like prop-wash, as it kicked up all kinds of dust, pelting me with fine pieces of dirt.

To Everyone's surprise, except maybe the pilot's, there was plenty of room on the H.L.Z. for both birds. Everyone boarded their assigned plane, and within a few minutes, the engines revved up, the propellers beat the air into submission, and both aircraft gently lifted off the pad.

24 July - The natives were getting restless, again. We had just finished making our morning rounds, and returned to the office to type up our morning reports. For you old military folks, you should remember the morning report. Who was at work, who was on sick call, who was on first, all that good stuff. I was filling out my sheets when Lunchmeat's head popped up over his computer screen.

"Did someone just call "duck and cover" over the radio?"

Ooh, more scar tissue on the heart. I got up from behind my desk, and started walking for the door. As I drew closer, I could hear the duck and cover alarm going off outside.

"Yah, that's the D&C!" I confirmed.

Opening the door, I stepped into the threshold to see if I could get a better feel for where the alarm was coming from. While trying to figure it out I did not hear Lunchmeat walk up, right behind me, and was not aware of his presence until he kept on walking out the door, to stand on the porch. Walking through the doorway he raised his radio, to call his guards, when we heard the words we had come to loath, "In-coming! In-coming! In-coming!" blast from the speaker hanging next to our building. The C-RAM alarm just activated.

Remembering he had, once before, been oblivious to the sound of the C-RAM, I screamed "Meat! Get your ass in here! That's the bulls-eye alarm!"

I think I already explained the C-RAM alarm indicated rockets were going to fall where you were, usually, and the duck and cover alarm just meant rockets were landing somewhere.

Meat did a fairly accurate impression of Michael Jackson as he moon-walked back through the door, and into the office. We waited for a few seconds, expecting to hear the explosion any minute, and when we did not, walked back outside to see what was going on.

Reports started filtering across the radios and all our venues reported they were green (no explosions, no injuries, all equipment accounted for, etc.) There had been explosions, but they were over by the old Chancellery building. I guessed the insurgents were not getting all their memos. Everyone had left from over there at the beginning of the month to move into the NEC. Better them than us.

25 July – Well, it was bound to happen. Last night, one of the guards was sitting outside his trailer when he got shot in the shoulder. I guess I should say, a bit more accurately, a bullet struck him in the shoulder. Remember that whole "happy fire" thing? Yah, it finally happened. One of our guards caught a round in the shoulder. The bullet pierced the skin and imbedded a few centimeters, not even an inch, into the top of his chest cavity.

No one saw it coming; there had been no national celebration. It was not like the day the Iraqi team won the soccer game that put them into the World Cup; nothing. Just out of the blue, a bullet fell out of the sky into this guy's shoulder. They took him to the CaSH to have the bullet removed and he was going to be alright. I bet, by the time he gets home, he will have a pretty good story to go along with it as well.

The mercury got up to 120^0 F today.

26 July – Here is the set-up. Since Iraq was a rather dusty place, and the American government was trying to prop up the Iraqi economy, we were creating jobs for Iraqis as well as paying them for doing them. This part was not all that hard to understand. We did this after every major war where we won and occupied the territory. OK, so that means WWII. Anyway, if a young Iraqi man, between the ages of eighteen and thirty, was employed the chances he would join the insurgency dropped significantly. I got that part, too.

Trying to make Iraq a cleaner place, and make jobs, meant we employed a number of crews who traveled around the I.Z. cleaning public areas – parks, roads, sidewalks, stuff like that. Today was Saturday, and that meant today was the day the street cleaning crew was cleaning the road in front of the Palace, the road all my CACs, and most of my search pits, were on.

In the beginning, the crew would show up with brooms, shovels, wheelbarrows, and believe it or not, palm fronds. Yes, that is right, palm fronds. They used these huge leaves like brooms to help sweep all the dirt and dust off the roads and sidewalks. The dirt would get piled up, in little mounds, on the side of the road and the guys with the shovels and wheelbarrows would come along to scoop them up and dump them in a truck. Not wanting to pass up the opportunity to increase productivity, while decreasing human effort (and this was the part I needed someone to explain it to me), the government, K.B.R. with government funds, went out and bought a couple dozen leaf blowers.

In the beginning, there was the crew, and they worked hard. The streets were swept clean and the dirt was taken away. Although it was primitive, it was efficient, and it was good.

Anon, the government, sitting in high places, looked down upon the crew, and seeing their toil, took pity.

"Lo be unto you." their voices broke from the heavens, "for we have seen the sweat on your brow, the break in your back. Upon you will be bestowed technology, and machines, to make thine labors easy, and more efficient. Your burden shall be made light and your wages shall be achieved effortlessly." And there was much rejoicing.

In the coming days, wise men from the west were brought forth, bearing gifts of leaf blowers, and managers. The managers cast their eyes upon the crew and proclaimed, "We are from the government, and we are here to help" whereupon a leaf blower was bestowed, one to each crew.

On this day, there is the crew, and they do not work so hard. The streets are swept with the air of blowers, and dirt is lifted into the air, and not taken away. It is advanced and technological, and fifteen minutes after the crew is gone the dirt settles right back down onto the street to start the cycle all over again.

Some ideas look better on paper. But hey, they sure do brief really well, right? The cloud of dust created by the leaf blowers could be seen a mile away. Good one, guys.

122^0 F on the thermometer today.

28 July – They got an early start today. Around zero-seven-hundred we began getting reports from the towers of explosions to the South, across the river, in the Kadhimiya district. There were three of them. Rak took the reports from his guards and forwarded them on to the TOC.

The source of these explosions most likely centered around today being the anniversary of the death of the 7th Imam (he died back in 799 AD, so they had been celebrating it for a while.) Several branches of both Shi'a and Sunni, although mostly Shi'a, celebrated this as a period of mourning and made pilgrimages to the Mosque dedicated to him. That mosque happened to be right across the river. Our towers could almost see it.

A little context may help you understand the scope of the situation better, and give an idea of some of the things we had to deal with here. I was not all that clear on this celebration myself, and I had been here for more than a couple of years, but I will do my best to try to explain.

Where Western religions have Priests, Bishops, or Cardinals as religious leaders, Islam has Clerics. Where Catholicism has Popes, Islam has Imams. Sunni Muslims use the word Imam for anyone who leads the prayer, so each mosque has an Imam. However, Shi'a Muslims believe to be an Imam, the person must come from the family of, or be a descendant of The Prophet Mohammed. Additionally, they are considered to be divinely inspired and therefore infallible, like a Pope, when giving religious doctrine. Keep this in mind because their dedication to their Imams will become very relevant in a minute.

Different sects of Shiites believe there have been different numbers of Imams, with the least number being seven, and the most being twelve. I am not going to try to delve into all the differences and nuances between these sects, that would take too much time, and to completely understand them would take earning a degree by studying them, or growing up in the culture. Suffice it to say, celebrating the death of an Imam was an extremely emotional event, rooted in deep religious beliefs, and would be equivalent to, annually, celebrating the death of a Pope or other pinnacle of religious leadership.

The short version of the 7th Imam tells he was arrested and captured by the Caliph of the time (Harun al-Rashid), brought to Baghdad where he was imprisoned and subsequently poisoned to death, and later buried.

Thousands make the pilgrimage every year to the temple built over his gravesite, many of them performing rituals of self-flagellation. If you are unfamiliar with this practice, it means to whip, or beat, yourself. The idea behind this is twofold: one, the person is trying to prove dominance over a perceived weakness or fault; second, through pain they are trying to induce a trance-like state, from which they will enter a deeper religious experience, and bring them closer to the Devine.

During the middle-ages a small number of Christian faiths used to engage in this ritual as well, using flogs made from knotted ropes or chains, but their practice has since widely fallen into disuse. Among many of these faithful, though, the practice is still very much alive. (See where the dedication becomes relevant?)

With all these pilgrims converging on one central location, many of them performing highly emotional rituals, you could see where the opportunity for something bad to happen may develop. Large groups of people, around here anyway, not only tended to attract Mr. Murphy, the author of Murphy's Law, they also tended to attract rockets, mortars, and suicide bombers.

In 2005, the main group heading for the shrine was approaching one of the bridges across the Tigris, not too far away from the I.Z.. Tensions were high, being only two years after the initial invasion, and emotions were at a fevered pitch from the wailing, flailing, and religious outpouring that accompanied the throng. From somewhere, deep in the crowd, an accusation was shouted announcing there was a person strapped with explosives in their midst. The reaction was immediate, and chaotic, as people rushed the bridge in an attempt to flee.

Throngs of people stampeded across the span, packing on numbers greater than the structure could hold. As the mass grew larger the narrow confines of the bridge packed them together, tighter, and tighter. The back of the mob pushed the front to move faster, inflaming the panic to escape. The pressure became so great that eventually the side rails failed and gave way. Some, those who had not already been crushed to death in the pack, or trampled, fell directly onto the support pilings, thirty feet below, dying instantly on impact. Some were drowned trying to escape the river's current. Others gave their lives attempting to rescue victims unable to help themselves.

American Army forces, supporting Iraqi military police, did the best they could to secure as much of the area as possible, but the sheer numbers of people involved in the migration made it an almost impossible task. The explosions we heard this morning were suicide bombers. Not just any suicide bombers, reports say it was women wearing suicide vests. This was something that used to be very rare around here. Popular opinion still held only men could be martyrs, but it was starting to get a little less prevalent. It was a tactic Al Queda used. They killed or wounded over a hundred with their detonations in Baghdad alone, more were set off in Kirkuk.

124^0 F today. Looks like we may not hit 130^0 F again this year.

30 July – This morning, I was sitting in the office with Rak, and a few of the guards. We were filling in our morning paperwork, getting ready to start our first set of checks, when the radio came to life. Out of the corner of my ear, I thought I heard Lunchmeat's voice, "OK, everyone duck and cover."

My inner Scooby Doo came to life. EEEERRRRR? All ears perked up, Rak and I looked at each other, then both of us looked at the radio. No one had heard the C-RAM alarm go off. From standing behind my desk, I walked to the front door to see if I could hear it blasting outside; nothing.

I reached into my pocket and pulled out my cell phone, punched up Meat's number, and waited for him to answer. "That's right, I got a duck and cover going on." he said.

"Oh man, do me a favor. Let someone know before you start conducting drills like that. OK? I don't need any more scar tissue on my heart!"

"This isn't a drill. I really do have a C-RAM alarm going off!" Crap. Wonderful crap.

I still could not hear any alarms going off, however, no sooner had I hang up my phone when I started to hear jackhammer Spanish come over my radio. All the CAC's were checking in with green reports – no damage, no injuries, all equipment accounted for. OOOH, double crap, maybe this was the real thing? We did not hear any explosion, but that did not always mean anything.

Rak checked in with his supervisors, and after a few short, staccato bursts of Spanish (remember, he hablas the Espanol) confirmed a C-RAM alarm had, in fact, gone off, but no one was able to pin-point the exact location. Additionally, the lack of booms did little to help us figure it out.

The rest of the day played out in relative quiet, and eventually this alarm was filed away as more of a curiosity than a threat.

122^0 F today. Sometime during the first couple of weeks in August would be the hottest day of the year. Do not let anyone kid you, it did not really matter how much hotter it got, once the mercury rose above 120^0 F it was just plain hot and miserable.

CHAPTER 8

10 Aug – I do not know if I told you, but my security clearance finally came through approved, and was reactivated. I started the process back in March when I first volunteered to work in the TOC. That was the place where all the information from all the State Department venues got funneled to, and all the notifications that needed to be made came from. It only took five months to finally be complete, and some people would say that was not a long time.

Since I had a Secret clearance for the last twenty-three years, you would think all it would take to reactivate it would be for someone to pick up the phone and ask if I had a clearance. Maybe they forgot the phone number. Anyway, my clearance came back approved, and I filled out the additional paperwork, so now I have a blue badge. The same as all the "special" people I had to deal with at the CACs. I was due to start working in the TOC tomorrow night at twenty-three-hundred (11:00 PM for you silly-vilians), that was if Security Managers coming back from vacation got in.

Our rotation was supposed to be four months in country, one month out of country. Every month we sent groups of people home, and brought others back so we maintained a constant number of Managers on the ground. It tended to work like this. Those who were returning from vacation flew into Amman, Jordan. Their arrivals were spread throughout the day, so people tended to arrive in waves. Because we did not show up in one big group, a rally point had been established at a hotel in downtown Amman, the same one I told you about earlier. This gave everyone one last night of relative freedom (read that as the last time for good food and strong drink) before heading back into Iraq. We spent the night in the hotel, hopped a shuttle to the airport before the sun came up, and got on a plane bound for Baghdad.

Arrival in Baghdad was usually late in the afternoon, and because we flew commercial we did not land on the military side of BIAP (Baghdad International Airport, for those that may have forgotten), we landed on the civilian side. The company had a representative at the airport (call sign Castaway) whose sole purpose was stewarding our people through customs, getting them over to Victory Base, and manifesting them for the Rhino shuttle to the Green Zone (my helicopter ride, at the beginning of the year, was the test run for an alternate transportation plan that never panned out.) You remember the Rhinos, right? The big, armored busses that ran Route Irish back and forth between BIAP and the I.Z. late at night (read that as "what flipping time in the morning?!)

From waking up in Amman to arriving in the I.Z, (The International Zone. I know you have not forgotten that one, I just wanted to be thorough,) the trip usually took around twenty-four hours. The incoming Security Managers tended to arrive with enough time to get a couple winks of sleep before they started in-processing back into the project, and started work by noon. There were a few hours in the afternoon when a turn-over was conducted between the incoming and outgoing Security Managers, and by fourteen-hundred the people going home started out-processing so they could catch the Rhino out that night. Crazy, busy, and chaotic were pretty good terms to explain it. With such a tight time line, it did not take much to throw a monkey wrench in the process.

As long as everything went according to plan, I would work for a couple of hours tomorrow morning, train my replacement for a couple more hours in the afternoon and start working in the TOC tomorrow night. It should make for a fairly long day. We will see how it goes.

The thermometer in the parking lot reached 131^0 F today. For the first ten days of the month it flirted with the one hundred thirty mark, but today it actually broke it. So far, this had been the hottest day, and if we were lucky, it would start cooling off from here on out.

11 Aug – Russia invaded Georgia. It had been a couple of days since the hostilities broke out. Between then and now the contingent of Georgian soldiers stationed in the I.Z. pulled out of Baghdad to go home and fight their invaders. Boy, did those guys look scared. They used to have a pretty easy gig here in the Green Zone; they were in charge of Checkpoint Eighteen, across the causeway behind the NEC. Being a conscript Army, they tended to lack a bit in the discipline category, and now that they left we were learning they had been running scams out there the whole time. Iraqi's paid money to the guards, and the guards would bump them to the front of the line. I did not think the Russians were going to go for the scams.

128^0 F. I hoped this was the beginning of the cooling trend.

12 Aug - OK, maybe this would be the hottest day of the year. We got up to 134^0 F.

During my first August in Iraq, after the invasion, a group of us had been watching the thermometer pretty closely then too. Someone had loaded one with the company gear, and every time we stopped for more than a couple of days it would get unpacked and set up by the troop billets. Starting on August First we checked it at different times to see just how hot it got throughout the day. It did not take long for us to realize the peak would occur around fifteen-hundred, and by the fourth, or so, we would all gather around it at that time.

Temperatures that year had already been unreasonably hot, and for this place that meant a lot. June, July, gearing up in our armor, vests, basic load of ammo, helmets, what have you, the mercury had risen into the one-hundred-forties as we rolled out on daily missions. Once August rolled around temperatures rose into the one-hundred-fifties, and about the tenth of the month, as our little group gathered around, the thermometer maxed out at 156^0 F.

I do not possess words capable of describing to you how hot that actually felt without telling you to crawl into an oven and turning it on. You would have thought the Devil himself was sitting outside, smoking a cigarette, asking "Hot enough for you?"

The only way I can describe this kind of heat is to tell you to cup the palm of your left hand. Now, cup your right palm in the same way, off set your hands sideways, and place right on top of left. Keep your fingers tight together, thumb along the side. Make sure you have a good seal around the edges so no moisture escapes, and count, slowly, to ten; one Mississippi, two Mississippi, and so on. On the count of ten, lift your right hand away from the left. The heat was so incredible, the cup formed by your left palms would only need ten seconds to be filled to the top with sweat.

Do not dump it out yet. With your left hand now full of sweat, keep your right hand cleared away, and count to ten again; one Mississippi, two Mississippi, etc. By the time you hit ten, again, the dryness of the heat would have caused all that sweat to evaporate, and your palm would again be dry.

And these people choose to live here.

19 Aug – Looks like we were beyond the peak temperature for the year. It had been a few days since the thermometer broke the one hundred thirty mark, and today was the closest we had gotten to doing it again, 127^0 F.

21 Aug – It had been a little while since the last time I was able to write about anything happening here. It was not like I had been busy, believe me, it was all I could do to keep from stabbing myself in the eye with a fork just to stay awake.

The rotation made it in on time, and all the handovers went as smoothly as could be expected. I started working in the TOC as scheduled, and was making the transition from the day shift back to night shift. Not just the night shift, but the midnight shift. After working twelve hour shifts as a Security Manager, I was now working an eight hour shift, and it did not start until twenty-three-hundred. Not a lot happened around here that late at night. I had heard a rumor, though. Someone was planning on opening a strip club on the other side of town. I heard it would feature full facial nudity.

Now that I had gotten into the routine of sleeping during the day again, it was not so bad. My shift only lasted eight hours, as opposed to twelve hours working the CACs, and I had gotten a bit of a pay raise as well. Having worked the past year and a half on twelves, I was not really sure how to fill up the extra 4 hours a day I had.

I was trying to stay busy by going to the pool every day, and swimming laps for a while. It was still hot enough for the bikinis to be out, which was nice, and the rockets had stopped falling with a frequency, so I was not all that worried about getting blown out of the water. But, from time to time, being at the pool reminded me of Angel.

It was still disappointing to me we did not have longer to get to know each other better. All the times Meat and I had cut through the pool, admiring her and Kayla as we walked, only to finally meet them, and strike up a conversation the day before they left was a little more than ironic. It almost bordered on depressing. I should probably explain a little something so I do not sound too pathetic; I was divorced, more than a couple of times. Each time was the result of infidelity, theirs not mine, so I already had a few trust issues where women were involved.

I realized I could have met her earlier, had I just found the courage to speak up, and my disappointment was more focused on me, and it being a self-inflicted wound. The thing that grinded at me more, however, was how she just disappeared without warning, after giving the impression she would like to see me again. It was difficult not to see that as reinforcement for my lack of trust in people. It also made me realize, with this being a war zone and all, people unexpectedly leaving may only be a medevac away. An echo back to what Chief had reminded us on prime rib night, not everyone left Iraq upright. People came, people went, and there was not always an explanation. Moving on would probably be the best way for me to deal with it, I guess, and dwelling on it only created roadblocks.

Having left the camaraderie of the Thundering Herd, more specifically knowing I had ready and willing backup during any incident, any crises, had also become more difficult in coming to terms with than I would have previously imagined. The team we created among ourselves, and our guards, had become solid, our own band of brothers. Our boss even commented, several times, on how our integration made his job a lot easier, and the support we gave him was indispensable. Our labors had culminated in creating something of a fiefdom at the Palace, spoken of with admiration by some of the other Security Managers and company staff, jealousy, if not outright contempt, by others. Nothing happened in our little world without us knowing about it.

No longer having Lunchmeat's constant backup, companionship, counsel, was something I felt more deeply. Since leaving the CACs I had felt slightly off balanced, like I was heavier on one side than the other. It was not so much the feeling I heard described by amputees, ghost pains in the missing limb, a phantom feeling the appendage was still there until they looked for it, and found it gone. It was more like part of me had faded. Been diminished. I still had all my arms and legs, but my center of balance felt like it had shifted more to one side, leaving me lopsided.

Walking posts several times a day, day in day out, had given us the opportunity to bond. Weathering the hazards of many uncertain, possibly explosive, incidents forged that bond into genuine respect. Refusing to allow the other to go alone in harm's way had made us brothers; Buffalo Brothers. Now, once again, I was back in a position requiring me to work more solo than as part of a team.

This was not to mean I was alone in the TOC during my shift, I was one of a small crew of people manning operations, it meant I was the one person in the TOC representing the team we had created. I was no longer out there with them, leading my portion of the group, heading up our operations and responses, organizing the left and right to maintain cover and security. Instead, I was removed from them not only by distance but by time, they remained on the day shift, and I had to try and adapt to this new team of which I had become a part.

Not ready to sever all ties I worked so hard to become comfortable with I still maintained contact with Lunchmeat and Rak. Sometimes, in the afternoon, before the end of day shift I went out to the parking lot, and shot the breeze with Meat. Every now and again I stopped by the office to chat with Rak. I did not check posts with them anymore, even though there was time in my new schedule to do so, because I did not want to cause difficulty for my replacement, or for the guards.

My replacement now conducted the checks with Lunchmeat and Rak, like we used to. If I were to show up at my old posts, along with the new guy, my presence may undermine his ability to take charge of them. It might also place the supervisors and guards in a moral dilemma; wanting to stay loyal to me, cast from the time, training, and incidents we shared, when they should be building loyalty to him.

I did meet with all the day shift Security Managers every evening though, after changeover, for dinner, and sit down with them in the Deli DFAC to eat and catch up on the events of the day. It still gave me a feeling of belonging with them, although to a much lesser degree.

Instead of being out on the ground during the busiest parts of the day dealing with issues, solving problems, my new job revolved more around coordination. The highlight of my night was to call the Security Manager responsible for notifying the dog handlers to go to the Rhino Staging Area and sniff the baggage (the dogs did that, not the handlers) of all the folks just arriving in the I.Z. That was it, nothing more.

Of course, every now and again, we got something different. Tonight I got a call, around zero-two-hundred, from some guy in the United States. "Hi, my name is Joe Schmuckatelly. I want a job in the I.Z. My qualifications are....."

"Whoa! Hold up there, high speed. You do realize you've called the Tactical Operations Center for the State Department in Iraq, don't you?"

"Yah, I want a job in Iraq. I speak Arabic. I…"

"Dude, this isn't Human Resources. It's the Operation Center. We don't do the hiring."

"Well, put me through to someone who does."
Yah, it did not work that way. Google the contracting companies in Baghdad, and send them a resume, just like the rest of us did.

Once I called the dogs for the Rhino, I tried to get out of the TOC and walk around the grounds for an hour or so. With the TOC located deep inside the north wing of the Palace, I did not want to start losing touch with the outside posts and activities. There were only a couple more weeks to go before I was to go out for my rotation, and there was no guarantee I would return to the TOC when I came back. For now, I was getting a lot of reading done, and a little lamenting over what I had given up.

26 Aug – We were notified a few days ago that two hundred insurgents were planning to attack the Palace and/or the NEC within the next four days. We were waiting for them, but so far nothing happened. Go figure. It was hard enough to get two Iraqis on the same sheet of music about anything. Getting two hundred of them together, figure the odds. We had a number of C-RAM activations at night since the warning was put out, but they all ended up being false alarms. That did not stop the heart from skipping a beat or two, though.

It had gotten to the point where, once I made the call for the dogs, I checked with the Watch Officer to make sure I was not immediately needed, grabbed the TOC cell phone, so he or any of the Security Managers could contact me, and went for a walk. My first stop was the staging area, to make sure the dog team got there, and chatted with the Security Manager while the dogs checked the luggage. Then I went for a fast paced walk around the

Palace grounds. Sitting for eight hours was about to kill me.

The temperatures were holding steady in the one-twenties during the day. Although that did not qualify as comfortable by any stretch of the imagination, the worst of the heat seemed to be behind us.

Night time temps, however, tended to drop into the low eighties, sometimes the high seventies. With nothing here that effectively retained the heat generated by day time temperatures, and no cloud cover to act as a blanket and keep the heat in, the warmth evaporated fairly quickly. When compared to stateside weather it may sound like it got comfortable over here after dark, but the reality was it got down right chilly. Anywhere else eighty degrees would normally be balmy, however, considering it was a forty degree drop from the day time high, having a light jacket available was not a bad idea.

28 Aug—Grown men could be such cry-babies. We had several Security Managers who worked at the Palace, and other near-by-venues, living in the basement of the Palace now that the Marine FAST team had moved out. I was

able to trade my trailer for one of those rooms, and now there were around a dozen of us living down there. However, trying to get a dozen grown men to clean up after themselves was like pushing a chain. Every one of them had at least fifteen years of military background, a prerequisite for getting hired for this project, with most of us being fully retired from the military.

Last night I finally had had enough. One of the pigs had moved all the garbage out of his room, and left it in the hallway for almost a week. I guess he expected someone to take it the rest of the way to the trash for him. Yesterday, the Complex Manager escorted some soldiers down here to show them the area. While they were looking around they commented on how trashed the place looked. We were down here with R.S.O.s permission, and making the place look like a pig sty was a good way to get kicked out. Some people just did not get it.

Frustrated and fed up with the childishness of others, I started clearing some of the stuff out of the hallway, and must have started something. Lunchmeat, Rak, and I wound up cleaning the whole area last night. Sweeping, mopping, cleaning the latrines, everything.

The pigs that made the place look like crap, none of them showed up to help with any of it. Thanks guys.

It had been four days since we were promised the two hundred insurgents who were going to storm the walls, and nothing had happened. During the day there had been a bunch of explosions out in the Red Zone, close to the I.Z. but nothing for us.

They had a saying over here. "Me against my brother. Me and my brother against my cousin. Me, My brother, and my cousin against everyone." These people could not stop fighting about anything with anyone. It was almost like it was in their blood. If they were not ganging up on the Americans, the Sunnis were killing the Shi'as, or one tribe was fighting another tribe. When Big Army pulls out in 2011, it looks like it is going to be a free for all over here.

30 Aug - A busy night last night.

It started out as a regular, slow night and I was going about my normal routine of looking for anything to keep me busy until the Rhinos arrived from BIAP. The R.S.O. riding in the lead vehicle had already called over the secure radio frequency telling us they were departing, so I was not going to have long to wait.

A small issue came into play here because once we got the call saying the Rhinos were moving, I was unable to pass that heads-up directly to the dog handlers because our cell phones were not secure, and most of the dog handlers did not carry radios, only the supervisors did (it had to do with not triggering radio-control detonated devices). Still having a little trouble seeing the problem? Let me pull the lens back a bit, and see if the bigger picture helps.

To underestimate the enemy was a classic blunder. With this in mind, remember the cell phones and radios the State Department had provided the Security Managers all operated on unsecure frequencies. To underestimate the enemy would be to assume (and you know what happens when you assume, you make an ass out of you and me) they had not gone to the local equivalent of Radio Shack, bought a programmable radio receiver, used it to scan for our frequencies, and were now listening to our broadcasts. With this new information, if I were to call on one of these unsecure frequencies, I would be defeating the purpose of the R.S.O. calling over the secure frequency, and alerting the bad guys that the convoy was moving so they could set up their ambush. Starting to get the picture?

Moving a little further down the time line. Not being able to call the dogs until the Rhinos were in the I.Z. meant we had a very small window in which to get the dogs on station, so they could sweep the luggage as soon as possible, and disperse the group so they ceased being a big, inviting target of people. In other words, we were totally reactive, had to respond quickly, and work effectively.

While monitoring the progress of the Rhino convoy, I got a call from my counter-part at the BDOC. He called to notify me there had been a Mercedes car, with a couple of Iraqis inside, over by the Gold Dome Gate, right next to the old Ministry of Defense – M.O.D. (you may remember it from the shock and awe videos showing the bombing of Baghdad. It was the triangle shaped building that looked like a pyramid with the top removed). The alarming part was they were driving around the IZ shooting pistols in the air. Remember how we talked about "Happy fire" and "Allah's fireworks"?

Now the thing that made it difficult to process this information, and alert all my venues in danger, was the fact that this was all they had; a dark blue Mercedes, no mention of the type, no mention of how many doors. Oh yah, they did mention it had Iraqi license plates on it, so I guess I could forgive them for not having the plate number. In case you did not know, Arabic numerals are not.

Let me explain that. When most people use the description "Arabic numerals", they are referring to the numbers we have become accustomed to in the west; 1,3,5,7, etcetera. This is not an entirely accurate description. "Arabic numerals" actually refers to the system of numbers containing a zero, used as a place holder, and a sequence of digits that are read as a numeral. Clear as mud, right?

Let me try this. Roman numerals have a different, unique symbol for every number in existence, starting with a base character, and positioning other characters around it; 1 = I (a base character), 3 = III, 5 = V (another base character) and 7 = VII. Arabic numerals only use ten different characters (0 through 9), arranged in different orders, to express every number in existence.

But, you ask, how does that explain how Arabic numerals are not? And the answer is; the system was originally invented in India, not Arabia, and because of this Arabic has its own symbols for numbers that look nothing like ours. For example; 1 = ١ , 3 = ٣ , 5 = ٥ , 7 = ٧. Get the idea? (To answer the follow-on question, the system was probably called Arabic because it was introduced to Western culture by the Arabs. Interestingly, in the Arab world, they do not call the system "Arabic numerals", they call it "Hindu numerals".)

Back to my more pressing problem, they could not even tell me if there were men or women in the car. Of course, being where we were, the good money bet was they were men. I guessed the bottom line he was trying to pass on was that there was a German car, with Iraqi people in it, driving around in the I.Z., shooting off guns. Not as strange an occurrence as you might think.

Of course, it could not be enough for me to have to get this information out to all of my Security Managers, especially the few within a couple hundred meters from the reported location, but the Rhino had entered the I.Z. around this time too, and I could not get in touch with the Security Manager responsible for bringing the dogs. And, just because I was not frustrated enough, I also had two other Security Managers calling with questions about matters completely unrelated to anything going on at the time. I could never have just one thing to deal with; they had to come in bunches.

As the unrelated phone calls came in, I asked the Security Managers if they had emergency information for me. They must have been confused by the question because they stammered and stuttered before spitting out that their calls were not emergency oriented. I gave them a quick rundown on the BOLO (pronounced like the long, curved machetes they use in the Philippines, it stands for Be On the Look Out), told them to call me back in an hour if they still needed an answer to their question, and quickly rang off with them so I could keep trying to call the dogs.

Time was dragging on, without successful contact, and I was doing my best to alternate calls between notifying Security Managers of the possible threat, calling for the dogs on the phone, and attempting to reach the Security Manager by radio. The Rhinos had been sitting in the staging area long enough I was sure the R.S.O. on site would soon be getting fidgety about the large cluster of passengers, whose safety he was responsible for, standing around in the open. It would not be long before he reached the end of his patience, called the TOC, and started chewing on someone's butt until the dogs got there. Since that butt was probably going to be mine, I decided on conducting a little pre-emptive damage control.. I turned toward the Watch Officer, and was about to ask him to contact the Rhino R.S.O. to let him know the dogs were running a bit late, when the phone on my desk rang.

Crap! I had not been fast enough. This was going to be the Rhino R.S.O. and he was going to kick my butt cheeks up around my shoulders like a back pack. With a fateful sigh of resolution, I picked up the receiver, and prepared for the onslaught I was sure I was about to receive.

"R.S.O. TOC, This is Rooster. How can I help you?"

"Rooster, it's Top. I hear you're looking for me."

It was the Security Manager in charge of contacting the dogs, not the Rhino R.S.O. Battling between frustrated rage at his being out of contact for so long, and relief this was not the butt chewing I had been expecting, it took me a second to get control of myself.

"Top! Where the hell have you been?" I cried. "Never mind, never mind. It's not important." I continued as I gained control over my frustration. "Get the dogs over to the Rhino Staging area, would ya'? They've been there for quite a while now, and I'm sure the R.S.O. is starting to get a bit antsy."

"Sure. No worries." He chirped, and hung up. What the hell??

A few dozen seconds later my frustration had down-graded to mild annoyance, and I picked up the hardline phone on my desk to call the last Security Manager in reference to the BOLO. I placed the receiver to my ear, and was about to dial the number when I realized there was no dial tone. None, whatsoever. Only dead air. Oh, what fresh hell is this?

"Hello?" I asked with great confusion.

"Hello?" Came the confused response.

It would seem I picked up the receiver before the phone had rung. How about that? Quickly recovering from my surprise, I shifted gears.

"R.S.O. TOC. This is Rooster. How can I help you?"

"Rooster, its Baldo. Up in the JDOC.

"JDOC? I thought you worked in the BDOC?"

"Six one way, half a dozen the other. Someone, somewhere, decided to change the name from Base Defense Operation Center (BDOC) to Joint Defense Operation Center (JDOC). Personally, I think some Officer just needed a bullet statement on their Officer Evaluation Report. Ya' know what I mean? Anyway, I just wanted you to know you can cancel the BOLO on the Mercedes. I.A. and Iraqi police just pulled a traffic stop on the vehicle, and took custody of three local nationals."

Because my curiosity was getting the better of me, I just had to ask. "What were they doing driving around the I.Z. shooting?"

"If I understand the interpreter correctly, they were coming from a bachelor party, drunk, and they still wanted to celebrate."

Stunned, I could only wonder. Where in the decision making process did it become a good idea to get rip snorting drunk, pile into a car, and start driving around a city, which currently happened to be in the middle of a war zone, and shoot guns in the air? No wonder Mensa did not have a chapter in Iraq, not a lot of geniuses around here.

One more time I hit the phones and called everyone to cancel the BOLO. Jokes? Everyone had one for this story. Hanging up the phone from my last notification, I checked my watch, and found barely an hour had passed since the Rhino first called they were moving. Now what was I going to do to pass the rest of the night?

CHAPTER 9

13 Sep – Not a whole lot going on in the beginning of this month. Working the midnight shift in the TOC did not lend itself to a busy work environment. It was not like working the midnight shift L&O (Law and Order) on a military post. Besides, this was Baghdad, not really a partying town. This was also the State Department, not so many loose party people. Additionally, just about everything that happened up here in the TOC was classified, so if I told you everything we did, I would have to cut your head off and put it in a safe. (Just kidding, that would make it a little difficult to convince anyone to buy this book.)

The time had come for me, and a few other Security Managers, to take some time off and head home for much needed R&R (Rest and Relaxation). Today, we started our out-processing. I already talked a little bit about this process, but just to recap; normally the Security Managers coming back from their rotation would arrive early in the morning on the Rhino (the same Rhino run I call the dogs to every night). They headed over to our project camp, got a little shut-eye, in-processed in the morning, walk around their venues with the out-going Security Manager in the afternoon and, bang, they got it.

I went to the Rhino area this morning to watch the Rhino come in, and unload the returning personnel; there were no Security Managers on board. Problem!

The company used to send us in and out through Amman, Jordan. When we took that route we would spend the rest of the day in Amman, and we would fly out the next morning. Bunches of wiggle room for those of us leaving on our rotation to make connecting flights. Now, we were flying through Dubai with only a couple of hours to lay-over between flights. Not so much wiggle room.

Not really knowing how this change-over was going to pan out, as soon as I got off shift this morning I went straight to bed. I woke up around fourteen-hundred, drank some coffee, dressed, and took all my stuff to the office on the Palace grounds in the hope the incoming Security Managers had arrived, and those of us leaving would be able to out-process. As luck would have it, all the other out-going Security Managers from the Palace had the same idea, and everyone was gathering, getting ready to head over to our project's Camp for out-processing. I love it when a plan comes together.

Loading into the few vehicles assigned to the Palace venues, bag and baggage, we made the short trip down Haifa Street, around 14 July Circle, and onto al-Khindi Street on the way to the camp. Unloading at the main gate, we turned in all our stuff – guns, bullets, radios, phones -- stored all the gear and clothes we were not taking with us, and returned to the Palace to relax and wait for our final out-briefing later that night. Still, no incoming Security Managers were boots on the ground. This part of the plan was not coming together. I hate it when that happens.

Later, less encumbered by our luggage, we loaded back into the vehicles and returned to the camp for our out-briefing. Arriving back at the main gate to the camp for the second time today, we were met by shouted greetings from the returning Security Managers, the incoming guys had just shown up.

Since having a ticket did not mean all that much in this part of the world, especially when bribery was still a common, if not expected practice, not all of the returning Security Managers were able to get on their originally planned flight. Some of them wound up having to take a later flight, at a less than convenient hour, and the company had to send a P.S.D. team (I know, it has been a while, so if you do not remember P.S.D. means Protective Security Detail, here is a reminder) to BIAP to pick them all up. Well, at least they were here. It also did not help that this was the time of Ramadan, and it appeared the entire Muslim world was trying to get on the same planes they had been.

How was this being Ramadan relevant to our travels? Good question. Ramadan is observed for an entire month, and is a time of fasting and sacrifice to gain greater religious understanding. Between sunup and the conclusion of sundown, Muslims are not allowed to eat or drink anything, so you can see how tempers may get a little short by the end of the day, especially after having had nothing to eat or drink all day long. Add to this the effect of fasting for an entire month, and you can guess how, as the month progressed, tempers could get even shorter. This also happened to be the most venerated month on the entire Islamic calendar, and judging by the numbers of travelers, It looked like everyone wanted to spend it with family. The headaches were much similar to those you would get trying to travel during the Christmas holidays.

The other good part about this rotation was we would not Rhino out in the middle of the night, only to have to sit around Victory Base for hours, and then BIAP, waiting for our flight. One of the company P.S.D. teams would be taking us straight to BIAP in the morning, so we got to sit around here and wait to leave instead.

So, here I sat in my room, my empty room. Having been working the midnight shift for the past month, and sleeping all day, I was not all that tired. Fortunately, I down-loaded a couple of movies to my computer, there was coffee upstairs in the little deli, and I could still nap before starting the journey home tomorrow. We would see how this one went. Oh yea, did I mention the dust storms started up again tonight?

15 Sep – Well, I guess no trip is ever without its problems. We all met over at the Palace office early in the morning to get a ride to our project's camp. Just to make sure there is no confusion, early around here meant zero-dark-hundred. I mean the birds were not even up yet. No sooner had we gathered then we got on the bus, and rode the

whole five minutes over to the company's main camp. When we got there, we met up with the dog handlers who were leaving with us, and we all sat around waiting for our P.S.D. ride to BIAP. The dust storm that had started brewing last night was still blowing lightly across the city. It had not grown in its intensity, but it had not yet blown itself out either.

Of course, one of the managers for the company's P.S.D. program spotted this large group of people lounging around his camp, and came over to ask what we were all doing there. We had been briefed on the plan. It was a good plan. We were confident in what was going to happen, and we knew what we were doing. "We're waiting to P.S.D. to BIAP" we chorused with great conviction.

"What? You guys were supposed to Rhino out last night. I don't know anything about a P.S.D. mission this morning." And off he stormed.

Confused, we stared at each other not exactly sure what was going to happen. I guess someone, somewhere, knew about us because the transport truck and escort vehicles arrived just a couple of minutes later. Earlier, I told you about the Rhino, it was basically an armored bus.

The transport they were going to put us in was just a little different. Imagine a five ton truck with the bed taken off. Now, take one of those big recycling dumpsters, make it taller, put thick metal plates on the outside, and benches along the inside. Add tiny, little windows down the side, a tiny, little air conditioner toward the front, and that constituted our ride. I will have to get back to you on how this is better than a Rhino.

We got everyone together, sorted out, loaded up, and started our convoy to the airport. Route Irish had changed a lot since the last time I had been on it. It also looked a lot different in the day time. All the T-walls that used to line the sides of the highway had been pushed back one hundred yards or so, and they had added checkpoints to every on and off ramp to inspect cars and control traffic flow. It was now pretty open and scenic. It looked like they were starting to make more changes out there, dare I even say progress.

Dawn finally broke as we were making our way down Route Irish, and now that the sun had crossed the horizon we could see how much the dust storm had settled in. It was blowing a bit like some of the snow storms you get up north, when the wind blows just lightly enough, and the snow falls just gently enough, it was more of a nuisance than a threat; conserving its strength so it could last all day.

Of course, BIAP was pretty much the hassle all airports were. For those of you who think the screening processes to get into an airport in the U.S. are excessive, boy, you do not have a lot to talk about. There was only one area at BIAP where passengers could be dropped off to catch their departing plane, only one for all of them, and this was where the gauntlet began.

Whether you arrived to catch a plane, or were accompanying someone who was catching one, everyone must process through the first checkpoint located outside the building. The first barrier was designed to funnel the throng into a single file line, and was only open long enough to allow a specific number of people to pass.

Once through you were directed to where the passengers lined up their baggage, checked and carry-on alike, in an area located between two rows of blast walls. Bags were lined up to allow easier access for the bomb dogs to sniff them, and the blast walls were to funnel any explosion up and away from the building. While the dogs were checking the luggage, all the people were shuffled around the corner where they underwent a hands-on pat down search, and visual inspection of everything in their pockets. There was no choice of a body scan, or an air sample test, everyone went through the hands-on-check.

Once the dogs were satisfied there were no explosives in the bags, and the pat-down search revealed nothing of significance on the people, everyone was allowed to retrieve their luggage and head off for the front door of the airport. No, there was no such thing as curb-side check-in in Baghdad. The flood gates opened and a mad rush of people cascaded into the search area to collect their bags, and rush off to be first in line at the next checkpoint.

The flow of travelers, bags in hand, slung over their shoulders, or pushed along on carts poured down the sidewalk along the front of the terminal only to be bottled up again at the main entrance. At the outer door of the terminal passports and I.D. cards were scrutinized before anyone was allowed to walk through the metal detector, and enter the building. All bags, baggage and the contents of every pocket were placed on a conveyor belt to make the slow progression through a scanner, before they could be retrieved on the other side by their owners. That is right, everyone and everything had been subjected to two separate searches before they ever set one foot inside the building.

Do not stop to take a breath just yet, so far we have only made it inside the front doors. Just like there was no curb-side check-in over here, the boarding pass counter was also located a little farther inside the airport than in the States. You could not just walk in the door, walk up to the counter, and get your boarding pass. That would be too easy, and access to this area could only be achieved by what? Yes, you guessed it, going through another security checkpoint, but this time only those that had a ticket in their possessions were allowed to process through and get their boarding pass. Tickets were purchased at a totally separate counter, well away from the terminals.

One more time, our passports and I.D. cards were checked, only this time they were checked against the name on our ticket. We were corralled into a maze of ropes that herded us to the next baggage scanner and archway. This time, the inspection was more familiar to any traveler who had gone through a U.S. airport. The contents of your pockets were dropped in one tray, your belt and shoes went in another, and any electronics went in a third. The whole lot went through yet another scanner, while we walked through the metal detector archway. For those of you not keeping track that made for three checks, and we had not even made it in to the terminal yet.

We were looking for the counter that would issue us the boarding pass for our flight out of Baghdad. Fortunately, all the signboards in the airport were written in English as well as Arabic. This was where tempers would usually start to wear thin, and folks began to show their agitation. Why, you ask? Because, as a society, Iraqis seemed to feel they did not have to stand in lines. The pushiest person tended to get to the front of the line, and the loudest person seemed to get served first. Additionally, social standing, class, and status were very important to this society, and if any one of the locals felt they possessed any one of those attributes they would not be seen waiting in line behind a bunch of infidels. At this point you should be realizing how this did not go over very well with a bunch of "Type A" personalities; hence, tempers. Fortunately, our company employed an American, known as an Expeditor, and a couple of locals to help the entire group speed through this process.

Iraqi Air flights were general seating flights, so the boarding pass did not guarantee you a specific seat, just that there would be enough seats for everyone on the flight. The trick for the Expediter was to make sure he was able to get enough passes for everyone. Remember that whole bribery thing I mentioned earlier? It was a real thing over here, and with the right amount of cash flashed to the right person boarding passes could be lost, found, or exchanged with ease.

With our coveted boarding pass in hand, we were now clear to move on to the terminal, and wait for our flight. Clear to move on, that was, after going through yet another security checkpoint. Boarding passes and passports were checked by passport control, this was where they logged us out of the country. One more baggage inspector got the opportunity to rummage through our luggage to see if there was anything in there he liked.

Having run the full length of the gauntlet, I collected my bags from the conveyor belt and walked into the terminal having been patted, poked, scanned, and processed no less than four times, and I had not yet made it to the plane. The inside of the terminal was fairly standard. A collection of chairs and couches were arranged for the traveler to lounge on while waiting for their flight to be called. The ubiquitous duty-free shop selling all the normal wares, with the exception of alcohol, was represented, and a few food stalls selling the local equivalent of fast food were there too.

I had lived through more than one combat zone, been shot at more than I liked, and had more than a couple of rockets explode uncomfortably close to me, but I still did not have the courage to eat any of the food they sold at those stalls. Instead, I slept. I had grown accustomed to working at night, and sleeping most of the day, and since I had not gotten a lot of sleep last night it seemed like the most productive thing I could do. I dropped my bags next to one of the couches, found a comfortable, out of the way spot on the floor next to my gear and barely remember lying down.

Five minutes. I could not have had my eyes closed for more than five minutes when one of the guys kicked me in the ribs. "Get your ass up or we're leaving you." He kindly growled down at me.

A less than ideal situation, in a less than comfortable location, I hauled my half sleeping carcass off the floor, tripped over my bags, almost hit a little kid with my backpack while trying to put it on, and headed off in the wrong direction three times before I was able to locate a familiar face. I stumbled my way over and got in line. Crap! How I had made it through rocket fest without getting myself killed was anyone's guess at this point. Having been not so quick on the jump was not helpful either. I was in the back half of the boarding line. With seating on the plane being general, not assigned, my place in line assured I was going to get a lousy seat for this leg of the flight.

The line shuffled and stalled, ebbed and flowed, started and stopped until I finally made it to the gangway entrance. Being a natural choke-point, what did I find sitting there but another baggage scanner and metal detecting archway. Off came the shoes, the belt, and the watch. On to the conveyor belt went the bags and trays. Through the scanner went my stuff, and through the archway went I. I will give you three guesses as to what happened on the other side of the archway and the first two will not count. If you guessed absolutely nothing happened, like the four times before this, you would be absolutely right. Go figure.

I walked down the gangway, glancing out the windows, and noticed the dust storm that had been quietly blowing all morning looked like it was picking up a little. Not too much of a problem, right? I mean, this kind of stuff happened in Baghdad all the time, and as long as we were boarding the plane that was a good sign, right? Doing my best to push all the negativity to the back of my brain, I picked up the pace and headed down the ramp. This was going to be my first trip back home since March and I really did not want anything to screw it up, least of all negative thoughts.

If we got the plane loaded, butts in seats, and out on the taxiway in a timely manner, we should be able to beat this storm. I ducked my head to walk through the porthole, into the plane, and as soon as I had the head room to raise my chin, I scanned my eyes over the passenger compartment to find the center isle completely chock full of people. General seating meant everyone was jockeying for the best available spot. Stuffing hags in overhead bins, shoving what was left under the seat in front of them, the cabin was an assault of sound and movement. So far this was not looking good.

I shouldered and elbowed my way down the aisle to the first open seat I could find, four rows from the back of the plane. Having dropped off my checked bag when I picked up my boarding pass, I only had my backpack to stow in the overhead compartment. The frantic scrambling for empty chairs was drawing to a close, and I was able to squeeze my way into an aisle seat. As I looked across the cabin it appeared there was a seat for everyone and everyone was in their seat.

The flight attendant was working his way down the aisle, checking the seat belts and seat backs, when he stopped just a couple of rows ahead of me. An Iraqi man had brought a large cardboard box on board with him instead of checking it in as luggage, and with all the seats filled and the overhead compartments stuffed he had decided to place the box in the aisle; and it took up the entire aisle. His left arm was casually draped over the box, as if it was a mere extension of his armrest, and he was happily chatting with the guy seated next to him. Anyone who had flown any distance at any time knew this was a no-no, and I could not believe my ears when the passenger started to argue with the attendant about it.

I did not speak a lot of Arabic, but it was not hard to figure out the content of this conversation, and the more the attendant spoke and pointed at the box the more the passenger would protest and wave his arms around. I sat in my seat, stunned, unable to believe what I was seeing and even less equipped to do anything about it. As the argument progressed I felt a small bit of relief as some of the other passengers seated close by joined in. It could only be possible they were just as aware of the dust storm brewing up outside as I was. Just like me, they must have had places they needed to be, and they must have wanted this plane to get in the air as badly as I did. I was sure with the overwhelming support of the other passengers the flight attendant would be able to quickly convince this guy to have his box put in the luggage compartment and we would be able to beat this storm into the air. Buoyed by this feeling of relief I started to settle back into my seat. That was until I realized the other passengers were not trying to support the attendant, but convince him the box should stay right where it was. How did this make any sense?

I did not know if it really was because the dust storm had grown in its intensity, or because the attendant was not making any headway with this unruly passenger, but after ten minutes of bickering an announcement in both Arabic and English came over the loudspeaker. "Ladies and Gentlemen, due to the weather we will be unable to take off at this time. Please depart the aircraft, and we will try again later."

With the memory of my last trip into Baghdad, and the two day dust storm that delayed every attempt jumping back into my mind, I collected up my pack and shuffled off the plane along with everyone else. With a low murmuring of "Insha' Allah" wafting across the cabin, we filed back up the walkway, and crowded into a waiting area to sit out the storm.

There we sat. The storm blew in, the dust blew around, and we sat. Some of the people napped, some read books. Children, being children, ran around the waiting area burning off the extra energy that came with being young while the rest of us sat some more. In flight food was brought for us to snack on, Halal food mostly, and water to drink. If you are not familiar with Halal food, just think kosher, subtract the Yarmulke, and you would be on the right track.

We watched the tarmac through the big windows along the side of the terminal, and saw the dust ebb and flow. It never seemed to grow in intensity, but we were not allowed back on the plane either, so we sat. For six hours we sat. Just about the time I thought we were not going to make it out today, people started to move and stir around the entrance to the gangway.

Without so much as an announcement, attendants were ushering small groups down the concourse toward the plane. Word of the activity began to spread throughout the waiting room, and once again people began snatching up their belongings and rushing to be first in line. By the time the boarding announcement was made, a mass of people had jammed themselves into a tight bundle at the door, jostling and jockeying their way to get to the front of the bunch.

Getting out of the waiting room and down the gangway was less organized, if such a word would even be close to appropriate, than our first boarding, but eventually everyone was back on board. Carry-ons were stowed, butts were put in seats, and as a hushed anticipation filled the cabin. I noticed there were no cardboard boxes anywhere in sight.

With a collective sigh of relief the plane was pushed back from the concourse, and we began to taxi toward the runway. Now, I was not a weather expert, but the storm still looked pretty much the same now as when we were taken off the plane. I guessed the only real difference was this time they were letting us take off.

The flight to Dubai was not all that long. A bit longer than it used to take to get to Amman, but all in all not too bad. The delay caused by the dust storm put us into Dubai with just enough time for me to wrench my way off this plane, speed the length of the terminal, and arrive at my departing gate just in time to make my connection. Thirty days at home is going to feel so good!

CHAPTER 10

15 Oct – I started the return trip to work, and the first hurdle came when I tried to fly out of Tampa to JFK, emphasis on try. As everyone loaded the plane, and the doors closed, we settled into our assigned places, and sat. We sat some more. We sat for a good long while. Long enough I was able to finish two chapters in the Tom Clancy novel I was reading, and if you have ever read any of his work, you know the man does not write short stories.

Finally, the pilot got on the intercom, and told us they were having a slight problem with one of the fuel valves. "We don't need this to fly." He said. "We just need it to transfer fuel between the left and right wings to level out the plane."

I knew I was not the brightest crayon in the box. I have even mentioned I had no clue when it came to knowing how to fly a plane, but don't we need to be level to fly? After an hour or so they finally got the valve working and we were able to taxi out and take off. I think they found the right size hammer to fix it. You know the saying; if you cannot fix it with a hammer, you have an electrical problem.

Yesterday, the company I worked for had emailed me the ticket for my return trip to Baghdad, and I started my journey by checking my bags in Tampa. The last time I flew to work I was only able to check my bags to JFK, the airline would not, or could not, I did not know which, check them all the way through the international flight to my final stop in Amman, Jordan. With this in mind, after landing at JFK again, I went straight to the luggage claim to wait for my bag. And I waited. Again, like sitting on the tarmac in Tampa, I waited some more. I waited long enough for them to turn off the conveyer belt, and yet, I had no bag.

On my last trip, my bags showed up in Baghdad a couple of days after I did. I knew they made it to Jordan. I had them with me at the hotel, and had given them over to the baggage handler at the airport before flying the last leg. Still, they arrived later than I did, and do you think I learned my lesson? Of course not, I even went out and bought a new suitcase for this trip.

Yes, I was a little tweaked about my luggage. This time, I was not even able to make it to my first stop without losing it, and being so soon into the trip it could be anywhere. With my luck, in the next couple of hours it could be basking in the sun on some Caribbean island while I was on my way back to the suck.

Staring at the empty, motionless conveyor, fuming at my dumb luck, a vague conversation wiggled its way out of the depths of my memory. Something about my final destination being Dubai this time, and not Amman, was relevant, but I could not put my finger on why. As the clue squirmed closer and closer to the surface, I partially remembered a quick snippet of information I had not paid much attention to back in Tampa. Wracking my brain, I tried to remember if the ticket guy had been saying something about getting my bag in Dubai. Self-induced stress, isn't it wonderful?

Wondering if this was a real memory, or something conjured by my imagination, I headed to the ticket counter responsible for my flight to Dubai for confirmation. Arriving at the desk, breathing just a little hard completely due to my exasperation, and having nothing to do with crossing the entire airport just to get here, I handed my ticket to the lady and asked about my luggage.

"Yes sir," She chirped, smiling broadly, "Your bags have already been checked all the way through to Dubai." How was it I could walk around on feet so shot full of holes? I also found there were no available seats in business, and first class had been overbooked by one. Great! Looks like I would be flying steerage, again.

Boarding time came, and I got on the plane. Walking down the aisle I scanned seat numbers, looking for mine. Further and further I walked, and the numbers grew, but I still could not find the one matching my boarding pass. This plane could not be that long, I thought, as my quest drew me deeper into its bowels. Finally, my search came to an end. I found my seat, and confirmed my worst fears; it was the outside seat, on the right side, center of the plane, last row.

Sitting butt-up against the bulkhead, there was no way this seatback was going to recline very much, promising nothing but torture for the duration of the twenty-hour flight ahead of me. Squeezing between the armrests, shoehorning my body into my seat like the proverbial ten pounds of rice into a five pound bag, I had to ask myself why don't they make these things in adult sizes? There were three empty seats to my left, however, offering hope I may be able to stretch out across them and catch a few winks.

Testing the armrest to my left I found, much to my relief, it lifted up and stowed in a tiny nook between the seatbacks. This little tidbit somewhat brightened my spirits, and I reached across the other two seats to swing their armrests out of the way of my future bed. A little more satisfied now, I settled in to wait for the doors to close, and the plane to get pushed away from the ramp.

A few of the passengers were still placing their carry-ons in the overhead bins, and only one or two people were left walking down the aisle, glancing from their boarding pass to the seat numbers. Not here, not here, chanted through my head as I watched one lone man, in the left aisle, approach the back of the plane. Looking from his ticket to the markers over the rows, he continued to advance. Closer he came, until stopping right next to my row. Crap!

He looked up to his right, stared back down at his pass, and shook his head. He then looked left, and a smile of satisfaction appeared on his face. Reaching up, he slung a backpack into the overhead bin, and sat in the other outside seat in my row. O.K., I thought, there were still two seats between us I could lie down on, it could be worse.

Grasping the armrest with his left hand, placing his right on the seat cushion, he scooted over, one seat closer. Me and my big mouth, it was getting worse. Without breaking stride, he repositioned his hands one more time, and scooted another seat closer to sit right next to me. Are you kidding me?

We sat in silence as the rest of the passengers completed stowing their gear and got comfortable in their chairs. Five minutes later, I felt the change in cabin pressure indicating the doors had been shut and sealed. Turning to the guy next to me I said, "Hey, buddy, move over to the other outside seat so no one else sits in this row and we can have some room. The plane is full."

The guy just looked at me, staring with a blank look, and did not move. I was about to try hand and arm signals to illustrate my point when I caught movement from a few rows up, a guy was climbing his way from his center row seat, over the passenger in the aisle seat. A sense of urgency pressed down on me, I had to quickly make the man sitting next to me understand. Quickly, I raised my right hand, and was about to make a pushing motion, indicating I wanted him to slide down a couple of seats, when the man I had seen climbing into the aisle sat down in the empty, outside seat in our row.

All I could do was hang my head, crestfallen. A sudden thought occurred to me and I snapped my eyes back toward the front of the plane in a desperate attempt to regroup. Staring across the rows in front of me, I looked for an opening in the seating arrangement I might be able to exploit. The center aisle of seats contained four chairs apiece, gazing over the seatbacks, I could see a head poking over the top of every seat, with the two center seats in each row completely empty. No good.

Switching to the outside, I first took inventory of the right. These rows contained three seats, and as my eyes darted up the aisle it was like looking down a furrow in a plowed field. The aisle and window seats were filled in each row, with an empty space over the middle seat like a plow had turned the earth in either direction. Quickly running out of options, I switched focus to the left side, only to find it a mirror image of the right.

Defeated, I gave in. Great, let the torture begin. For the next twenty hours I would be stuffed, right here, having to cram my six and a half foot, two hundred fifty pound self into a single, airplane seat. Thanks buddy (again, only half a word). At least I had an aisle seat so I could kick my legs out, but with my seatback in its upright, locked position, there was not going to be any reclining. If I did not already have back problems, I was going to have them by the end of this flight.

I did not know if my exceptional communication skills were to blame, or if it was the way I completely ignored the guy sitting next to me, but no sooner had the "fasten seatbelt" light gone out than he finally did shift over, even if it was only one seat. From time to time I would glance over at the two, and see them carrying on in great conversation like two old hens. Grumbling, I did my best to keep my frustration in check. I was not very successful. Despite my best attempts all I could think was; dude, in the middle of the flight I hope he spoons you.

Flying conditions must have been better than expected. What should have been a twenty hour flight turned out to only take sixteen. Thank God for little blessings. Always traveling with a little vial of ibuprofen proved to be helpful, too. In between naps I popped them like M&Ms. How did I know they worked? Simple. After the plane landed, and we were allowed to leave, I was able to walk, not without a certain amount of pain and stiffness, but at least I was able to walk.

Since I had a checked bag to claim, I was not allowed to go straight to the gate for my connecting flight to Baghdad. I had to go through baggage claim to pick it up, and that meant leaving the security area inside the terminal. The airport in Dubai was not run quite like the ones in the States. For one thing, they did not open the ticket counter for any particular flight more than two hours before takeoff, and since it was going to be fourteen hours before my flight was scheduled to depart, I was not going to be able to get back in the terminal for twelve of them.

Because of this practice there were no shops, no restaurants, and very few chairs outside the ticketing area. Why have them, everyone knew not to show up too early. Luckily, I was able to snag one of those rare empty chairs, so I sat. And then I sat some more. I sat outside security for twelve whole hours while the rest of the guys I had flown in with got to stay inside the terminal and do things like, well, eat. I think I learned my lesson about checked baggage.

Of course, by the time we hit Baghdad, I was pretty hungry. Still, not hungry enough to eat any of the food they sold in that airport. Luckily enough, as we were collecting our bags, shuffling through customs, and pouring out the front doors, we had a ride already waiting to take us back to the I.Z. Remember the P.S.D. trip to BIAP: They had the same thing for us to go back. Joy! Joy!

16 Oct – I was back, working at the Palace, only this time I had the P.X. parking lot, H.L.Z. Washington, and the Rhino Staging area, the areas that used to be Lunchmeat's.

The new system for rotation, through Dubai instead of Jordan, had also forced the creation of a new change-over procedure. Before, returning Security Managers arrived in the morning, and had time to conduct a handshake on venue. Conducting a procedure called "left seat, right seat ride" (it's a car metaphor and should, necessarily, be taken literally) the out-going Manager would start on the left (driver's) seat and take the new guy around (occupying the right passenger's seat) to observe posts while the driver explained them. During the second round, the new guy would occupy the driver's seat, and demonstrate what he learned during the first trip, with the out-bound Manager along for the ride in the right seat. Once complete, the handshake was over, and the out-going Manager would depart. Now, the out-going depart first, causing the returning Managers to have to hit the ground running.

This rotation was Meat's turn to get out of the suck for a while, and go home for a much deserved rest. Knowing how closely he and I had worked together, someone in the chain-of-command realized it would probably be a good idea to put me in his spot while he was gone. It would have been nice, however, to see him before he left, walked posts one more time like the old days, go through a formal change of responsibility with his supervisors, but this new rotation made that impossible. It made me a little disheartened, this was Lunchmeat's world, I was just living in it.

I talked over my assignment with the Complex Manager, the same one Meat and I used to work for, and we both agreed this would be the best place for me to go. I also knew the Manager who took over CAC's from me, when I went to the TOC, was scheduled for his rotation next month so, trying to lay a little ground work, I suggested my assignment only be considered as "caretaker" for the time Meat was on rotation. I offered the idea of, when he returned he should come back to the parking lot, and I should be slid back over to the CACs. After quick deliberation, he agreed. We were getting the band back together, with Rak still covering Towers and Grounds, the Thundering Herd would roam the plains again, and the Buffalo Brothers would return for an encore performance.

Single occupant change-over was not as terrible as you first might think. The guards and Guard Supervisors tended to provide a decent amount of continuity during the change-over. They did not rotate as often as we did, and when they did it was offset to ours, so they were able to maintain a good amount of procedural knowledge, and incident history.

Both Lunchmeat and I, having come from a shared military background, were very familiar with this kind of handoff. And way back when I was still on CAC's we made preparations for just this sort of thing to happen at either of our venues. It was called a continuity book.

You would be surprised just how much people learned about their particular job the longer they stayed in that job. Just how much they really knew about that job. Most people did not think about it. This was what they did, so they just did it. Military mindsets were just a little different. We were painfully aware the person in a particular job position today, may not be the person in that job tomorrow, and working in a war zone only served to emphasize that.

To help ease the transition for anyone tagged to replace us, either due to normal, mundane reasons, or something more catastrophic, we had taken to writing down everything we knew about our venues. As we learned something new, or encountered new situations, we would add this knowledge to the book. Emailed questions to the R.S.O.s, and their responses, were printed and added to the book. Just like we had been taught, we made every attempt possible to set the new guy up for success, not failure, and now that Meat was gone I would be the one benefiting from the work he had done. Additionally, working as closely as we had did not hurt things either.

Meat left big shoes for me to fill. Fortunately, my feet are not all that small themselves. You know what they say about guys with big feet? They have big hands. You know what they say about guys with big feet and big hands? They wear big shoes and big gloves.

18 Oct – I had been covering Lunchmeat's venue for a couple of days. I still found it difficult not to look at it that way, and I got the impression his guards and Supervisors secretly thought the same thing.

Conducting my first post check, on the first day, had almost been like returning to family after a very long hiatus. As I approached each post I could tell when one of the guards spotted me, because the others would turn to look. As I drew nearer, big grins would break across faces when they recognized it was me, and I could not help but grin back. Finally, stepping onto their posts, guards and supervisors alike would rip the glove from their right hand and thrust it out for me to shake.

Removing my glove, in kind, I would grasp their hand, palm to palm, and they would shake it vigorously, squeezing so hard I thought my fingers would pop. I knew almost all of them by face, and was able to call most of them by name. Only those who had been newly assigned after my assignment to the TOC did I not know or recognize.

Their greetings were emphatic. "Mr. Rooster! So glad to see you! You work Parking Lot now?" And when I confirmed I was, in fact, their Security Manager their grins would broaden into full-fledged, toothy smiles, spreading from cheek to cheek.

At many of the posts this was how it went, with cheerful reintroductions and re-acquaintances, and after getting all the niceties out of the way, we settled down to work. I drilled them on the responsibilities of the positions they were working, the equipment they used to conduct the job, and general guard knowledge (most of the time with help from the Supervisor for translation). I asked questions about their families, they in turn about mine, and generally we eased back into the full swing of things.

At some of the posts, however, their happiness over my being their boss only lasted for a few seconds before being replaced by a look of concern. I was expecting this to happen, but not to the level some of the guards expressed. As their face transformed, their handshake would slow, their grip would relax, and as we broke hands they would look up into my face, their concern mixed with confusion, and ask, "Where is Mr. Lunchmeat?"

I explained to them he was on his vacation. How he had gone home to spend time with his family and friends, and for some of them this would be enough. The look of concern would fade, their confusion cleared away, but for most of them who pressed for this additional information the answer seemed insufficient.

Their concern may have been relieved, it certainly appeared their confusion was sated, however the next emotion to cross their face was the one that bothered me most; hope. Almost as if it were welling up from their tear ducts the anticipation would fill their eyes, brim over the lids, and wash across their face. The first guard I saw this happen to caused me to become the one who was confused, and then concerned. Worried over where this was going, I stared at him anxiously until, in a hesitant voice, the guard asked, "Will he come back?"

The first time I heard this question it caught me off guard. I understood the words coming out of his mouth, even though they were in Spanish, but was completely taken by surprise at the intensity with which he spoke them. I had no idea exactly what emotion was driving this question, what unspoken motivation spurred him to ask it, or what the combination of words and emotions could unintentionally be implying. Was he asking if Meat would ever return to Baghdad, or just the Parking Lot?

The question never dawned on me when I walked onto his venue. This was simply a rotation, he would be back in a month. But now that it had been asked, I had to ask myself the same question, and found I could not answer it. I did realize I was taking just a little too long formulating my answer, so I decided to punt. Stalling for time, I turned to the Supervisor and asked for a translation.

He confirmed I had heard the guard correctly, but offered nothing in his tone that helped me solve my problem. Not too sure which way to go, I opted for something noncommittal, yet reassuring. Wrenching a broad grin across my face, I placed my hand on his shoulder, and looked him in the eyes.

"I hope so." I told him. "I really hope so."

After a few more guards, and one or two supervisors, asked the same question I came to the realization that these were Lunchmeat's core supporters. Many of these guys had served in their own country's militaries, and of those who had not many came from the law enforcement community in their native land. Regardless of their differing background, the one thing they did have in common was he had earned their respect, much as he had earned mine, and most of this group was feeling his absence with a sense of loss.

As I made my way, from post to post, I would be asked these additional questions by one or two at each stop, and after doing my best to be honest and reassuring with each of them I would head off for my next check. With each stop, experiencing the intensity of their stares, hearing the emotion in their voice, I grew a little more concerned the shoes I had agreed to fill were getting a little bigger, and with each step I took I wondered if my answers were causing my feet to shrink or get larger.

20 Oct – We got a new guy in on this rotation. He did not have any military experience, but he did have some time as a cop under his belt. He was put on the WPPS camp, working the day shift, a fairly easy venue to learn and work so he should do alright.

E.O.D conducted a controlled detonation this morning. They were blowing up some stuff they needed to get rid of, and as usual they announced the detonation over the big voice. Broadcast all over the Palace grounds, the announcements were made thirty minutes, fifteen minutes, and five minutes before the shot. Standing in the P.X. parking lot I could hear them as clear as a bell.

Remember how I used to complain I could never understand those announcements when I worked at the WPPS camp? Well, it appeared things over there had not gotten any better. Right after the shot went off the new guy came running through the front gate of the camp. Wild-eyed and frantic, he stopped next to the outer gate shack jerking his head and eyes back and forth. Spying me, standing by the bus stop, he ran over. Almost out of breath by the time he got there, he stammered, "Rooster! What the hell was that?!"

"Relax. It was just E.O.D. blowing up a bunch of rockets and stuff they've collected and needed to get rid of. Didn't you hear the announcement on the big voice?"

"Yah, but I didn't understand what they were talking about."

The learning curve over here was set at right around ninety degrees.

22 Oct – It had been a little over a week since I returned to work, and the guards were beginning to act like they felt more comfortable. I certainly was.

I did have a couple of false starts at first, a few incidents Meat never talked about with me, or covered in his notes, and a few times I questioned the validity of the information the General Supervisor gave me. Since then, I had learned my lesson, and thankfully the Supervisor had been very professional about the whole thing. Our biggest explosion came about because of a vehicle placard, think of them as I.D. cards for vehicles.

That morning I was walking around the parking lot checking on guards. I was standing off to the side of the main gate, observing operations, when an armored Mercedes Land Rover from the Danish Embassy was waved through the entrance. There was nothing special about the action, nothing out of place, but I casually glanced over to watch the vehicle drive by anyway. (Yes, there was a very tall, very blond, very beautiful Valkyrie in military uniform who worked at that embassy. But she has nothing to do with this story. Only because she wasn't in the car).

As it drove by me, I peered through the windshield and saw a placard on the dashboard I had never seen before. Unlike I.D. cards, placards were issued from a lot of sources. Like I.D. cards, only placards issued from a select few of these sources were allowed entry into the parking lot. That was not to say only a few, individual placards were allowed to enter, oh no, that would make our job way too easy. Instead, only a few sources were authorized to make the specific placards granting access, and sometimes it seemed like they churned them out by the ream.

Having never seen this particular style of placard before, I followed the vehicle as it entered the search pit. Brake lights flashed as it came to a halt toward the front of the pit, and were shortly extinguished after the sound of the transmission lever traversing the steering column ceased, indicating it had been put in park. By the time I reached the back of the truck the driver had already turned the engine off, opened the door, and was stepping out onto the pale blue, short pile carpeting replacing the fine Persian rugs that had once laid here.

Stopping behind the driver's door, next to the handle of the rear door, a leg dressed in military trousers, bloused into the top of highly spit-shined black combat boot, stepped out and firmly planted itself on the ground. The thickness of the ballistic window in the rear door made it difficult to look into the driver's compartment to see who was trying to get out of this vehicle. The tinting applied to it did not do much to help either, but by the way the person had to rotate on their heel, so their second leg could be extracted from the foot well, told me they were not going to be short.

The second foot hit the carpet with much the same authority as the first, and from the depths of the front seat the driver began to unfold themselves. Camouflage pants gave way to a camouflage blouse, and by the time the whole uniform finished unfolding from the truck, standing the rest of the way up, I found I was standing face to face, staring into the face of Thor. Some guys got all the luck when it came to the right genes. The Bastard.

Standing just a little taller than me, this guy must have bought his uniforms one size too small, either that or had them tailored. His B.D.U. (Battle Dress Uniform) pants fit more like jeans, less like a uniform, and the sleeves of the jacket were rolled, cuffed in the style U.S. soldiers do, to mid bicep. I thought if he tried reaching across to touch the opposite shoulder, every stitch in the cuff would have snapped as a result.

Uniforms were supposed to hang loose from the body, presenting a little bulk to break up the outline of the torso. I did not know how this guy did it, but his blouse looked like it actually tapered at his waist, giving the V impression you only got with body builders. He did not wear a pistol belt to create this illusion, in fact he carried no weapons at all. Not even a hammer. Close cropped, golden blonde hair cut well within military regulations topped a smooth shaven face, and only a master stone mason could have shaved that chin that close. This guy certainly gave new definition to Great Dane.

Staring at this bulk it took me a second to remember I was the one with a pistol and seventeen rounds of ammunition strapped to his waist. And another second to wonder, if this guy really took a disliking to me, would they be enough?

"Excuse me sir, may I see your placard please?" I asked, getting back to business.

For a second he just stared at me. I did not know if he was transposing my question into Danish, or my question had caught him off guard, but eventually he seemed to understand what I wanted and shrugged. Tectonic plates move more perceptibly than he did, although I doubt they were capable of as much destruction as this guy would be able to master on a good day.

Turning toward the driver's compartment he grasped the top of the open door with his left hand, causing the suspension to moan and creek a little as this side of the vehicle dipped an inch to support his weight, as he leaned in. It took him three tries just to capture the laminated paper resting on the dashboard, between two of the sausages jutting from his right hand. Turning back to face me, he held it out for me to take.

Reaching for his offering, I grasped the placard from the side of beef that held it. That hand was big enough, had he been holding a fifty caliber Desert Eagle pistol, it would have looked like a B.B. gun in his grasp. Holding it low, not quite in front of my face so I could still keep my eyes on him over the top, I perused the surface of the card. He may have looked like a Norse God, and move like a continent, but if he decided to take issue with my questioning his placard I did not want to become the fault line he was going to grind against.

So intent had I been on paying attention to this soldier's movements, I never noticed the parking lot Supervisor walk up behind me, and the suddenness of his voice almost caused me to fumble and drop the placard.

"Mr. Rooster, this is new." Came from over my shoulder.

"Yah, I know. I've never seen one of these before, either."

The placard looked official, but was printed in a pattern I had never seen before. All the stamps and seals looked about right, but were not affixed in the traditional spots like all the other placards. The lamination itself was also brand new. It still had some of the curlicues hanging off the edges from being freshly trimmed.

"No sir, I mean this placard is new for the Danes." My Supervisor clarified.

I did not think so. It certainly was not the Danish placard I remembered from before I went on leave, and Meat had made no mention in his continuity book of the Danes getting issued new placards. The deciding point for me, however, was I had not received any new information from the pipeline warning me to look for new placards.

"No, I don't think so." I replied. Turning to my Supervisor I added. "If this is new, show me the message authorizing it."

One of the things Lunchmeat had gone to great pains with was teaching these guards the benefits of having printed orders and authorizations. All of the guards and Supervisors in the parking lot came from Peru or Chile, and possessed hot, quick, Latin tempers. When Meat first took over, more often than not, shouting matches would erupt between the guards and people violating policy when they failed to follow instructions. The guards took it personally when these violators refused to comply. Eventually, he was able to get them to understand their authority came from the policies, not from their personalities, and that had started them down the road to greater professionalism.

Knowing this was what I was getting at, the Supervisor relented. "I have no authorization paper, only I know this O.K." as he took a step back.

Turning back to the soldier, I found him still standing in the exact same spot where I had last seen him, stoic, motionless, patient, like a mountain. I did not even think his expression had changed. "I'm sorry, Sir. I need to check on this real quick. It will only take a moment."

Another shrug was all I got, and I turned away to pull out my cell phone. My first call went to the JDOC. Working in the parking lot they were my point of contact instead of the TOC, and Baldo picked up the phone. For several heated, confusing minutes we discussed the placard I held in my hand until, eventually, we realized we were both describing the same thing, just using different words to go about it.

The short answer was this was the first issue of the newest run of placards for the Danes. Earlier, before I arrived in the parking lot that morning, Baldo had cut through on his way to the P.X. Being a native Spanish speaker, he had flagged down my Supervisor and told him about the new placard that would be starting today, and gone off about his business forgetting to include me in the loop. The Supervisor, not expecting to receive information directly from the JDOC Rep that I did not know about, never said anything until this incident started to unfold, and only realized I had no knowledge of it when I started to contradict him.

I could not rightfully be angry with the Supervisor. Growing up in his culture had taught him the boss was always right, even when he was wrong, and in the end the junior always supported the senior. So it was with Baldo who I had a few heated words regarding information flow.

Returning to the search pit, twenty frustrating minutes later, I handed the placard back to the soldier, apologized for the inconvenience, and assured him this would not happen again. I was fully expecting to be on the receiving end of a titanic tirade, but one more time all I got was the shrug of epic duration as he replaced the placard in the vehicle, and wandered over to the waiting area so his vehicle could be searched.

Returning to my Supervisor, I found him still standing on the carpet, looking a little sheepish.

"Pinguino," that was his call sign, it was Spanish for penguin. He was Chilean, and since the southern tip of the country lies just off the coast of Antarctica they tended to have penguins in the area. "Come, take a walk with me." It was time for me to eat a little crow.

"I apologize for doubting you. I should never have done that. You've always given me good advice, and

I can see why Mr. Lunchmeat always talks very highly of you. Are we good?"

I must have used all the right words because he looked up at me with a big smile on his face (Pinguino never smiled).

"Si, Senior. Estamos bien, Muy Bueno." (Yes sir. We're good. Very good.)

I can see why Lunchmeat liked these guys.

24 Oct – They shut down the road running between the P.X. and the H.L.Z today so they could make some major repairs to the surface.

It was odd how, when a routine was changed from its normal state of being, people suddenly lost their minds, and their brains. For example: All day we had Americans and Iraqis trying to drive through the road block so they could get to where they wanted to go. Never mind the fact that when they had to stop at the road block, they could see the road in front of them was being torn up, and there was no path through the construction. Still, they tried to drive through. Most of the Iraqis tried, failed, turned around, and quietly left. The Americans, of course had to get angry about the whole thing as well.

Most of the Americans had to stop, and ask directions on how to go around the block to get past the construction. The detour they needed to use was not a road normally traveled by the Americans, and until four months ago had been T-walled off in a dead end, so I guess I could understand their confusion. What I did not understand was how a bunch of soldiers and civilians who lived and worked in a combat zone could get so upset when the normal routine of their day had been interrupted. I thought these were the kinds of people who lived for challenges, and thrived on adversity.

25 Oct – We had our first big rain of the year today. Now I understood how this place could flood after forty days and forty nights, they just waited for the sewers to back up. It was almost like someone had explained the concept of storm drainage and runoff to the Iraqis. They thought it a great idea, in theory, but decided it was an activity best undertaken by other countries. Let me explain.

As I walked down the sidewalk I would notice storm grates, along the gutters on the sides of the road. Growing up in the United States, I would naturally have thought they also had large, unobstructed drainage pipes under the roads to go along with those grates like we did. Well, not so much. There did exist a system of pipes and plumbing, but since it rained so infrequently here those pipes tended to fill up with the blowing dust more than water. Because the total accumulated amount of rain was so slight, and the occurrence of storms were so far apart, the pipes did not get flushed out all that often either. Hence, the little bit of precipitation they did get tended to turn the dust in the pipes into a thick mud, and without enough water to flush all of it out, the mud then dried inside the pipes to a hardness close to cement.

Remember when I told you Iraq was not a sandy desert, but a dry, moisture free dirt desert? That had a lot to do with the runoff problem as well. The dirt here was not like the top soil we had in the U.S. It could not even be described as loam because the clay content was too high, and the clay was the source of the issue. Top soil allowed for a certain amount of ground seepage to occur, letting the water drain directly into the earth until it reached an aquifer, or the water table. Loam did pretty much the same thing.

Clay, on the other hand, did not do this. Do not forget, some buildings around here were still being built with bricks made from this same soil. Also, there was a ziggurat in southern Iraq with bricks made from this soil, and some of them dated back to the 21st century B.C. Quick, hard downpours were rare here. Most of the time storms began as slow drizzles. That did not mean it would not rain like someone opened the flood gates, it was just that they usually started out slow. Once started the top layer of soil, about an inch or two, would soak up the moisture until it became saturated.

If that was all the further the process went, fine. The ground had been moistened, and the worse thing to happen was having to walk across it. Why was that so bad? Because after less than a half dozen steps your boots would be covered with that top layer of goop, and weigh an extra five pounds apiece. The wet clay not only stuck to everything, but while it remained on the ground it became a top coat lining, protecting and shielding any dirt underneath from getting any of the moisture. In fact, turn around and look back at the steps just taken. Every step, everyplace a boot touched the ground the top clay would be gone, stuck to the boot, and a dry, dusty print about the size of the boot would remain.

Should that light drizzle turn into a real rain storm, however, that inch thick clay top would now act like a barrier to the deeper soil. Sealed tight, like it had been covered by a clay pot, the rest of the rainfall would not penetrate to the deeper layers of dirt. Unable to penetrate, it would run across the surface instead of soaking in. And, water being water, followed the force of gravity and sought its own level, its lowest level. This was why it did not take more than a couple of inches of rain to cause some serious flooding.

It only rained one day, fairly lightly, for about two hours, and the roads were turned into canals. There was barely a dry piece of roadway poking above the surface of the water anywhere, not to mention the lakes and ponds that formed in the parking lots and open spaces where no drainage existed. This could not be the same culture that created the plumbing and engineering required to build the hanging gardens of Babylon, not by a long shot.

I realized the rainy season only lasted for about two months, but it was going to be a long two months. Construction seemed to suffer from the lack of rain as well. The chow hall behind the Palace was a couple of years old now, and you would have thought it was fairly water tight. Not so much. As we were sitting inside eating our lunch, we heard a loud splash of falling water. All of us looked toward the front of the room and saw one of the bullet lights had been pushed out of the ceiling by the sheer weight of the huge volume of water backed up behind it. Now, water was pouring through the ceiling, all over the plates, utensils, and food in the serving line.

If that was not enough, the connection between the chow hall and the kitchen had sprung a leak as well. Where the two buildings were joined together, the water was flowing from the ceiling in spouts as big as my wrist. It was almost like it had never rained over here before.

29 Oct – October was almost over, and even though I had only been back in Baghdad for half of it, the time moped along slowly enough to almost make me feel like I had never gone on leave (or maybe it was just me).

Like when I used to work CACs, I still met the other day shift Managers for breakfast in the chow hall. Rak was still working Towers and Grounds, and the new guy on CACs, the one who replaced me, was Bammer. As his call sign implied, Bammer hailed from Alabama, graduated from the University of Alabama, and looked like he once played line-backer for The Tide. It would seem not a lot of imagination was wasted in deciding his name.

One thing to note about him was; do not let his country attitude, the slow easy way he talked, and his mild southern drawl fool you into thinking he was not all that quick. He earned his Masters' degree during the twenty plus years he spent in the Corps before retiring from the Marines. Having been a Marine was what should tell you he is not all that quick. (O.K., maybe I still harbored a little animosity over his having the venue I wanted back.)

From breakfast we went to formation, just like we used to, and from formation we ambled over to the office. Paperwork was filled out, Dailies were completed, and everything got emailed off to the boss, just like we used to. Then, came post checks, not like we used to.

Do not think Bammer was not a good Security Manager, that would be a wrong assessment. I kid him about being a former Jarhead, sure, but he was not a bad Manager; he just ran things differently than I had. In the month and a half since I left CACs he had formed them in accordance with his vision and leadership. They still did good work. Missions got accomplished correctly, and it looked like the guards had accepted him.

The Thundering Herd, on the other hand, did not seem to have weathered the change so well. Rak was still Rak, quiet most of the time, prone to fits of raucous laughter when he found something humorous that went as quickly as they came. He and I still talked like we used to, traded information on a regular basis, and his guards still stopped me to have a talk when I came by. Now, however, he conducted his post checks on his own, or with his Supervisor, not with us.

For the first couple of weeks I was back the three of us always seemed to be on different sheets of music. Bammer usually completed his paperwork first. When done he would scoop up his radio, and with barely a word, head off to make his rounds. Rak never seemed to take much notice when he left, and after a week of this I could not stand it any longer.

One morning, several minutes after Bammer had already slid out the door, I finished sending my reports and looked over at Rak. Sitting at Lunchmeat's old desk, I was directly in between Rak's and my old desk, now Bammer's, (the two of them face each other and Meat's desk faces out, completing a U shape, with Meat's chair in the bowl of the U). Leaning back in the chair, I turned my head and looked over toward Rak.

His computer and monitor blocked any view I had of him, but off to the left I could see his right hand furiously moving a mouse around the pad, and every now and then a finger would click one of the buttons. The action alone told me all I needed to know, Rak had finished his report, too, and was now doing a little, light web surfing.

"Hey Rak," I questioned. "What's Bammer's deal? Nobody seems to talk anymore and everyone looks like they're trying to keep out from under everyone else's toes. It's been two weeks and the Thundering Herd has yet to stampede."

The plastic rattle caused by the mouse's motion stopped. Slowly, it slid up and to the right. One, solitary click sounded, and Rak removed his hand from the device. The cushions of his chair lightly sucked air through the stitching in their pleather covers, only to rapidly expel it again as he adjusted positions. I heard the creek of the casters and the crunch of the wheels as they rolled over the linoleum for a second before his face came into view.

Gliding to the end of his desk, so we would easily be able to maintain eye contact, Rak turned the chair to face me, leaned back, laid his arms along the armrest, and lifted his feet to the top of his desk crossing his ankles left over right as he placed them on the surface.

"I don't really know." He started. "After you went to the TOC, and Bammer came on board, things seemed to go O.K. at first. We made checks like we used to when you were still here, but it just wasn't the same. It didn't take long before Meat would take off for rounds on his own, or he would hang back here as me and Bammer left. Pretty soon Meat wasn't even coming back to the office for breaks, he just stayed out in the Parking Lot, or somewhere else on venue."

Lost in thought at this new information I looked away from him, and tried to make some sense of this. Rak's story did not sound anything like Lunchmeat. He tended to be more extraverted than either Rak or me, and I found it hard to believe he would push Bammer out for any reason. Unfortunately, with him still on leave, there was no way to really ask him what was going on.

I took the rest of the day to mull over that bit of information, unable to make heads or tails from it. The next morning I told Bammer to hold up before he could make it out the door, quickly closed out my paperwork, and scooped up my gear for post checks. Maybe I could deduce something by walking around with him.

We left the office in the same way Meat and I had done so many times before, followed the same routes he and I once walked, but it was not the same. I had known Bammer for over a year now, even though we never worked this closely before, and I figured even though we were at the start of a new routine the core of what we were doing should not be too unfamiliar. So we walked, we talked, we joked, but the easy, familiar flow just was not there.

It had been about a week since then, and things were getting better. Rak still did not join us with the frequency he accompanied the Thundering Herd, but he did join us from time to time. Bammer and I started establishing our own new routine. Of course it was a little different from the one Meat and I had. Even though I was still Rooster, he was not Lunchmeat.

Today, we were in the process of making the last check of the day, and I was heading out of the South CAC to cross over into the Parking Lot. Bammer was still inside talking with a couple of the guards, and the Supervisor was standing outside next to the sandbagged bunker guarding the vehicle gate. As I walked by, just about to step into the street, I heard him call my name.

"Mr. Rooster," he said in a quiet respectful, almost reverent tone. "You do good work making Mr. Bammer ready for CACs."

His words brought me up short, and I stepped back away from the crosswalk. Turning, I nodded my head to him in acknowledgement of his compliment, and said the only thing I could think of. "Thank you."

Nodding back, he cocked his head slightly to the right, and pressed on with the thought it looked like he really wanted to talk about.

"You walk with him like Mr. Lunchmeat, only not like Mr. Lunchmeat. You are not Buffalo Brothers. I think you miss him." Damned Peruvians, they get so emotional about everything, and by far are too perceptive for their own good as well.

That was the first time it had been said out loud, and by the same Supervisor who first called us Buffalo Brothers to boot. Memories flooded back in an instant, the suspicious package right across the street from where I was standing. Coordinating between venues the several times we had to shut the area down due to positive responses for explosives at the mid CAC, just up the road. Layered over the top were memories of shooting the breeze, conducting post checks, and hanging around the living area in the basement after work.. No, he was right, this was not the same. I just had not been able to admit it until now. Or maybe I just did not want to. A blank stare washed over my face, pushed by the force of my reverie.

"Yah, I do." Was about all I could muster, and turning on my heel I crossed the street to finish checking my posts.

CHAPTER 11

2 Nov – And I had to ask myself, did these people remember there was a war going on here? This morning I was walking through the Palace with Bammer, we were on our way to make the first post checks of the day. As we walked through the Palace we passed by the service desk for K.B.R. (Kellogg, Brown, and Root. The maintenance company here in Iraq). You probably remember them from the news as a part of Halliburton. Passing the desk, a commotion caused us to stop and take notice. Standing there was a young female Air Force Captain, palms flat on the counter, bent slightly forward so her nose was mere inches from touching that of the K.B.R. worker, raising seven kinds of hell.

"I can't wait around all day. I have to be in court. If I have to stop by this desk every morning and put in a work request until you guys come out and fix my TV, then that's what I'll do. I cannot watch my football!" Yes, that was right, football. This woman was almost in tears because the TV in her trailer was not working, and she could not watch her football game. Air Force, they sure did know what was important when they went to war.

Later in the day I was walking through the parking lot, checking on my guards, when a man came huffing and puffing over to me. Let me paint you a picture. This guy was around six feet tall, and had to weigh over four hundred pounds. Clad in light colored slacks, dress shoes, and a white button-down shirt, complete with tie, he kept trying to hitch up the computer case that kept trying to fall off one slopped shoulder while doing his best not to fumble the cell phone pressed against his ear with the other. Fifteen or twenty file folders were pinned against his body by his bicep, just below the phone, and every one of them was trying to escape in a different direction. To top it all off he was sweating like he had just finished running two miles (ten feet) across the parking lot to get my attention.

"Excuse me," he puffed as he shuffled up. "Excuse me."

There was really no need for him to address me in order to get my attention. The menagerie unfolding in front of me had already done that.

Stopping a few feet to my front, he rotated his chin slightly away from the mouthpiece of the phone, and asked. "Are you the Security Guy?"

Several of the folders took this opportunity to make their break, and sprang from his arms. As he scrambled to capture them, the cell phone decided to create a diversion by squirting out of its trap, and flying in the opposite direction. What resulted was the most interesting juggling act I had ever seen as folders, phone, and computer case arched from hand to hand to shoulder.

Watching his performance I came to the realization I had been on this project for a couple of years now, and apparently had become fairly well recognized in the Baghdad area. Let's face it, when you were almost six and a half feet tall, weighed over an eighth of a ton, shaved your head shiny bald, and sported a dark bushy goatee you tended to stand out in a crowd. But I certainly did not think of myself as "The Security Guy."

Fully out of breath, and sweating like it was July, not November, his gyrations gradually gave him dominion over his unruly equipment. By thwarting each and every escape the phone was eventually re-holstered on his hip, the computer case became slung over his neck, bulging across the expanse of his belly, and the folders ended up secured tightly in the grip of both hands. Recovering from his exertion, now that everything was back in order, his breathing became less labored, and with his distractions brought to task he composed himself, little by little, until he was finally able to level the full measure of his attention back on me.

Looking down at his intent face I replied to his question. "Yes, sir, I work for the security company here. How can I help you?"

"You have a guard over at Ocean Cliffs, (the Iraqi Government Building area, remember that place?) and he is much too aggressive."

Not being too sure where he was going with this, and wanting to give my brain the opportunity to cycle a little faster, I asked what I thought would be an obvious follow-up question. "Begging your pardon, but did I hear you correctly?"

"Yes," he seethed, readjusting a few of the more uncooperative folders. "You did. We were driving up to Ocean Cliffs, and one of your guards told us to stop. When we didn't, he stepped into the street, reached down, and put both of his hands on the weapon at us."

Judging by his look, his demeanor, and his outrage I had a bad feeling I knew where this was heading. Still, not being overly sure I fully understood his statement I asked for a little more clarification. "Sir, are you saying he pointed his rifle at you?"

"No, no. He didn't raise his rifle. He put his hands on his rifle. Then, he glared at us."

I had never seen such a look of righteous indignation over being glared at in a menacing and intimidating manner before in my life, but this guy had it. Here we go again.

Doing my best to maintain a calm, professional manner I attempted to assume the most neutral look I could. I cocked my head slightly to one side as I formulated my next statement, and asked. "Sir, you realize this is a combat zone, and some people actually do try to blow us up by running checkpoints with car bombs, don't you?"

"Well, yes." He exasperated. "But there was no need for him to be so aggressive with US! We're Americans after all."

And there it was. That "obviously American " thing. Did I mention how much I did not understand that one?

Staring at his red, puffy, sweat-covered face I came to the understanding, in my own mind anyway, there was no way I was going to be able to talk any sense to this guy. Nothing I could say was going to make him understand the dangers and constant threat those guards worked under every day. To him, only one possible course of action would ever be able to correct the insult he had just suffered. Acquiescence to his bruised ego. I chose the road to appeasement.

"Of course not, Sir. I'll make sure I talk to his Security Manager about that. Is there anything else I can do for you?"

Pausing, for just a moment, he actually looked like he was searching for another outrage he had been forced to endure.

"No, that will be fine. Thank you." And off he went, still struggling with his belligerent belongings. Probably on his way to write a scathing memo. Some people just did not have a clue.

5 Nov - Things had been suspiciously quiet around here lately. As usual, there were a boat load of weapons violations; people leaving their weapons unattended in their parked vehicles while they shopped in the P.X. I was still not sure how that one made sense.

Some people seemed to believe just because their vehicle was armored it could not be broken into. How did they think we got their weapons out so the I.Z. police could log them in their reports before they get back? A coat hanger, thirty seconds, and I was in your car taking your guns. Some people never learned.

Walking posts today the guards seemed to be in fairly high spirits, at every stop I was met with smiles and enthusiasm.. My first few checks went quite smoothly, and everyone was on their game when I quizzed them on recent changes to policy and their new responsibilities because of them. I chalked it up to their pride at being quick on the draw with the answers, and getting all the questions right. It was not until my third or fourth stop that I discovered the real source of their reverie.

I was just finished with grilling the two guards stationed at the walking gate between the main K.B.R.

camp and the Palace. Unable to trip either of them up during the questioning, I was congratulating them on how in-depth their knowledge was of the policy changes. Beaming over their success, both guards smiled at each other. Then one turned back to me and said.

"Mr. Lunchmeat will be happy with us on his return."

Turning back to his partner, he made the statement one more time in Spanish, and received a vigorous nod of agreement from the other guard.

Not exactly sure how to respond to this, all I could do was look at him and say, "Really, you think so?"

"Oh, yes" He chirped back confidently. "On his return he will come here, and you will return to CACs. Again, we will be big, good buffalo team."

His broken English made it a little difficult for me to wrap my brain around what he was trying to say, but once it did I realized the cat was out of the bag. I should have known, eventually they would learn of our plan to have Meat return to the Parking Lot and my transfer to CACs. In hindsight this probably should not have surprised me as much as it did; after all, we were the ones who created this monster. Guards, like soldiers, tended to hear a little bit about everything, and as soon as one of them knew something juicy, or thought they had puzzled something together, they lit up the switchboard at rumor control like a pinball machine.

I looked into his beaming face, and did not know what to say. Of course, my lack of command of the Spanish language did not help this feeling any either, so I did what I could do. Nodding conspiratorially, I gave him a sly wink and said, "O.K."

In this new frame of mind I continued my checks, even going back to the posts I had already visited. While talking with the rest of the guards no one else mentioned they were privy to the information that had inadvertently been shared with me. But hanging around the periphery of the posts I paid close attention to the little bits of conversation they exchanged when they thought I was not listening.

We both know my Spanish was not all that good, even on a good day. Fortunately, I did not have to be fluent in the language to pick up on key words or phrases. Some words, like Lunchmeat or CAC, did not have a direct Spanish equivalent, so the guards pronounced them the same way we did. Those were easy to spot. Others, like those that provided context, were a bit more difficult to identify. By the end of the day I had a massive headache from trying to figure out who was talking about what, and how much they thought they knew.

Just prior to shift change I realized I was not going to figure this one out, not with my limited understanding of Spanish, and went looking for my General Supervisor. I figured the information was already out there, so it was not like asking him questions was going to cause too much more damage. Besides, his command of the English language was as close to fluent as I had heard from any of the other supervisors, except for Toro maybe.

Not wanting to raise any kind of alarm throughout the posts, I did not use the radio to call him to me. Instead, I continued strolling from post to post in the hope I would run into him while he was conducting his checks. Walking away from the gate at the Rhino Staging area, toward the North CAC, I was cutting across the asphalt slab where the dogs check the baggage when I saw him walking in my direction. As the two of us got closer, I stopped next to a duck and cover bunker while he finished walking over to me.

"Hello, Mr. Rooster." He greeted me.

"Hey Acero," I replied. Acero was his call sign, in Spanish it meant steel, as in man of. "One of the guards said something odd to me earlier, and I was wondering if you could explain it to me."

A stern look immediately covered his face, and he quickly shot back. "Who was it and what did he say to you?"

Judging by the look on his face, and the tone of his voice, I thought he was expecting for me to tell him a particular word in Spanish I did not understand. It also looked like he was expecting that word not to be the kind used in polite company, or toward the boss.

"Talking with some of the guards today a few of them mentioned how Mr. Lunchmeat, when he returns from rotation, will return to Parking Lots. What can you tell me about this?"

Almost instantly Acero's look of concern vanished to be replaced by a look of great enthusiasm. "Oh, yes Sir. We heard this morning, and all of the guards are very excited about Mr. Lunchmeat coming back. When he returns you will go back to CACs, and we will be the big Palace Team again like before."

Oh boy, this was only a suggested plan when Manny and I talked about it earlier; but now it looked like the plan had taken on a life of its own. "Really, where did you get this information from?"

"Toro, at the CACs, we were talking about it at formation this morning. They are also looking forward to it with great enthusiasm."

"O.K. thanks." Was all I could come up with. Stealing a quick look at my watch I saw I would have to hustle back to the office if I were going to have time to talk this development over with Manny before he left for his afternoon briefing with the company leadership. Looking back at Acero, I made an excuse instead. "I have to head back to the office and close out paperwork. See you at formation."

"Hasta Mañana." he replied with a smile, and turning, headed off to the Rhino gate with what can only be called a spring in his step.

Heading back to the office I mulled over the guards reaction to our plan, and how they may have heard about it. I knew I had not said anything to anyone, and I was pretty sure Manny did not either. So deep was my thought over this I barely remember walking through the north CAC, waving at the guards as I passed, and only finding I was too late to catch Manny before he left brought me out of it.

Later that night I was returning to the office, in the hope of catching him at his desk, when I found him standing in the driveway outside the main palace doors, right in front of the portico. We had just received two vehicles full of V.V.I.Ps (one V was not enough for DoS, so they added another V) and he was babysitting their Iraqi drivers.

I stopped to tell him the news I discovered that day, and the guards' reaction to it, only to find out he had not told anyone either. Now, this just did not make any sense. I was not the leak. He had not been the leak, and between the two of us we discussed the possibilities of how this may have happened. We tossed out scenarios, we discussed viable options, we even talked about things that were probably ridiculous. Right up to when the duck and cover alarm went off, then we stopped talking and ran.

Halfway to the bunker I pitched a look over my shoulder to make sure the Iraqi drivers were keeping up, only to see them standing, stock still, right where we left them. They had not moved an inch. I guessed it made sense the Iraqis had not reacted to the sound of the alarm, since they did not have duck and cover alarms in the Red Zone.

Yelling at them, and swinging my arm in the traditional "Follow me" gesture, the Iraqis finally got the idea and made a mad dash after us. What time they lost off the blocks, with a slow start, they more than made up for during their sprit, and we all made it to the bunker at about the same time. Once we realized everyone had made it under cover before the booms, there was some stress-relief inspired chuckling, and a little back-slapping.

We waited inside the relative safety of the bunker for quite a while, but did not hear any explosions. Either the rocket had been a dud, or had landed so far away we never heard the impact. Either way, we were fortunate enough to catch a break on that one. Without realizing it, we had all been standing just thirty yards away from Death Valley.

8 Nov—OK, help me with this one. I had been back for almost three weeks now. In the twenty-one days I had been back from vacation, I had completed fifteen incident reports. All but one of them had been for P.S.D. Teams

leaving their weapons in their vehicles while they went into the P.X. to shop.

Today took the cake. Some of the teams used Ford F-350 pickups. They put a big metal box-like compartment in the bed of the truck, with a turret on top for a machine-gunner, and armored the rest of the truck. Today, one of the guards found an AK-47 sitting on top of the turret. Not locked in the vehicle. Not secured inside the big metal compartment. Just lying on top of the turret with no one in sight. A closer inspection of the vehicle revealed the hatch, which sealed the opening the gunner stood in from the rest of the compartment, had been left unlocked, and we were able to climb into the box where the rest of the team's weapons were.

I had already called the JDOC to have the I.Z. police respond, and my guards were removing the weapons from the vehicle and laying them out on the ground, so they could be inventoried and documented when they arrived. As the last machine gun was being lifted from the turret, the P.S.D. team arrived back at the vehicles, led by their Team Leader. He was not happy. Fortunately, the I.Z. Police showed up at almost the same time, so I did not have to deal with him.

As the patrolmen were cataloging the weapons, and placing them in the trunk of their car, the Team Leader was arguing with the Patrol Supervisor. He could not understand why they were taking his weapons. He was quite convinced he and his team had done no wrong. His argument was that since nothing had happened to the weapons while he was gone, and now he was back, we should just give the weapons back to him. No harm, no foul, regardless of the fact anyone, not just the guards, could have come along and taken their guns while they were gone.

"Well, why don't you just use some common sense on this?" He finally spat at the Supervisor.

When it came to something like this, I would like to know what the definition of common sense really was, since it certainly was not common and, when it came to this, sure as hell did not make any sense.

14 Nov—The guards and Supervisors appeared to have a pretty good handle on the calendar of rotations for the Security Managers. Today was the first time in a week any of the guards asked me about Meat coming back from rotation, and the few who did started the conversation by

saying his leave should be over in a couple of days. Although I wanted him to come back, as much to put our plan into action as missing having someone I trusted that much watching my back, I had heard nothing through official channels, or back channels (unofficial) for that matter.

Making post checks with Bammer, I also noticed the guards in the CACs, as well as the Parking Lot, were all working just a little harder, smiling just a little more, and moving with a greater sense of purpose. Bammer mentioned something about it when he noticed it, and not wanting to create an awkward moment, I changed the subject.

15 Nov—It had been a busy week. Again, someone decided to leave their weapons in their vehicle, sitting on the front seat in plain sight. Dutch Embassy this time. I guessed these people looked at their armored vehicles like they were safes or tanks. With all that armor on them, how could someone break in?

Things had also been pretty noisy in the Red Zone for the entire week. There had been a bunch of suicide bombers, and a lot of automatic weapons fire. Al Sadr made a statement this weekend that any agreement made between the U. S. and the Iraqi government, that did not call for American troops to immediately pull out of Iraq, would result in his boys shooting at us again, or still, depending on how you looked at it. Sounded like rocket fest was about to start up again. But then again, we never did get that ground attack we had been promised.

16 Nov—It was official, Lunchmeat would not be returning to the project from leave. A thing I was not wanting to deal with on a number of levels. Manny called me back to the office this afternoon to give me the news. Sometime during his leave, Meat was approached with a job proposition back in the States, something to do with firearms and training, and from the way it sounded the offer was too good to pass up. Steady work in the States, minimum travel away from his family, along with a decent paycheck. Regardless of how much the guards, Supervisors, and I wanted him to come back, I guessed I could not really blame him for accepting.

      Now, I had to crush the rumor the guards had been hanging onto for the past week. Not only did I get to stomp all over their hope, I would also be rubbing a little salt in the wound as well. When the rotation comes in tomorrow I had two hours to train my replacement before going back to the TOC to work second shift. With Bammer on CAC, Rak on Towers and Grounds, and the new guy in the parking lot the chance of getting the band back together was officially dead, and no more Lunchmeat meant no more Buffalo Brothers as well.

18 Nov – Yesterday, the Iraqi Cabinet voted on the SOFA (I'll explain SOFA in a second) that applied to U.S. Forces, and approved the bill. All that was left was for the bill to pass through Parliament, and it would be good to go. We were expecting to receive rockets after that vote, especially if it gave favor to our military.

Tuesday, the Stars and Stripes reported that a source close to the Iran Ayatollah professed how Iran approved of the agreement, and said the Iraqi government had done well in negotiating it. After that announcement, we did not expect to be rocketed, since Iran had been the prime instigator in the insurgency. (They deny it, and investigations were still on going to prove it, but most everyone over here lived in the real world.)

Today, the paper reported that MPs (Members of Parliament) loyal to al-Sadr were trying to stall The House so they would not vote on the measure, meaning the bill would not be passed before the dead-line in the UN resolution allowing US troops to be here. The resolution I am talking about was the one passed in the United Nations giving U.S. and coalition forces the authority to be in Iraq. Without it we lost our approved mandate, and would have to leave.

Al-Sadr had been a mouthpiece for Iran for years. (Again, not necessarily proven, but it was hard to overlook all the evidence to the contrary.) He would not even live here in Iraq, but stayed nice and safe in Iran. Even though the government of Iran approved of the bill, which meant problems of a different kind I am not going into just now, Al-Sadr still wanted to protest it. Children.

For those of you not familiar with it, SOFA (pronounced like the long, comfortable seating structure in your living room) stood for Status of Forces Agreement. For Service Members who have spent any time in countries like Germany, South Korea, Japan, or England, a SOFA was old news. For the rest of you, here is the gist. SOFA is an agreement between the U.S. and any country that hosted our armed forces, giving our military permission to be on their soil, and established a few ground rules. It laid out the legal status of American Service Members while they were in the host nation, what was considered a crime, legal proceedings, and the rights and privileges a Service Member could expect.

Here was where the SOFA got a little sticky. While in broad strokes the SOFA set up agreed terms under which the military was allowed to operate, it also established the civil and criminal jurisdictions under which the military was allowed to operate. It also established the civil and criminal jurisdictions under which the military would fall should laws be broken. Civil matters were not usually all that worry-some, since they were normally settled with a fine. They were not presenting much of a problem.

Criminal matters, on the other hand, were a whole other kettle of fish, and the issue that had everyone worried. Here was why. Normally, the host nation would agree for U.S. courts to have jurisdiction over crimes committed by one U.S. military member against another. They also normally allowed the same jurisdiction when something happened as part of the military member's duty. See the sticky part?

While stationed in Europe, Service Members had a well-defined on and off duty time. A distinction which was not so clear in a combat zone, and this opened the door for a very troubling question; would there really be part of this agreement that allowed U.S. military personnel to be charged and tried in the Iraqi court system?

For us, the big question was where did the contractors fall. Most of the supply convoys, dignitary, and V.I.P escorts were now being conducted by civilians, not the military. State Department properties were also being guarded by civilian contractors. Who was going to conduct the investigation if we had to pull triggers to defend these places? The Iraqi Government wanted to see all contractors subject to Iraqi law, and only Iraqi law. For now, the U.S. Government had not cut us loose to swing on our own, and we hoped that lasted.

Another part of the SOFA that was holding up the process was the inability for everyone to agree on the date for U.S. Forces to withdraw from Iraq. Right now, U.S. Forces still had authority to be in Iraq through a mandate from the U.N. Without a SOFA, U.S. and coalition forces would be forced to withdraw when the mandate expired at the end of December. The Iraqi government had already stated publicly unless the SOFA was signed by both sides they would not seek an extension of the mandate, and would pursue legal means, as well as world wide support, to expel the Coalition Forces. You can see how things were getting a bit tense around here.

19 Nov – I had been in the TOC for a couple of days, and was settling into my new routine. It was a lot different working the second shift than it had been on the midnight shift. The room was full when I came to work at fifteen-hundred, and empty by the time I left at twenty-three hundred, so there was finally something to do up here other than read and watch TV. Now that I was working the second shift though, I found my mornings to be a little less busy than they used to be. I woke up around zero-seven-hundred, instead of zero-four-thirty, went upstairs to grab some breakfast at the deli, eat, and watch some TV I had recorded on my computer. Later, I went for a quick walk, for about an hour, and hung around until lunch.

I would like to tell you my talk with the guards, a couple of day ago, went well. It did not. The first one I told was Acero. You would have thought I had kicked him in the crotch. After gathering himself back together, he and I walked posts and broke the bad news as we got to each one. Reactions were pretty much the same at every stop. First they thought we were kidding, but the look on Acero's face as he translated for me convinced them we were not. Once they got over the shock of realizing we were telling the truth, some of them actually got angry he was not coming back.

A lot of questions were asked as to why he was not coming back. Guards with families waiting for them to return home from their contract understood better than the single guys did, but that did not stop most of them from moping around for the rest of the day. With the state of mind the majority of the guards had been in after receiving the news, I was glad the rest of shift went off without incident. I was not overly positive what type of response the guards would have given had there been a serious incident to respond to, but I was sure it would not have been restrained, and more than a few of them would probably have taken out their frustrations in reaction.

Toro took the news a little harder than most. I think most of it had to do with his having to tell the rest of the guards without the support of a Security Manager. To the best of my knowledge, Bammer never knew about the rumor, or the guard's anticipation of it.

Today, I went to the Palace office a little early so I could join the other Security Managers for lunch. The whole crew was preparing for a V.V.I.P. who would be coming in around noon, and they had to make sure the motorcade got into the Palace before they could eat. With nothing else to do, I figured I would spend the time hanging out with Bammer, and we strolled over to the Main CAC to wait for the activities to begin. It would be a nice change for me to watch one of these operations from the outside instead of being knee deep in it. We had not been inside the gate shack for more than a couple of minutes when a loud bang erupted from out front.

Confused, and a little surprised, Bammer looked at me, and I looked at him. "Man, I think someone just shot your clearing barrel."

A clearing barrel was basically a fifty-five gallon drum filled with sand. It was usually placed on a stand that slanted the barrel at something close to a 45 degree angle, and was used as a back-stop when anyone was unloading and clearing their weapons. It provided a safe place for them to point the muzzle while they completed the process.

As we walked through the front door we could see the Guard Supervisor running over to the clearing barrel, telling someone "Sir, Sir, just put the weapon down!" in heavily accented English. Rounding the corner of the front bunker, an Air Force Colonel came into view standing in front of the clearing barrel, staring at his weapon with a very confused look on his face.

"We were going to the range today." He explained, his face still looking down at the weapon grasped in his right hand, as he turned away from the clearing barrel to look us in the face. His shoulders sagged in defeat. "I forgot I loaded my pistol." Some officers should not carry guns.

In his own laid-back, country comfortable, slow drawl kind of way, Bammer walked over and placed his left hand, reassuringly, on the Colonel's right shoulder.

With the other, he gently pressed his palm against the back of the Colonel's shooting hand and slowly, with gentle even pressure, turned the officer in the direction of the clearing barrel until the muzzle of the pistol was pointed in a safe direction again. "Not to worry, Sir. We'll get you through this."

Needless to say, Bammer did not join us for lunch. Once the convoy had been ushered through the gate he had to fill out an incident report covering the Colonel's negligent discharge of his pistol.

Tonight we had a lot of noise from across the river in Rusafa. Thirteen reports of small arms fire, explosions, and smoke. I did not know what it was all about, but they certainly were making a lot of noise about it. Rusafa was the district due east, and a little north, across the river from the I.Z. We used to get some rockets from that area back during rocket fest. Most of the noise was coming from one particular area, around the Sheraton Hotel, right on the border with the Karadah district, and I did not know what that meant just yet.

Chances were we never would find out exactly what was going on either, since random gun fire in the

Red Zone was a pretty common occurrence. Explosions, on the other hand, were a little less frequent, but still happened often enough that news agencies did not bother themselves with mentioning most of them, and rarely sent reporters to the blast site unless it was something spectacular.

21 Nov – I went for my walk this morning. I usually took a fast paced walk for about an hour. It killed some time, and was easier on the joints then running. I could usually make two figure eights around the Palace grounds in that time, which meant I covered almost five miles.

Today, as I was walking through the North Drop Arm, the barrier dividing the Palace from Camp Travis, I heard a very loud, very familiar bang right behind me just as I passed through the gate. It was the sound of another clearing barrel being brutally cut down in the prime of its life. That's right; I was less than five feet from another clearing barrel murder. I will tell you what, I was glad soldiers were using the barrels correctly, but I thought I was going to wind up getting shot next to one of these things. And once again, you guessed it, it was an officer.

An Australian General Officer to be precise. Did I mention how some officers just should not carry guns?

The WPPS guys decided they wanted to start some controversy tonight, too. The Ambassador's Protection Detail (A.P.D.) decided to come roaring through the main gate without identifying themselves to the guards. His convoy looked just like most of the other convoys operating around here. The reason was so he did not stand out so much, and became an easier target. It seemed since the A.P.D. boys knew who they were, we all should too.

Approaching the lane designated for V.I.P.s the first vehicle in the convoy did the right thing and showed the proper identification to enter the checkpoint, so the guard lowered the popup barrier, letting them continue down the bypass lane toward the gate. Published procedure required the lead vehicle to tell the guard if there was more than one vehicle in the convoy, no signal and the vehicle was a solo. There was no signal.

Unfortunately, there was more than one vehicle in the motorcade. The second vehicle rode through the checkpoint on the bumper of the first vehicle, but did not show their identification. When the last vehicle tried to roll through without his identification showing, the guard raised the barrier and stopped the vehicle. You would think he had just insulted their mothers by the way they started screaming.

Guys, this was easy. Show your credentials and you were through. Follow proper procedure and everyone would get out of your way. As Spike Lee would say, do the right thing. Failure to prepare on your part, however did not constitute as emergency on my part.

After they got through the checkpoint, they went straight to the Ambassador's detail leader, and cried. I think it went something like this. "The big mean security guard stopped big, aggressive, WPPS killers and would not let us through the checkpoint until we showed them our proper credentials to enter the Palace" or something like that. I guess it did not take a lot of brains to pull a trigger.

23 Nov – Went to the NEC today. They opened the new PX over there so I decided to see what it was all about. They had beer. They had Sam Adam's Boston Lager, which meant they had good beer. I had been buying my

beer on the economy for a while now, and it had all been Tuborg or Carlsburg, Danish. Both were a pilsner, very light. Tomorrow night, I got lager.

In case this sounded confusing, I will explain. The P.X. across from the Palace, next to the WPPS camp, was a big general purpose P.X. Soldiers, Marines, any service member assigned to, or traveling through, the I.Z. had access to this P.X. State Department direct hire, contractors, and Coalition Forces are also allowed inside. Right after the invasion a general order, known as General Order #1. G.O. #1, was issued to the military saying Service Members were not allowed to drink alcohol while they were in theatre, and since this P.X. was used mostly by the military they do not stock any.

Hurray for supply and demand. A couple of enterprising and capitalistic Christian Iraqis (no, not all of them were Muslim) found a way to import beer and liquor into the I.Z., and opened a liquor store around the corner from the NEC. State Department folks, and those of us who were contracting for DoS, did not fall under this General Order, and this was where we went to buy the stock for our liquor cabinets. With a P.X. being opened inside the New Embassy walls, this P.X. was able to stock beer and liquor. Of course, the P.X.s on the Army FOBS did not.

Now, I see a few confused faces out there, so I will go ahead and voice the question I am pretty sure some of you have been thinking any time I have mentioned we had a beer or two from time to time. Your question is; where in the decision making process did it become a good idea to have liquor in a combat zone: Guns, booze, bullets, beer, rockets, liquor; throw in a couple of disgruntled postal employees and you have got yourself a real party, right?

Believe it or not, it did not really work that way. We were all very aware of the environment we were in. Each one of us knew life could get very real, very fast. Those who would not normally pick up a beer when they were at home did not normally pick up a beer over here, and those of us who would normally have an after dinner drink at home, had an after dinner drink here. Trust me, if anyone understood sobriety and moderation it was the people over here, and I had yet to meet someone who was willing to risk their life, and their job, just so they could get drunk. That was one of the reasons I took a job with this company.

Parliament will vote on the SOFA on the 26th. I think everyone was expecting the worst. Tomorrow, we will have a D&C drill since it had been about six months since the rockets stopped falling regularly, and we had a bunch of new folks arrive since then. We will see how it goes.

24 Nov – So it begins. This morning I was out for my morning walk when I heard a very loud explosion. Not the typical shooting the clearing barrel type of bang, but a boom from a bomb, a bomb placed under a bus carrying Iraqi government employees to work to be exact. It exploded just outside one of the outer I.Z. checkpoints, killing thirteen Iraqis who worked for the Trade Ministry.

A little while later, I heard another boom. This one was rather close, and brought back memories of rocket fest. Come to find out, a female suicide bomber blew herself up right outside checkpoint three, the entrance to the I.Z. right next to the Iraqi Government Building/Ocean Cliffs. Remember the two people from earlier who thought they had been treated aggressively by the guards out there? Yah, about that.

25 Nov – They decided to vote on the SOFA referendum today. Well, not really. CNN and Yahoo put out a story saying Parliament was going to wait until tomorrow to vote, but really they voted today. I did not know if this was someone's idea of misdirection, or just bad information, but the story came out right after I got on shift today.

Around seventeen–hundred, one of the Intel guys came into the TOC and said they had passed the referendum by a simple majority of fifty-four percent. One hundred forty-nine of the two hundred seventy-five Members of Parliament (M.P.s) voted yes. Thirty-five M.P.s voted no, but that was to be expected since they were loyal to al-Sadr, and ninety-one members did not vote at all. Know why? Reports said they were "in fear of our lives" if they voted. How could this be called a stable government?

I did not know what this vote meant for us, but it would probably take the insurgents a couple of days to get their rockets in place, and now that the government had voted for us to stay for three more years, I got the feeling we would be seeing rockets pretty soon. Whether they would be shot at us or the Iraqi Government Building would be anyone's guess.

The general Iraqi public was not all that happy about the vote either. Protests had broken out all over the city decrying the agreement. Thousands of Iraqis also gathered all over the country, with one group massing in one specific traffic circle in central Baghdad where they were burning American flags and effigies of President Bush. Are you ready for this one? Remember the film footage of American soldiers in a M88 tank retriever helping Iraqis pull down a statue of Saddam Hussein? Remember how the Iraqis were all waving American flags, hugging the soldiers, jumping up and down on the statue, and generally singing praises for the U.S.? Remember the traffic circle in which all this happened? That was the same place they were now protesting our presence. The stench that just crawled up your nose is the smell of sick irony.

How quickly these people forgot about being helped. Oh, they would remember for years, decades, even centuries any insult they had to endure, any oppression forced upon them, any perceived injustice they had suffered, but help seemed to be another issue. I guess some people were comfortable in their misery, and were only able to define themselves with it.

28 Nov—Tonight ended up a little busy, even though things started out rather slowly.

Around seventeen-hundred, an hour or so before the day shift Security Managers finished their shifts, two R.S.O.s came running into the TOC asking what the big explosion they had just heard across the river was. Because we sat pretty deep inside the Palace, and did not normally hear sounds from outside the building, none of us had any idea what they were talking about, or what to tell them. Earlier, I had been sitting at my desk, reading, and heard a soft, low thud-like boom sounding more like someone on the other side of the wing slamming a solid door into a heavy frame. I had not thought much about it at the time, and went right on reading. If this was the boom they were talking about, enough time had passed since I noticed the sound that phone calls reporting the blast should have come in by now. They seemed pretty excited, and shook up, over the size of the explosion, yet I had nothing. No reports about anything.

Being the company that employed all the guards who manned the towers and gates around the Palace, everyone tended to look at us to be the eyes and ears when it came to everything regarding the perimeter. Being the person in the TOC who represented the company responsible for all those eyes and ears meant I was the single source that was supposed to know what was going on out there, and so far I had not received a single report.

When I was working outside, with Lunchmeat and Rak, we were at the core of a notification and information network so interwoven hardly anything escaped it's notice. Working within the team we created, teaching integration between guards and supervisors, training them to report quickly, as well as accurately, notifications seemed to come in almost as the events were happening. Sitting apart from them now, with Lunchmeat gone and Bammer coordinating CACs, I could only trust in what we started was still in place. But the thing beginning to concern me now was, if the sound I mistook for a slamming door was actually the explosion they were asking about, the time lag between the incident and the report was dragging out far too long.

The R.S.O.s crowded around the Watch Officer, the guy at the top of the TOC food chain, and began to pelt him with questions. Where was the explosion, how far away was it, was it inside the I.Z., and was anyone injured? Rapid and intense, they jackhammered him with questions. Questions he could only address with a blank stare. Quick on his feet, and sharp with his mind, what do you think he came up with for an answer? Slowly he rose to his feet, removed the glasses from his nose, turned away from the R.S.O.s and said with a thin, sly grin, choosing deflection over confrontation, "Rooster, What do you have to report?" Oh, Crap!

Both R.S.O.s immediately turned their attention away from the Watch Officer, and focused it entirely on me. Out of the corner of my eye I could also see the rest of the TOC pause, interested to see how I was going to handle this. My brain scrambled for just a second, tried to come up with a good answer, and drawing a blank decided to jump behind my instinct for self-preservation to hide instead. Self-preservation kind of shrugged its shoulders and said "Eh, I got nothing. Here. Try this. Tell them you'll make some phone calls." Great: that was no help.

Much to my surprise, with the eyes of both R.S.O.s boring holes through my skull, a low throaty answer popped up from my butt, and I heard a voice that sounded incredibly like mine say "The Security Managers are collecting reports from the guards right now. As soon as they have coordinates they'll phone them in." Now where did that come from?

The last thing I wanted to do was jump on the phone, and start calling for reports. Like what had happened to me in the past. Nothing was more frustrating than receiving a phone call demanding information you did not yet have. On the flip side, I had seen Managers sit on information, and neglect to pass along reports for a number of reasons… Some good, some not so good. With no way of knowing which scenario I was currently facing, all I could do was trust the data was actually being collected, and would make it to me shortly. If not, I had just talked myself into a corner. Good job.

Uncomfortably, I stared back at the R.S.Os as my brain continued to scramble. Seconds ticked by like minutes as nothing happened. All alone, I watched as one R.S.O. shifted his weight from one foot to the other, while crossing his arms over his chest. And the silence stretched on. Nervously, I tried to shift my gaze away from their glare, only to find I could not focus on anything other than the intensity of their speculation. My entire universe instantly shrank to encompass nothing more than the distance between us. Standing on the brink I almost gave in.

From its place of hiding, my brain was working hard to convince me I would be fully justified in picking up the phone to make the calls I hated to get when I was a Security Manager. As time dragged on self-preservation joined in, adding weight to the argument, screaming for me to save myself.

Standing before the onslaught of my own mind, I felt resolute. Part of my brain told me their argument had credibility, but my professionalism would have no part of it. Small pockets of gray-matter analyzed their thesis, and found a logical consistency buried in its terms. Action on my part would make me look competent to the R.S.O.s, like I was doing something to get the information they wanted. But my aversion to hypocrisy and dedication to the competence of the Security Managers would not back down. Unfortunately, caving to peer-pressure, my disloyal hand broke faith with my will, and started to move.

The phone on my desk started ringing before my fingers had moved even an inch, and I dove at it like it was a life preserver. The Lifeguard on the other end of the line was Rak, calling to tell me his towers were reporting a flash and huge explosion had just occurred directly south, across the river from the Palace. An explosion big enough, and loud enough, that it shook the dust loose from the rafters in the office. My belief had been justified. My faith renewed. Although not as timely as their notifications used to be, they were still passing information.

Repeating out loud, so the R.S.O.s could hear, the words Rak was telling me on the phone I relayed the blast had taken place in the Red Zone, not the I.Z., in the Karrada district. A row of buildings obstructed the line of sight between the tower reporting and the actual blast, but they had seen massive debris thrown in the air by the force of the blast. Rak also conveyed, for minutes after the initial explosion, reports of continuous small arms fire (S.A.F.) around the point of detonation.

This was not uncommon for the Iraqis to start panic firing after a VBIED explosion. I did not know why, they just did, and for the next twenty minutes I got calls every two or three minutes of more S.A.F. from multiple location in the Red Zone. It was almost like they were taking their gunfire show on the road. With steady reports flowing in the R.S.O.s seemed to relax, and we started charting the hot-spots on our maps.

If this had not been enough excitement for the night, I also got a call from the JDOC with more information. The military liaison up there had called around through his people, and found out one of the Army units patrolling in the same general area as the initial blast had decided to conduct an unannounced controlled detonation to destroy a bunch of ordinance they had captured. Thanks for the heads-up guys. No one was able to determine if this had been the blast that started all the fireworks, or if it was just a part of the chaos being reported in the aftermath. One thing was for sure, though, there were a lot of nervous trigger fingers out there.

Victory Base also got smashed with a couple of rockets tonight. No reports of any injuries, but I finished my shift before any reports like that would have come in.

29 Nov – The day started out plain enough. I got up, went for a walk, hung out in the room until lunch, came back from lunch, and waited for shower time. Around fourteen-hundred, I had just stepped out of the shower when I heard a rather loud, and very long, boom. It lasted too long to be a rocket blast, so it had to be thunder. All morning the sky looked like it was trying to decide whether or not it wanted to rain. I guess it made up its mind. I could hear the rain coming down hard outside, and had visions of the flooding we had last month when it rained. Boy, I was not ready for what was about to happen.

Finished with my shower, I had gone back to my room to get dressed for work. I was a little early, so I thought I would head upstairs, and grab a quick cup of coffee. As I opened my door, one of the Palace Guards was standing in the hallway in a state of bewilderment. He truly looked like he did not know what to do. He looked at me, then at the floor, then back to me again.

"Boss! Boss! Look!" He said, and pointed at the floor in front of him. The corner of the hallway was blocking my view of what he was pointing at, so I walked to where he was standing, and saw water gushing from under the bathroom door and flowing down the hallway. Great!

I ran upstairs to the K.B.R. help desk and told them a pipe must have burst in the basement, and it was now flooding. As I ran back downstairs I started calling all the Security Managers I could to tell them we were flooding again.

I got back to my room, and started picking up my footlockers, shoes, and anything else lying on the floor. Everything went on top of something high, the bed, the desk, my wall lockers, anything in an attempt to keep it from getting wet. The last time this happened I did not get a lot of water in my room, so I did not think this was going to be too bad either. Boy, did I figure that one wrong.

After moving all my stuff off the floor curiosity started to set in. Walking back into the hallway, I peeked my head through the doorway of the bathroom to see if I could determine the source of the flow. Peering into the first room, where the toilets and sinks were, I could see water gushing over the step from the raised back room where the shower was; the shower I had been in just ten minutes ago.

Sloshing upstream I stopped below the step, and surveyed the watery scene before me. Dark, thick liquid bubbled up from the center of the room. A slight lip at the top of the step had turned the floor into a small pond, and water, thick with mud gurgled and spewed from the drain in the center of the room replenishing the little lake as the excess spilled over the short dam. Wherever that drain emptied was not only filled to capacity, it was being force fed by the runoff from the rain pressuring the overload back up the pipes. This certainly was not a simple case of a broken pipe.

Heading back into the hallway I looked toward the front stairs and discovered water gushing through two more doorways, the other two bathrooms. Huge puddles were forming on the floor, and as they rushed from door to door they crept closer to each other covering the tiles with their soupy mess. Stopping at each of the bathrooms, I poked my head into the shower room of each to find water bubbling up out of the drain holes in the floors in each one. This was way too much water for a simple water pipe break.

Since the last rain a lot of dirt and filth must have built up in the drainage pipes, somewhere out in the gutters and sewers, and dried into a plug. Now that the pipes were clogged, the water draining from the roads outside was going the only place it could, into the basement. The run-off from the palace grounds had no place to go either. Seeking its lowest level, the water wound up draining into the sumps around the basement windows.

Eventually, those started leaking as well. It was not until much later I learned it had also hailed for almost ten minutes on top of all the rain. That was the hard sound I heard when I was getting out of the shower. Not just rain, but rain mixed with hail.

All afternoon the water kept rising, and I returned to my room a couple of times to stack my stuff higher. By the time it was all over there were six inches of water flooding the entire basement, not just the area where we were living, but the entire basement under the Palace. They had to turn off power to the entire building because the water was flowing in and around the generators, and they were afraid they would short-out and electrocute anyone standing in the water. The flood caused the Palace to shut down for a day and pretty much soaked everything.

Oh, by the way. We got hit with a rocket just to the west of the Palace this morning, too. I wound up sleeping through the D&C alarm. As expected, the C-RAM did not go off, again. For some reason, the damn thing had not been working right. It seemed to be at its worse if it had been a while since our last attack. We also never seemed to find out it was not working until we got rockets, and it did not sound.

30 Nov—They sent some love our way again this morning. About the same time as yesterday, zero-six-thirty. This time the C-RAM and the D&C went off. The rockets hit around the same place as yesterday.

The flood waters have stopped rising. They pulled port-a-john sucker trucks up to the back of the Palace and were trying to suck the water out of the basement with them. At its highest, the level rose to just over the bottom step of the stairs. It was going to be a bitch to clean all that stuff up. Since the power was still shut off, I had not ventured into the depths of the watery abyss, so I was not sure how bad the damage was just yet, but I should get a better look in the morning once they have turned the power back on down there. They got the power turned back on in the rest of the Palace, but not so much down stairs yet.

CHAPTER 12

4 Dec—They said the attacks around Baghdad dropped to an all-time low in November. I did not know about that because it seemed like I got eight to ten reports of either small arms fire (S.A.F) or explosions in the Red Zone every night. The guards in the towers, both here at the Palace and over at the NEC, that looked out over the Tigris called them in.

Tonight, in addition to the tower reports, I got a call from the Security Manager at the al-Khindi Street Checkpoint on the west side of the NEC. His call sign was Shadow. He called to report he had seen someone with a flashlight walking around under the bridge just to the west of his position, sweeping the light back and forth across the ground like they were looking for something. He told me he had originally called the JDOC, and asked for the I.Z. Police to come out and take a look, but by the time they arrived the light had been doused and the mysterious person had disappeared. Typical, right? Cops. A day late and a dollar short.

Of course, it came as no surprise when the cops came back to his checkpoint and told Shadow there was no one under the bridge. They did say they had found a place where it appeared someone had cleared out an area where they could lay down, though.

As interesting, not to mention confusing, as this information was I had to remind him there was not much I could do for him. With fewer and fewer combat troops inside the Green Zone, the I.Z. police were the only ones actively patrolling, and they were under the direct control of the JDOC, not the TOC. All I could do was pass this on to the duty R.S.O. and make a journal entry of the information. Neither one of us was all that happy that more could not be done.

Coincidently, last night he had called to report shots being fired from the other side of the same bridge, in the Red Zone. To give you a little idea of where this checkpoint sat, I need to explain a little geography. Not far to the west of Shadow's checkpoint, maybe half a mile, was checkpoint twelve, the entrance to the I.Z. from Route Irish. Originally named the Khadamia Expressway, the road entered the Green Zone and climbed up, onto a bridge that crossed Al Khindi Street (this was the bridge

Shadow saw the flashlight under), and continued on to central Baghdad. Where west-bound Al Khindi passed under the bridge, and made a sharp left turn to merge with the expressway, the right side of the road was lined with T-walls that separated this part of the I.Z. from the Red Zone. From the top of the bridge you could look out across Indian country. Yah, I know calling it Indian country was not politically correct, but being part Native American myself, I liked to think the description meant wild, untamed, and dangerous.

The I.Z. Police responded to his first call about the shooting, and fifteen minutes later I got a call from the JDOC reporting the shots had been two cars, in the I.Z. racing down the road shooting at each other; no further information. Only in Baghdad, right?

It had been about a week since the flood. The basement had been cleaned up fairly well, however they wanted us to move into the trailers over on Camp Travis. When the extent of the damage had initially been realized, rooms were made available for us at the project camp next to the NEC. They were nothing fancy, but at least they were dry. Fifteen feet by fifteen feet, the rooms were big enough for a couple of beds, two wall lockers, and not much more.

These trailers did not come equipped with bathrooms or showers, so a trek over to the AB unit a few rows away was required to take care of those specific needs. Simply stated, the AB unit, or ablution unit, was a trailer with sinks, showers, and toilets. The whole setup was a lot more rustic than living in the basement, but it was warm and dry.

Only those of us who worked in the TOC had to move over to Travis, though. I guessed it made sense because the Operation Center was still located in the Palace. The caveat to this was the fact that the TOC was due to move into the NEC in about a week, and it would have made more sense for us to just stay there.

5 Dec – Peace was breaking out all over Iraq. At least, to listen to the DoS folks, you would think that.

On the first of the year, the Palace would be handed over to the Iraqis, and DoS would withdraw into the NEC, which would then officially become the Embassy, and the Army would move into their FOBs. In preparation for this we got our transition briefing today, but the company still wanted all of us who had been living in the Palace to move into Camp Travis, located on the north-east side of the Palace. The camp would be secure from the Palace grounds when they were turned over to the Iraqis, but we would have to drive to the other side of town to go to work. That may not sound so bad, except the only vehicles allowed to leave the secure compounds had to be armored, and right now we did not have enough of them to go around.

About those trailers, remember rocket fest? Same type of trailers. Not hardened, some sand bags, and D&C bunkers for when the rockets came. Unfortunately, most of the DoS and DoD personnel who were here now, had not been here for the fest.

6 Dec – Today, I received fifteen different emails advising us there was a threat of I.D.F. (indirect fire) in the I.Z. for the next couple of days. You would think people would remember this was a war zone. There was always a threat of I.D.F. in the I.Z.

Last night, around zero-three-hundred, the C-Ram went off. Clanging alarms, flashing lights, but no booms, just the alarm. I hoped it was only a false track.

7 Dec – It was a false track. Another way to say it was a false positive.

I moved into the CHUs today, again. (CHU, pronounced chew – stood for Container-Housing Unit). It was almost like a shipping container, the small ones, with electricity and insulation. A CHU was a bit different from what I lived in when I was in Edgewood back during rocket fest. Those had been more along the lines of a no-frills trailer home, gutted of everything except a common bathroom, shower, toilet in the middle, and two rooms on either side with two twin beds. It was a complete trailer, and all you had to do was hook up the water, electricity, and plumbing and you were ready to move in.

The kind I was in now, well, some assembly was required. They were put together in an H pattern. The legs were the bedrooms, and the center span was the entrance way and bathroom. The living area was an open space about seven feet wide, and fifteen feet long. The cross piece containing the bathroom area was small, and the shower was even smaller. They had these things sandbagged pretty well, but they were still soft sided when it came to big booms. Maintenance folks told me they had installed thin Kevlar sheeting on the roofs and sides to help protect the occupants, but I was not going to bet my life on how resistant they were to shrapnel, let alone a direct hit. I had seen a little too close, and a little too often the havoc those rockets could wreak.

Also, the C-RAM went off again today; another false track. I just hoped the thing worked for real when the time came.

9 Dec—Tonight was the second night of the "Festival of the Sacrifice" and it sounded like a war zone out there (I crack myself up). Last night was the same, gun fire all over the place. Shadow even called in some from around the west side of the IZ.

For those of you unfamiliar with this holiday let me lay down some knowledge. The Festival of the Sacrifice, also known as the Greater Eid, was the lesser of the two major religious holidays in the Muslim Faith, almost in the way Christmas was the lesser to Easter for

Christians, but not quite. Celebrated in remembrance of Abraham's willingness to follow God's orders to sacrifice his son Ishmael, it lasted for three days.

Traditionally, Muslim families with the ability to do so were required to sacrifice their single best piece of livestock as a way of paying homage to Abraham's intention to sacrifice his son, with the beast representing the sheep that was sent to replace Ishmael on the alter. Normally, it was a cow that was slaughtered because of its size, but rams, goats, and sheep were acceptable as well. Once sacrificed, the meat was distributed among the family who owned the beast, their immediate friends and family, with the last third of the portion being given to the poor and needy. And, as with any other celebration in this part of the world, gunfire seemed to play a major role in the festivities. Remember that happy fire thing?

I was sitting in bed this afternoon, reading, when the D&C alarm went off. Good thing it was cool enough I could keep my window open all the time now because the sound of the alarm was pretty faint. I could only hope the low volume meant the intended P.O.I. was well away from where I lived, and not that loud speakers were not mounted close to my trailer. Either way, I thought it a good idea for me to take a walk around the area to see if I could find where they were. It may have been annoying, but in a small way it was comforting to have the C-RAM speaker right outside my trailer when I lived in Edgewood. No idea where they were over here. Oh Yah, no booms came with that alarm.

10 Dec—The C-RAM was going wild today. No less than five false tracks. If you have been keeping track, like I had, there seemed to have been a lot of false tracks lately. I wish I could tell you why these kept happening, but the answer was; I had no freaking clue!

Rumor had it the anti-heat-seeking missile flares launched from the helicopters would produce a false track. I did not know if that was true, but the premise sounded a bit dubious to me. Stories had also circulated saying the radar would lock onto small flocks of birds, but that sounded even less likely. Either way, I thought the C-RAM would be going down for maintenance soon.

I got a call from Shadow tonight. It was always interesting to get his calls. He reported there were a couple of individuals, possibly Iraqi soldiers, up on the overpass watching his check point. Once again, the I.Z Police showed up right after they got in a car and drove away. Wasn't that just like the cops? When everything was over, that was when they decide to show up.

The powers that be were moving us again. I got an email from my boss today telling me to move back into the project camp. No sooner did they kick us out then they told us to move right back in. Good thing I had not taken the time to unpack.

11 Dec – A year and a half after it was supposed to be opened, and I was now living in the New Guard Camp. Officially named Camp Condor. Not to give you the wrong impression, but the camp had actually been open, and occupied, since somewhere around July, so it was only about thirteen months late in opening.

Originally built as the base of operations for the Embassy guard force, it also housed the majority of the American Security Managers, all of the Administrative personnel, and the men who guarded the Embassy and other properties closely related to the Embassy.

Remember the trailers I described way back during rocket fest? The trailers here were exactly the same, if not a little smaller, and were packed in like sardines. And, of course, we had our own chow hall, medical clinic, and a small gym.

The camp had been plagued with construction problems too numerous to talk about since its inception, and they were still building the overhead cover to protect us from the rockets, yet it seemed to be alright for the time being.

14 Dec – President Bush came to town today, his last trip of his administration. Since Big Army was running the show, they decided not to tell the TOC anything about the visit until he was already on the ground in Baghdad.

The Army was notorious for doing things in a big way, and in keeping with this theme, they shut down all the roads in the I.Z. in preparation of his arrival. M-RAPs (The M is pronounced separately from the RAP. They were Mine Resistant, armored personnel carriers) and Bradley fighting vehicles (lightly armored fighting vehicles designed to deliver infantry to the fight), Humvees and Armored Security Vehicles (heavily armed and armored wheeled vehicles that replaced the old Vietnam era V-100s used by the MPs) were stationed at every intersection. The reason for the visit was so President Bush could put the final signature on the SOFA (Status of Forces Agreement).

Once all the official stuff had been concluded, they went on to have a news conference at Prime Minister Maliki's residence. During the conference one of the Iraqi reports started throwing shoes at President Bush. Rumor had it, the reporter yelled "Here's a goodbye kiss from the people of Iraq" and he started flinging footwear.

To give this a little context: Remember the news story from right after the invasion when an American M88 Tank Retriever helped pull down a statue of Saddam Hussein? If you recall, a bunch of Iraqis jumped up on the fallen statue, and started hitting it with their shoes. In this culture that was one of the worst insults you could give someone. The bottoms of the feet were dirty, and showing them to someone was a great insult. By extension, the bottoms of shoes were just as bad. Get the picture?

Security scrambled to protect both Presidents, and when the dust finally settled do you know who brought the tennis shoe-tosser down? An R.S.O. agent and one of the WPPS guys. You know, the same folks who had not been informed that POTUS was going to be in town. Go figure.

15 Dec – Yah, they knew what they were doing when they put Camp Condor together. All year, while I was working at the Palace, we had been seeing emails from the Camp Manager about water outages in this new camp. They were pretty funny then, but not so funny now that I lived here. This afternoon, I went to lunch, and when I was leaving the chow hall I almost walked into a flood of water behind the building.

Unlike the flood in the palace, this one was caused by the main water line servicing the camp blowing a seal. Pressurized water exploded out of the buried pipe and had dug its way to the surface where it cracked the pavement next to the D-FAC, and burst through the seam in a pretty good impression of Old Faithful. I did not think much about it until I tried to take my shower before work. No water. Nothing.

This evening, my relief showed up one and a half hours early for shift. Reports of the water main catastrophe made it around camp fairly quickly, and everyone was adjusting their schedule around the need for finding alternative shower sources. The absolute failure in the line resulted in five hundred gallons of water spewing out of the ground, soaking everything. It was going to take them until tomorrow morning to dig up the pipe, fix it, bury it again, and test it.

The Iraqis started to protest this afternoon. For those of you who have spent time in this part of the world, that should come as no surprise. The reason for the protest was the incarceration of the journalist who threw his shoes at the President yesterday. It looked like most of Sadr City turned out for the event.

The reporter, a journalist named Montadhar al-Zaidi with the Egyptian based al-Baghdadia television station, had become quite the celebrity over here. The T.V. station reported receiving hundreds of phone calls from a vast majority of their viewers, and almost all of them had been in support of al-Zaidi's actions. Al-Baghdadia Television had even gone so far as to issue an ultimatum saying, "Al-Baghdadia Television demands the Iraqi authorities immediately release Mantadhar al-Zaidi, in line with the democracy and freedom of expression the American authorities promised the Iraqi people."

Maybe it was just me, but I could not quite figure out how "freedom of expression" covered the act of assault committed against another person, let alone the President of a country. I also did not quite understand the reference to "American Authorities", especially now that Iraq had its own legitimate government, elected by its people. Fortunately, the Prime Minister had a firm grasp, and denounced al-Zaidi's actions as "a shameful, savage attack".

17 Dec—The C-RAM shop and maintenance personnel were conducting a lot of tests today. Wouldn't you know, we got a track in the middle of the test, no boom though. It took C-RAM almost twenty minutes to call it a false track. Until then, all the alarms were going off around the L.Z. and no one knew what was going on. For those of you who recognize it, the word for this was SNAFU (pronounced Snafoo). For those who had never heard this before, it stood for Situation Normal, all Fouled (or any other F-word you cared to use) Up.

18 Dec—A couple of things today. First, we received Intel saying some of the guards at checkpoint eighteen, the checkpoint at the end of the causeway behind the NEC, may have taken a bribe to allow a vehicle with explosives to enter the I.Z. through their checkpoint. Follow-on attacks were considered likely. Later today we caught three Ugandans taking pictures of the NEC from the same causeway. It might have been nothing, but you never knew.

I guess I should explain this causeway so there won't be any confusion. First of all, the NEC sat on land next to the al Sijood Palace, one of the many Saddam built in Baghdad. This Palace sat on the right bank of the Tigris, downstream from the Palace where I used to work, and had a number of smaller villas that spread out to the east and west from the main grounds. In the area between the river and the Palace complex, Saddam had an artificial lake built so he and his guests could have a place to fish, swim, and generally do whatever it was that dictators did when they recreated.

A long causeway separated the south end of the lake from the bank of the river, and a road had been built on top of it, running the length of the dam. At the west end of the causeway was checkpoint eighteen, one of the few checkpoints dedicated to the searching of semi tractor-trailers, construction vehicles, and any other large trucks. Once a vehicle had gone through the inspection, determined it was clean and passed through, they had free access to anywhere in the I.Z.

We also got Intel saying Al-Quida in Iraq may try to bribe someone, at a different location, so they could get two more vehicles through another checkpoint carrying weapons and explosives. Again, follow on attacks were expected. It sounded like life was going to get a little sporty around here when we turned things over to the Iraqis after the first of the year.

20 Dec—Not much happened today. Stars and Stripes had a story about the shoe-man. Apparently everyone was outraged he had been "beaten up" during his capture. The story went on to say no one had seen him since the attack, and that had to mean he was obviously tortured and beaten while in custody. Obviously.

Have I mentioned how emotional this society was, and how quickly they jumped to conclusions? Here were a couple of examples of how rumors and wild speculation abounded here. When the invasion first rolled over the berm into Iraq, a rumor was started by the locals, and spread throughout the country like wild fire. The rumor said our sunglasses were actually X-ray vision, and we could see through their clothes with them. A rather cool, James Bond-like thing to have but, obviously (did I use that word right?) we did not quite have that level of technology yet. Never the less, we did not do very much to try to dispel that rumor.

For another example, when I had been on active duty we were rounding up captured insurgents and combatants, and taking them to holding centers for further evaluation and questioning. While processing a group of these detainees, at one of the confinement facilities, one of them began talking, pleading to our interpreter. Not being functional in Arabic, I was forced to watch the conversation and wait for a translation.

What I saw was the detainee ask the Interpreter a question that caused the Interpreter to screw up his face in confusion. Tentatively, the Interpreter asked a question of his own, and waited for the response. The detainee started into a long rapid fire explanation only to be cut short when the Interpreter began to laugh so hard I thought he was going to choke.

It had been during August, and we were reaching temperatures in the one hundred forty - one hundred fifty degree range. Being one of the hotter summers on record, the detainee had asked if he could have one of our "cold pills". Iraqi soldiers, and the general public, had been told by Saddam how Americans were weak, and would not be able to stand the heat of an Iraqi summer, much less be able to fight. Because of this, obviously (they kept using this word. I did not think it meant what they thought it meant), we had invented pills to keep us cool. They also thought our body armor was really personal air conditioning suits.

Kind of makes you proud that people could think we were capable of that kind of technology doesn't it? It should also make you wonder what kind of society would actually believe these stories, let alone consider their conclusions as being obvious, especially when they came from an area known to the world as the cradle of civilization.

22 Dec – Remember the water pipe that blew the other day? It blew again yesterday, this time in a different spot, around fifteen-hundred, and we had been without water ever since. They seemed to believe they would have the water turned back on around midnight tonight though. We would see about that in the morning.

Of course, until they turned the water back on the toilets did not work, there was no taking of showers, and you could dry shave, if you wanted to. Once again, we were back to peeing in bottles, and using bottled water, not the warm kind, if you wanted to take a shower in your own bathroom. If you wanted a hot shower, you had to go looking for one.

Fortunately, someone was smart enough to hook a water truck up to the chow hall so they could still cook for us. I thought we would have a riot on our hands if the chow hall had to shut down. Personally, that would not bother me too much. The chow hall tended to serve its own take on the three major food groups, breaded, fried, and greasy.

23 Dec – We received new intelligence tonight. Word had it three land cruiser trucks had made it into the I.Z. Not a

big accomplishment, except all the makings for three VBIEDs had reportedly made it in as well. Folks were in a big scare about this one. I guess it meant the source was fairly credible. Either that, or we had a bunch of newbies who did not have a lot of time in country yet, and were reacting a bit over the top. One thing I learned while working with the State Department was, if reaction was good, over reaction must be better.

An attack was supposed to take place sometime over the next couple of days. I was thinking the likely times would be Christmas day or the anniversary of Saddam's hanging. These guys loved holidays and anniversaries.

D.D.M.s (Designated Defensive Marksmen – some people would call them snipers, but that was no longer P.C) had been requested to sit on top of a few of the buildings in the NEC to overlook the 215 apartments. The Khindi Street check points were a little fidgety, and I could not say I blamed them too much since they were the first line of defense for the NEC. If something was going to go boom on the NEC, they had to get through those check points first.

24 Dec—Apparently, they are taking this VBIED thing very seriously. Today D.D.M.s at the NEC observed a couple of guys standing on a balcony to one to the 215 apartments, acting suspiciously. It looked like they were talking on their cell phones, but were trying very hard to be inconspicuous about it. It was possible they were just very intent on their conversations. It was also possible they had camera phones, and were trying to photograph the NEC in preparation for an attack.

The Two-Fifteen apartments were one of those anomalies I told you about a long time ago when we talked about how normal Iraqi civilians lived in the I.Z. Located directly across Khindi Street from the NEC, it was an apartment complex inhabited solely by local civilians, at least I hoped it was only local civilians since I seriously doubted the original tenants, post invasion, still lived in them. Squatters and opportunists probably made up the majority of the residents.

The major point of concern lay in the fact that the southern wall of the apartment complex paralleled the northern wall of the NEC for more than one hundred yards, and the apartment buildings were tall enough to give a pretty good view of the inside of the NEC. Me being me, if I were an intelligence agent working for a rival country, this would be the spot I would set up to watch the comings and goings of the Americans.

There were a whole bunch of additional soldiers in the I.Z. right now, so they conducted a raid on the apartments. Ten buildings, give or take. Seven stories per building, give or take. Three or four apartments per floor, give or take. I did not know if they checked them all, but it sounded like they had a pretty full day.

Somewhere in the I.Z. a raid turned up a vehicle that looked like it had been prepared for use as a VBIED. I did not get the full story on the results of the raid, but it sounded like the car had been prepped, but the explosives had not been loaded yet. Tensions seemed to be running a bit higher now that they found something like this.

Since the find, normal shuttle bus service between the Palace and the NEC had stopped running. Instead, armored Rhinos, the same kind that made the run down Route Irish from the I.Z. to BIAP, had been substituted for the soft-skinned busses. In addition, the extra soldiers who were transferred here have set up internal checkpoints all over the I.Z. and they were searching everyone and everything. A message had been put out to all DoS personnel to stay off the streets, and remain on the FOBS and camps until further notice. If we did leave the base, it would be in an armored vehicle.

We also received, and you are never going to believe this one, an unspecified increased threat of I.D.F. to the I.Z. from now until the end of the month. Now, there was something new. With all the C-RAM activations over the past week, or so, I was wondering if they were false tracks or if we were really getting shot at and the rockets were not detonating on impact.

Since tomorrow was Christmas, a completely Christian holiday, I was sure they were going to send some holiday greeting to us. You know, the noisy, booming, shrapnel producing kind. And I did not mean party poppers.

Merry Christmas to all and to all a good night.

25 Dec – Nothing much official happened today. The attacks we thought we were going to get never materialized. That was a good thing.

RUMINT (pronounced Room-int) said another one of the reported VBIEDS had been captured today. Found in the heart of the I.Z., it had been nabbed during a raid by Big Army. We had not received any reports on the action, and were still waiting to get the official word on the raid and its results. This was why it is being accredited to rumor.

You know the Army has all kinds of acronyms for all kinds of stuff, right? When it came to intelligence (yes, I know, that statement is rife for parody), Big Army broke it down like this:

SIGINT (pronounced SIG-int) was signals intelligence, or intelligence gathered from electronic signals (known as ELINT), communications systems (further broken down as COMINT), radars, and radio.

HUMINT (pronounced Hume-int) was human based intelligence, or intelligence gathered from talking with people. Sometimes this was conducted during a conversation with operational personnel as part of a mission debriefing, sometimes it was through the interviewing of prisoners or suspects.

TECHINT (pronounced Teck-int) was technical intelligence gathered from technical media and scientific sources.

RUMINT as you can guess, was rumor intelligence, or as others may call it, rumor control or scuttlebutt.

There was a pretty big boom tonight from somewhere west of the I.Z. It sounded big enough to be a car bomb, but nobody found it important enough to call in.

Oh yah, I almost forgot. We received another unspecified threat of I.D.F. directed against the IZ. sometime between today and the end of the month. Big surprise, right?

26 Dec—The TOC finally moved into our new office in the NEC today. It was about time. Things were a little slow, and a little hectic, but what would you expect. There were always growing pains when you started something new. Everything worked, wonder of all wonders, the only problem was we did not know how to operate all of it yet.

I guess RUMINT got it wrong. They did not find the suspected VBIED vehicle yesterday, they found it today. It was somewhere on the north side of the I.Z.. Believe it or not, they found it on a FOB. FOB Honor, to be exact. Nobody knew how it got there, and fortunately my company did not run the security for that base.

Big Army was setting up to raid the place when I left work tonight, so I had no information on how it went. I guessed if nothing went boom over the next couple of hours they had a successful raid.

Lots of S.A.F. across the river tonight, which was pretty much normal for this place. Some nights it was light, some nights it sounded like, well, a war zone.

27 Dec—I guess the Air Force was not all that intelligent when it came to everything flying. Tonight the I.Z. Police decided to have a check point. I think I talked about these guys already; they were all Air Force Security Police. Well, that was not completely correct either. The Air Force Police used to be divided into two separate camps. There were the LEs (law enforcement) and Security, and their missions were completely different.

As you can guess, the LEs were cops. They rode in marked police cars, patrolled the bases, and enforced the laws. Security did everything security related, and this mostly dealt with providing protection for the planes, the flight line, and SCIFs (Secret Communication and

Information Facilities). A few years ago they combined the two branches into one group, and renamed them Security Forces, SF for short. You know, SF, like Special Forces, except during this incident the "special" may only refer to the short, blue bus these guys rode to school.

So, there they were, with a checkpoint set up on the road running between the H.L.Z and the P.X. parking lot. They set it up with up-armored Chevy Suburbans (subs for short). Concertina wire, guns, and generators with long poles that had huge spotlights attached to the top, pretty standard stuff for any checkpoint. The only problem was the huge spot lights were pointed up and down the road that paralleled the helicopter approach to the H.L.Z.

I know a lot of you have never flown a helicopter before, and even fewer have flown in a military helicopter, let alone flown in one at night. For those of you that have, do not spoil this part of the story for everyone else. Military helicopter pilots had a little something extra to aid them in night flying that civilian pilots did not have. We call them N.V.G.s or NODs (Night Vision Goggles or Night Optical Devices).

If you never used one of these before, they could be a little tricky. They took what little light there was, and amplify it hundreds, if not thousands of times. Just a little bit of star light in the deep desert was more than enough illumination for a set of N.V.G.s to light up the whole area for you to see. Because they used the ambient light for magnification, if you were to take a set of N.V.G.s into a cave, well, they just would not work. You would have to bring a little bit of light in with you for the goggles to amplify.

The other problem with them was the fact they generally only saw in two dimensions, more or less. For those of you who have become used to binocular vision, this meant that depth had pretty much been removed from the equation. A pretty nasty thing for someone, especially a pilot, not to be able to judge depth when he was (oops, almost forgot, or she was) trying to land a helicopter. Fortunately, these folks practiced and trained with their equipment over and over and over again, making sure they got it right every time.

Now, add to this problem two or four huge, bright spotlights pointed directly at your piece of equipment that was already designed to magnify light's intensity. If you were lucky, your N.V.Gs would sense the light was too bright, and shut themselves off. You were only lucky because an eight-thousand dollar piece of equipment had just saved itself. But now you were wearing the equivalent of a two pound blindfold and, oh yah, were currently trying to land a helicopter. If you were not so lucky, the N.V.G.s would completely burn out, costing you the eight thousand dollars to replace them, and you were still trying to land the helicopter with a big, heavy blindfold on.

Needless to say, a bunch of the pilots got a little upset about the check point, and since the first person of authority they ran into was one of our Security Managers, we got the call in the TOC to fix the problem. Good thing we knew the right people to talk to.

28 Dec—Got a call from the JDOC (Joint Defense Operation Center – it used to be called the BDOC, but someone decided to change it). They called to tell me that checkpoint number two was closed due to two double dog sits. That was right, two dogs were not enough, they had to call in a third. And when that one sat too, they called in a fourth just to confirm what the first three had done. Unbelievable. It turned out to be nothing, and no

explosives were found on the vehicle. I did not know how that one was going to get explained.

A bit of tracer fire was reported to the south, across the river tonight. And, once again, we did not have any water in the camp today. I loved this place.

29 Dec—Had to do an hour's worth of training on the new SOFA (Status of Forces Agreement) this morning. The SOFA was officially named "Agreement between the United States of America and the Republic of Iraq on the withdrawal of United States Forces from Iraq and the organization of their activities during their temporary presence in Iraq." Quite the mouthful, wasn't it?

There were a number of provisions in this agreement that did not apply to what the military, or contractors, were doing over here but needed to be put in writing anyway. Things like information technology, communications, health care, exchange students, and education. I do not know about you, but I did not think I would be in a hurry to jump into that exchange student program.

What it did outline, that was relevant to my situation, was the withdrawal of U.S. combat forces from

Iraqi cities by 30 June 2009, and the complete withdrawal of U.S. Forces by 30 June 2011. This last part was subject to further negotiations, and probably should be looked at real hard since Iraqi Security forces did not appear to have too firm a grip on things. For the Defense Contractor there were two stipulations.

First, U.S. Contractors working for the Department of Defense (DoD) would be subject to Iraqi criminal law. Not exactly the best status for them since some DoD contractors worked directly with military units. My last deployment with Big Army had us teaching at the Baghdad Police Academy, and we had contractors teaching some of the classes alongside of us. On the second half of that deployment we worked with the Iraqi Police out of their police stations, and there were contractors working with us then as well. Plus, not all translators working outside the wire were military. Some were contractors.

Additionally, there was not enough military units to escort all the convoys necessary to feed and supply all the FOBs. So, the majority of the life support convoys were escorted by contractors instead of active duty military units. The bottom line for those guys was they worked outside of the relative safety of the FOBs, and were subject to ambushes and gunfights. One stray bullet hitting a bystander while they were defending themselves could result in murder charges, incarceration in an Iraqi jail, and a trial in an Iraqi court.

Second, for the U.S. Contractors working for the State Department (DoS), we fell under U.S. jurisdiction. Exactly how the status of each Contractor would be determined on the ground was anyone's guess, and none of this addressed the status of the non U.S. contractors who were over here supporting the effort, like our guards. I figured the best thing for any of us to do, if a situation developed, was to hall ass to the U.S. Embassy, and let the Diplomats hash it out.

We still had the threat of I.D.F. in the I.Z. but nothing had fallen on us, yet. No boom today. Maybe boom tomorrow.

30 Dec—Well, we finally got some of that I.D.F. they had been promising. Around nineteen-thirty we were looking at the big board in the TOC when a message of I.D.F. came across the screen. The big board was a huge, flat screen T.V. that displayed messages and conversations in

one of the chat rooms all the operations centers were hooked into. Sorry, you would not be able to log into this chat room because it was held on a closed, secure network of computers. This way all the TOCs around the Baghdad area were able to share information with each other without fear of being looked in on. It was kind of like the local area network of computers where some people work. It was not connected to the internet.

Anyway, as the POO (Point of Origin. Pronounced pooh, it was from where the rocket was launched) and P.O.I (Point of Impact. Each letter is pronounced separately, and this was where the rocket was predicted to land) were being reported on the big board my phone began to ring. It was Shadow.

He was calling to report a rather loud explosion approximately eight hundred meters south of his position, beyond Camp Fernandez. He said the blast was loud enough to make him think it actually had blown-up somewhere on the camp, until one of his towers reported it was across the river. Good information, but at the time I was not sure just what to do with it.

Making a quick note before hanging up the phone, I turned back toward the plotting map where a small team was gathered. Coordinates from the big board were being charted and the results showed the shot had been fired from an area a couple, five, kilometers southwest of the I.Z.. The impact site was calculated and found to be just shy of a click (military speak for a kilometer) south of Fernandez. That must have been the boom Shadow just reported.

No sooner had we completed plotting the I.D.F. report then I got a phone call from the guys at the JDOC. They were reporting another explosion at Adnon Palace resulting in two Saber guards being wounded, with the possibility of up to six more; they only had confirmation of the two. Saber was another contract security company, but where we hired mostly Peruvians and Chileans they hired Iraqis.

Adnon Palace was located directly north of the NEC and East of the huge, crossed saber monument shown in a lot of pictures of Baghdad. That Palace was kind of in the Green Zone, kind of in the Red Zone, and was primarily used by the Iraqi Army's Intelligence guys (now there was an oxymoron if ever I had heard one.) Even though Big Army worked there too, it was mostly

Iraqi, and was guarded by the Iraqi Army and Saber Security.

Long story short, the shot to the south had been tracked by the C-Ram. They said it was a mortar round, and since it was not going to hit in the I.Z. no alarms had gone off. The round that hit over by Adnon had been a one hundred-seven millimeter rocket. It had been fired from the north/northwest of the I.Z., and if it had a little more oomph it might have hit the NEC. No explanation as to why the alarms did not go off for that one. Also, both rounds had been fired within minutes of each other. Sounded a bit like a coordinated attack to me. We would see what they threw at us next.

31 Dec –New Year's Eve. Tomorrow started the new world order in Iraq, and they already started T-walling off the Palace. Getting ready for the Iraqis to take over. In the morning the Iraqis were going to have a flag raising ceremony over there and did not want to see any Americans within two hundred meters of the place. All the guards would stand inside the CACs, and no American vehicles would be allowed to enter the Palace grounds all day.

They also T-walled off all the grounds behind the Palace as well. It looked like we are only giving them the Palace building, and the front of the grounds for now. We were still taking all the classified stuff out of the North Wing, and reconditioning the rest of the building back to its original layout. It seemed like only yesterday we were taking this part of Baghdad, and now we were giving it back.

Tomorrow also began the drawdown of U.S. troops from Iraq. That should be interesting to watch as well. The Iraqis could not keep things from going boom anywhere else in this country, what made them think they would be able to secure this place?

Happy New Year!

www.ingramcontent.com/pod-product-compliance
Lightning Source LLC
LaVergne TN
LVHW021753060526
838201LV00058B/3076